William Byrd Consort Music

Anne Martin

Peacock Press

William Byrd Consort Music

ISBN 978-1-914934-53-7

Published by Peacock Press, 2023
Scout Bottom Farm
Mytholmroyd
Hebden Bridge HX7 5JS (UK)

Design and artwork by DM Design and Print

Front cover by Roger Williams

William Byrd
Consort Music

Anne Martin

William Byrd Consort Music

Table of Contents

William Byrd Consort Music; the beginning of English chamber music

Introduction

Today we accept without question the notion that a piece of music can exist and be played in its own right and does not have to serve any other purpose. Until the sixteenth century, music was mainly seen as serving a particular purpose such as for liturgical use, for formal occasions, for dancing or telling a story. Vocal music, particularly liturgical music or music with sacred texts, was held in higher esteem than instrumental music. William Byrd (1539/40–1623) was one of the first English composers to change the status and perception of instrumental music through his compositions for viols and keyboard. His surviving textless consort music consists of 33 works out of his significant body of compositions, which number around 500, of which vocal compositions make up the largest part. Yet this small body of work is diverse, consisting of different musical forms, and written over a time span of around fifty years. They range from student works to mature, reflective compositions. The intention of this book is to provide background and insight into Byrd's consort music for those who enjoy playing it and a handbook for those who wish to study it.

Scholars, such as Pieter Dirksen, recognise that Byrd 'was perhaps the first major composer who took instrumental composition as seriously as he did the composition of vocal counterpoint'.[1] Kerry McCarthy writes, 'if every note of his vocal music had been lost, he would still be considered a first-rate composer on the strength of his instrumental works alone'.[2] This book is solely concerned with Byrd's textless consort music, examining the musical forms he explored and identifying the emergence of his own idiomatic instrumental style.[3] It does not look at his consort songs. (Any reference to 'consort music' will refer to textless music.) The order in which Byrd composed his consort pieces is considered and for whom he might have written them. His consort fantasias are among the earliest examples of true chamber music and abstract music. They should be recognised as playing a distinctive role in the history and development of English chamber music.

Byrd's consort music is probably the least studied of all his music, the last major study being undertaken by Oliver Neighbour in 1978.[4] It is time to re-examine it. Since

1978, Early Music studies have developed and changed the way we look at sixteenth century music. There are now a far larger number of musicologists who are performers and have brought music back to life. There is greater knowledge of instrument construction and ranges, particularly of viols. Significant studies, helped by advances in technology, have been carried out on manuscripts, particularly looking at identifying the dates of manuscript paper, analysing handwriting and identifying scribes. Studies have been made of the use of voices and viols in the sixteenth century and how that affects the range and compass of music. The use and significance of particular clefs has also been considered by performers of the repertoire. All of these factors justify looking again at Byrd's consort music, as does examining how he exploited the opportunities offered by improvements in instrument making and the instrumental skill on offer to him. Looking at the music, we can see the musical skill and understanding he developed through its composition and confirm the place and importance of this music in the overall development of abstract instrumental music.

All of Byrd's 33 consort pieces were edited by Kenneth Elliott in 1971 as volume 17 of the Byrd Edition.[5] His textual commentary lists every variant in the sources he was able to access.[6] Where there are significant differences between the original sources, this is discussed in the appropriate chapter, for example in that looking at Fantasia 6/g1, which exists in different forms; one manuscript contains only the first 89 breves. In most cases, the original manuscript copies of Byrd's consort music do not diverge significantly from one another where there is more than one source. The titles used for each piece relate to Neighbour's classification as it is well established, making referencing easier and ensuring consistency with earlier studies.

Byrd spent the majority of his working life associated with the Chapel Royal. Little of his early life is documented. We know he must have been a chorister and received a musical education and believe he became a pupil of Thomas Tallis (*c.*1505–1585), at the Chapel Royal.[7] As a young boy, he may have followed his brothers into the choir of St Paul's Cathedral or he might been a chorister at St George's Chapel Windsor. A 'Byrd' is listed as the seventh boy in a list of St George's choristers made in 1548.[8] As a chorister, he must have learnt to play the viol, and the understanding of the viol's possibilities displayed in his consort music would suggest he was an excellent viol player. After completing his musical training and likely acting as assistant organist to Tallis, Byrd left in 1563 for a position at Lincoln Cathedral, where he remained until 1572; he then returned to London as a gentleman of the Chapel Royal filling a vacancy left by the death of Robert Parsons. Byrd served there until he began to withdraw from public life around 1592. With the exception of a six-part pavan and galliard, it is thought he had written all of his consort music by the 1590s. In spite of being a Catholic, Byrd was a loyal servant of Elizabeth I and he survived relatively unscathed until his death at the age of 83 in 1623, having lived through most of the reign of Elizabeth's successor, James I.

Byrd's surviving consort pieces consist of five categories of composition: Latin-titled hymn and Miserere settings (11), written without text, In Nomines (7), two sets of variations based on a ground and a popular tune, fantasias (10) and dances (3).[9] The first of these works was likely written around 1555, when Byrd was about fifteen, and the last in the early 1600s, when he was in his sixties. Included among this music would appear to be some of the most intimate of his compositions. Byrd probably wrote at least some of his consort pieces specifically to explore different structures that could support textless instrumental and autonomous music; some of his consort works may have been written for a particular patron or group of players. No original manuscripts of consort music in Byrd's hand are known to survive. He published just two consort works in *Psalmes, Songs and Sonnets* of 1611.

There are several things to consider when assessing the development of truly abstract instrumental consort (i.e. chamber) music by Byrd, and the emergence of his particular style. Firstly the historical context of his music needs to be understood, in particular the impact of the Reformation on musical composition, looking especially at the education of choristers and the growth of viol playing in England, which led to the need for suitable music for performance. The question of the role of musical theory in sixteenth century English music also needs consideration, in particular the influence of mode on Byrd's musical structures and how far he had moved away from modal theory towards a new tonal language. It will become clear that Byrd was on the cusp of the transition from the music language of the Renaissance to that of the Baroque.

Another question to ask is how much consort music was actually composed for specific instruments, in Byrd's case for viols. Some textless music was also intended for performance either by instruments or voices, the latter using solfa syllables. Identifying whether music without text was written for instrumental performance or for voices can be helped by looking at how it is notated, examining clefs, signature accidentals, and the ranges of individual parts and the overall range, known as the compass; this refers to the complete range of notes (pitches) from lowest bassus note to highest cantus note found in a piece of music. Byrd himself was concerned with the overall range of his music and the individual ranges of voices and parts. In his introduction, 'Epistle to the Reader', in *Psalmes, Sonets and Songs of sadness and pietie* (1588), the first printed collection containing music only by Byrd, he refers to the overall pitch range as the 'compasse'.[10]

Looking at the 41 sources of Byrd's consort music also provides information. Dating the manuscripts and sources and identifying their places of origin, scribes and owners is of significance in trying to establish the order in which Byrd composed his consort works. Exact dating of manuscripts and placing them in chronological order is difficult but for a significant number there is sufficient evidence to place them within a range of years through the identification of scribes, owners, paper and contents. For example, the manuscript GB-Ob MS Mus. Sch. e. 423 can be identified as belonging to John, first Lord Petre (1549–1613), a friend and patron of Byrd. It was copied between 1577 and *c.*1589. This gives us the earliest known date for the second of Byrd's six-part fantasias. A small number of manuscripts can be placed more accurately and there is the definitive date for the publication of two of Byrd's consort works in the *Psalmes, Songs and Sonnets* of 1611. What kind of music is found in a manuscript collection and where Byrd's pieces are placed, can provide us with useful information as to how they were perceived. It can also us help to confirm which composers influenced Byrd.

Different genres found in Byrd's consort music are individually examined in the book, starting with his Latin chant-based works and In Nomines. A chapter is devoted to Byrd's first known fantasia, a six-part work which has strong links to vocal music, but is undoubtedly an instrumental work. The next chapter is devoted to his consort works in variation form. Chapter Eight looks at his first great consort work, the first six-part fantasia in g. Chapter Nine covers Byrd's consort works not mentioned in previous chapters including his last known consort work, the Pavan and Galliard 6/C.

Chapters follow the route Byrd took with his compositions. Using the dating information from the sources and some musical clues, pieces are examined in apparent order of composition, relating them to genre, suggesting the order in which Byrd explored different structures for composition. Each genre is covered although Byrd's Latin-titled works are only mentioned briefly, as they do not contain a significant number of instrumental characteristics. Some pieces are examined in greater detail than others because they are the first example of a genre used by Byrd or because of the significant features or new traits they contain. Instrumental characteristics are noted as they appear in the music. Consideration of pitch, note range, structure, tessitura, texture, tempo and rhythmic complexity and the use of intervals all contribute to analysing Byrd's music as does assessing the influence of other composers.

Finally, the last chapter makes an assessment of Byrd's contribution to instrumental consort music, confirming what he achieved and determining whether it is possible to identify if any of his consort pieces were written for a particular purpose, group or patron.

1 Pieter Dirksen, *The Keyboard Music of Jan Pieterszoon Sweelinck* (Utrecht, 1997), p. 518.

2 Kerry McCarthy, *Byrd* (New York, 2013), p. vii.

3 The term, 'consort' is taken as referring to a small group of musicians playing or singing.

4 Oliver Neighbour, *The Consort and Keyboard Music of William Byrd* (London, 1978). Neighbour did not include Byrd's consort songs in his study.

5 William Byrd, *Consort Music*, ed. Kenneth Elliott, The Byrd Edition 17 (London, Stainer and Bell, 1971).

6 Ibid., pp. 152–65; Elliott was unaware of one set of partbooks, *D-Kl* MS mus. 125 and four lute and keyboard books are omitted.

7 See John Harley, *William Byrd Gentleman of the Chapel Royal* (Aldershot, 1997).

8 Kerry McCarthy, *Tallis*, (New York, 2020). p. 46.

9 The latter a single pavan and a paired pavan and galliard.

10 William Byrd, *Psalmes, Sonets and Songs* (1588), ed. Jeremy Smith, The Byrd Edition 12 (London, Stainer and Bell, 2004).

William Byrd's consort works listed by genre

Titles given for each piece relate to Oliver Neighbour's classification in *The Consort and Keyboard Music of William Byrd* (London, 1978). The first number refers to the number of parts in each piece, and any letter to the final (the finishing note that determines the key of a piece). Upper or lower case indicates major or minor. The second number provides a means of distinguishing between pieces of the same genre, in the same number of parts and with the same final. The numbers in brackets locate each piece as it occurs in the collected edition of Byrd's consort music, William Byrd, *Consort Music*, ed. Kenneth Elliott, Byrd Edition 17 (London, Stainer and Bell, 1971).

Dances	(Byrd Edition 17)
Pavan 5/c	(14)
Pavan and Galliard 6/C	(15a and b)

Fantasias

Fantasia 3/C1	(1)
Fantasia 3/C2	(2)
Fantasia 3/C3	(3)
Fantasia 4/a	(5)
Fantasia 4/g	(4)
Fantasia 4/G	(34)
Fantasia 5/C	(8)
Fantasia 6/F	(11)

Fantasia 6/g1 (12)

Fantasia 6/g2 (13)

In Nomines

In Nomine 4/1 (16)

In Nomine 4/2 (17)

In Nomine 5/1 (18)

In Nomine 5/2 (19)

In Nomine 5/3 (20)

In Nomine 5/4 (21)

In Nomine 5/5 (22)

Latin-titled works

Christe qui lux (I) (24)

Christe qui lux (II) (25)

Christe qui lux (III) (26)

Christe redemptor (27)

Miserere (28)

Salvator mundi (29)

Sermone blando a 3 (23)

Sermone blando a 4 (I) (30)

Sermone blando a 4 (II) (31)

Variations

Probable chronological order of Byrd's textless consort works and date of earliest source

The number in brackets refers to the order manuscripts are listed in Chapter Four. Manuscripts that can be accessed digitally are marked * below. (See Appendix 4)

By late 1550s

Sermone blando a 3	GB-Lbl Add. MS 29246 (14)*	early 1600s
Sermone blando a 4 (I)	GB-Lbl Add. MS 29246 (14)*	early 1600s
Sermone blando a 4 (II)	GB-Ob MSS Tenbury 354–8 (15)	early 1600s
Christe qui lux (I)	GB-Lbl Add. MS 29246 (14)*	early 1600s
Christe qui lux (II)	GB-Lbl Add. MSS 30480–30484 (1)*	*c.*1570 –1590s
Christe qui lux (III)	GB-Ob MSS Tenbury 354–8 (15)	early 1600s
Te lucis (I)	GB-Lbl Add. MS 29246 (14)*	early 1600s
Te lucis (II)	GB-Lbl Add. MS 29246 (14)*	
early 1600s		
Salvator mundi	GB-Lbl Add. MS 29246 (14)*	early 1600s
Christe redemptor	GB-Lbl Add. MS 29246 (14)*	early 1600s
Miserere	GB-Lbl Add. MS 29246 (14)*	early 1600s

By 1563

In Nomine 5/1	GB-Lbl Add. MS 31390 (2)*	*c.*1568–1578
In Nomine 4/1	GB-Ob MSS Tenbury 354–8 (15)	early 1600s
In Nomine 4/2	GB-Ob MSS Mus. Sch. d. 212–6 (25)	by 1610
In Nomine 5/2	GB-Ob MS Tenbury 1464 (3)	*1570–1575

1562– *c.*1565

In Nomine 5/3	GB-Ob MSS Mus. Sch. d. 212–6 (25)	by 1610
In Nomine 5/4	GB-Lbl Add. MS 31390 (2)*	*c.*1568–1578
In Nomine 5/5	GB-Lbl Add. MS 31390 (2)*	*c.*1568–1578

After 1567

Fantasia 6/F	GB-Och MMS 979–83 (4)*	*c*.1575–1581

(Motet version *Laudate pueri* found in *Cantiones Sacrae 1575*)

***c*.1570**

Prelude and Ground	GB-Lbl Add. MS 32377 (8)*	1585–1590

after 1572

Pavan 5/c	GB-Lbl Add. MSS 37042–6 (21)	completed after 1606

(Keyboard version found in *My Ladye Nevell's Booke* 1591)

1570s

Browning Fantasy	GB-Lbl Add. MS 31390 (2)*	by 1578

1580s

(?)Fantasia 4/G	GB-Lbl Add. MS 29427 (27)	*c*.1612–18

(Motet version *In manus tuas* found in *Gradualia 1605*)

***c*.1585–6**

Fantasia 6/g1	GB-Ob MS Mus. Sch. e. 423 (6)*	ms completed 1589

***c*.1586–9**

Fantasia 5/C	GB-Lbl Add. MSS 17786–91 (24)	1610–1620s

(Keyboard version *A lesson of Voluntarie* found in *My Ladye Nevell's Booke* 1591*)

***c*. 1588/9**

Fantasias 6/g2	GB-Ob MS Mus. Sch. e. 423 (6)* (added at completion in 1589)	

***c*. 1589/90**

Fantasia 4/a	GB-Lbl Add. MS 29246 (14)*	early 1600s
Fantasia 4/g	GB-Lbl Add. MS 29246 (14)*	early 1600s

Published in *Psalmes, songs and sonnets* 1611

c. 1590

Fantasia 3/C1	GB-Lbl Add. MS 29246 (14)*	early 1600s
Fantasia 3/C2	GB-Lbl Add. MS 29246 (14)*	early 1600s
Fantasia 3/C3 (possibly 1580s)		
	GB-Lbl Add. MS 29246 (14)*	early 1600s

After 1600

Pavan & Galliard 6/C	GB-Ob MMS Mus Sch. C 64–9 (34)	*c.*1635–*c.*1640

Chapter 1

The impact of the Reformation on chorister education and viol playing in sixteenth-century England

Byrd was born around the beginning of 1540 and his formative years coincided with the upheavals of the English Reformation.[1] This had a significant effect on his music education and his development as a composer. The Reformation changed the demands made on choristers and opened up opportunities for new musical activities such as viol playing and the composition of music for viols. As ensemble playing increased during the sixteenth century so did the need for appropriate music to perform.

Just five years before Byrd's birth, Henry VIII had broken away from Rome, and the Act of Supremacy was passed in November 1534. Initially this had little effect on church worship and the lives of church musicians, but this changed radically with the two Acts of Dissolution (1536 and 1539), which abolished the monasteries, where a substantial part of England's musical life and education had been centred. The last Abbey to close was Waltham Abbey, and among those losing their position was a young organist Thomas Tallis who is thought to have saved a fifteenth-century manuscript of music theory[2] and became Byrd's teacher.

The impact of the Reformation

The initial impact of the Reformation on music was the disbanding of most monastic choirs. Only monastic houses that were seats of bishops survived, becoming diocesan cathedrals. Where this happened, choirs, including boy choristers, were retained and monks often became secular clergy. Specific provisions were made for the selection and education of boy choristers. Henrician statutes for Canterbury Cathedral state that ten choir boys should be 'of tender age, both with musical voices and apt for singing, who shall serve, minister and sing in the Choir'.[3] The statutes directed that a minor canon or clerk of good character should be appointed to educate the boys in singing and playing artistically on keyboard instruments. The loss of the monastic choirs between 1535 and 1540 was counterbalanced by a number of new choirs, including those established in the New Foundation cathedrals created by Henry VIII after 1538.[4] By the early 1540s there may have been around 200 professional liturgical choirs in England.

Under Henry VIII, worship, church music and chorister education did not radically change. It continued to be based round the existing liturgy and liturgical chant. This necessitated a study of Latin, the ability to memorize Latin texts and psalm tones and the learning of solmization to memorise intervals.[5] Choristers needed to be able to improvise round a known chant and understand the rules governing cadences. They started at the age of seven with 'song', a combination of Latin grammar and chant. The boys learnt to read and write and to memorize psalms with their associated psalm tones and liturgical texts. This was followed by the introduction of improvising against a chant or 'faburden', which at the simplest level involved doubling a chant at an interval of a fourth above and a third below. At the next stage, choristers progressed to reading notes through the Gamut, a combination of the six hexachord syllables (ut, re, mi, fa, sol and la), and learning note letter names. They could then sing notated music when given the starting note and the clef. This enabled them to read a chant and develop more advanced improvisation skills. Finally, boys learnt to read mensuration or 'pricksong' in order to reach advanced levels of vocal improvisation and to sing polyphony. Older boys transferred these skills to playing the organ. Improvisation still played a key role in liturgical music in the final years of Henry's reign, when Tallis, John Sheppard (*c.*1515–1558) and Christopher Tye (1505?–1572) were producing some of their finest polyphonic music. Two significant changes to the liturgy came in 1543, from which time lessons at Matins or Vespers had to be read or sung in English, and in 1544, when Archbishop Cranmer replaced all the Latin processional litanies, using English texts to fit some of the existing chants. He followed the principle of one note to one syllable and his *First Litany* in 1544 was based on one chant, the Sarum Processionale.[6]

Henry VIII died in 1547, succeeded by Edward VI with Edward Seymour, Duke of Somerset (*c.*1500–1552), as Lord Protector. There was rapid, significant change in church worship. Not a great deal is known about Byrd's early life, but it must have been about this time (aged around seven) that he became a chorister perhaps in the choir of St Paul's Cathedral or he may have been the chorister called Byrd mentioned in the 1548 list from St George's Chapel Windsor. The records for the years Byrd would have been at St Paul's have been lost.

Under the Protectorate of Edward Seymour, Thomas Cranmer was able to pursue more significant reform. Worship in English was immediately introduced and the role of the clergy changed. With the passing of the 1547 Chantries Act, the majority of collegiate and non-cathedral choral foundations were abolished or converted 'to good and godly use', such as in the creation of grammar schools and enlarging of universities.[7] A special clause exempted existing educational establishments from being abolished, these being the university colleges and Eton College, Winchester College and St George's Windsor. The Act of Uniformity of 1549 contained the orders of service to be used everywhere, and Cranmer's first *Book of Common Prayer* was published. This reduced regular church services to three: Matins, Evensong and the Eucharist. The Eucharist remained in content much the same as the Latin Mass that preceded it, but was now in English. Most previous church music became unusable and a great deal had been lost at the time of the dissolution of the monasteries. Suitable choral music was urgently needed for the new services. Several solutions were found. Some pre-Reformation music, such as four appropriate movements from two of John Taverner's (*c.*1490–1545) five-part Latin Masses, was adapted to English words from the 1549 *Book of Common Prayer*. Efforts were made to adapt Latin plainsong to English texts. In 1550, John Merbecke (*c.*1510– *c.*1585) set whole sections of the 1549 *Book of Common Prayer* to music, putting Cranmer's words to melodic phrases based on plainsong. There was new music, free from the constraint of plainsong, written by composers such as Tallis, Tye, Sheppard and William Mundy (*c.*1529–1591). This included complete settings for the new services and motets or 'anthems' with English texts. An anthem was allowed at the end of both Evensong and Matins. This new music was simpler than that of the pre-Reformation, reflecting the demand for straightforward word setting.

These developments were short lived. John Dudley (1504–1553) replaced Seymour and the Calvinists gained influence. The 1549 *Book of Common Prayer* was withdrawn and a replacement was issued in 1552. It was far more Calvinistic and references to singing were removed. Some bishops, such as John Hooper (*c.*1495–1555) of Gloucester and Worcester, went beyond this, banning polyphony and ordering church organs to be removed. The Church of England appeared to be inexorably moving towards strict Calvinism in which there would be no place for professional choristers. King's College Cambridge, for example, had no choristers by 1552.[8] If Edward VI had not died in 1553, it is likely that the English choral tradition would have vanished. But Byrd's experience as a chorister was to change radically for four years with the accession of the Catholic Queen Mary.

Mary immediately repealed all of Edward's reforms, restored the Latin rite and its music and banned all music with English texts. Choristers had quickly to master the old Latin Mass and Offices. Polyphony was revived, choirs reinstated and composers were expected to produce music for the old rite. The Gyffard Part-books, GB-Lbl Add. MS 17805, contain music for the Catholic Liturgy written by composers active in the 1550s or earlier (although it is now thought the part books were compiled in the 1570s).[9] They encompass almost all the surviving four-part Latin works of Taverner, Tallis, Sheppard, Tye and William Mundy. The fact that the collection is mainly of four-part music is most unusual and the music seems more typical of Protestant church music than ornate Catholic liturgical music.[10] Perhaps this is indicative of the immediate demand for readily accessible music with Latin text. The music in the Gyffard part books comes from repertoire sung in the Oxford college chapels, St Paul's Cathedral and the Chapel Royal.[11] It is likely that, as a chorister, Byrd was familiar with this repertoire. He would have been thirteen when the Catholic revival occurred and would have participated in singing ornate polyphony which had re-appeared in important services.

By his teenage years Byrd seems to be have been associated with the Chapel Royal and probably became an assistant organist. Byrd considered himself a pupil of Tallis, who served at the Chapel Royal from around 1543. Early writers such as Ferdinando Heybourne and Anthony à Wood assert that Byrd was Tallis's pupil.[12] John Harley suggests that if Byrd was a chorister at St Paul's, then the master of choristers Sebastian Westcote could have sent him to Tallis for further musical studies.[13] Byrd's earliest known vocal composition is his contribution to *Similes illes fiant*, a psalm setting in three parts for four men's voices written around 1558 at the end of Mary's reign. The other contributors were Sheppard and William Mundy. Sheppard was a member of the Chapel Royal. Mundy was not but he was parish clerk at St Mary-at-Hill, a London church which had connections with the Chapel Royal and its singers. Although Sheppard died in 1558, he had a lasting influence on Byrd as can be seen in Byrd's *Great Service* which, as Richard Turbet writes, reflects Byrd's 'interest in rhythm, melodic outline and, to a lesser extent, scoring' found in Sheppard's *Second Service*.[14] The *Great Service* was probably written many years later for the Chapel Royal.[15]

With Mary's death in 1558, the pendulum swung back again. Elizabeth I's coronation was in the Latin rite but the new Queen had grown up a Protestant. (The Roman Catholic Church considered her illegitimate.) She rejected the Marian settlement, resulting in a return to the reformed liturgy and a new *Book of Common Prayer*, which was almost identical to Cranmer's 1552 edition. Elizabeth probably would have preferred a return to the 1549 version but, while she accepted the 1559 book, she insisted that music should be maintained in cathedrals and in some churches, thereby steering a path between Catholicism, which she fought all her reign, and extreme Protestantism. The 1559 *Book of Common Prayer* was accompanied by a set of 55 Royal requirements of which the forty-ninth stated that in collegiate churches (including cathedrals) and some parish churches, choirs of men and boys and music in services should be maintained. By 1560, thirty-four cathedrals, chapels and churches were managing to maintain choirs, most singing Matins and Evensong daily, although not all managed to continue due to the increased influence of Puritanism, financial problems or occasionally the poor calibre of the choir master.[16]

The post-Reformation education of choristers

The changes in Church liturgy were reflected in the education and activities of the boy choristers. In the first half of the sixteenth century, with the emphasis on Latin, Christian morals and music for the liturgy, rather than a curriculum specifically geared towards producing professional musicians, the education offered to choristers was a general one. It was a practical, rather than an academic education, that trained choristers to take part in daily services. After the Reformation, with the founding of Grammar Schools at the beginning of Edward's reign, secular education and that of choristers began to diverge and distinct differences emerged.

As general education and specialist music education began to separate, the curriculum offered to choristers had an increased musical content. This provided the opportunity for some choristers to be educated specifically for a musical career. Although they continued to receive a general education, including Latin, the new chorister curriculum contained much more emphasis on written music, musical literacy, the studying of composition techniques and playing instruments, normally viols and organ.[17] The reduction of the number of services choristers were required to sing from the Mass and the daily offices (Matins, Lauds, Prime, Terce, Sext, None, Vespers and Compline) to just the three services in English, Matins (which Cranmer derived from the old Matins and Lauds), Evensong (taken from Vespers and Compline) and Communion, which replaced the Mass, created space for the increased musical content in the curriculum. Choristers were no longer required to improvise over plainsong. With the advent of the new services, notated composed music became much more important, as did the ability to read music. Choristers were also expected to copy and compose music.

As well as an increase in musical activities, there was also more time for another aspect of choristers' education, dating back to medieval times: their involvement in acting, which became more widespread from the 1540s.[18] At the beginning of the century, Chapel Royal choristers are recorded as having appeared in court pageants, the first noted example being those that were part of the celebrations of the marriage of Catherine of Aragon to Henry VIII's elder brother, Prince Arthur, organised by William Cornysh (?1465–1523) in 1501. Cornysh became Master of the Children of the Chapel Royal in 1509 and under him the choristers progressed to acting roles. Records from 1515 show the choristers acting out stories before the king at Christmas.[19] Cornysh is known to have written at least eight plays. From Cornysh onwards, successive Masters of Choristers of the Chapel Royal and St Paul's wrote and produced plays, developing the boys' acting skills. Choristers effectively became professional actors and plays became an important part of their activities, particularly after the Reformation.

Masters at choral foundations were also using ballads and songs, usually based on classical stories with a Christian focus, to reinforce Latin grammar and moral education. The plays written for choristers were usually morally based and incorporated some of these songs. One such example is *Wit and Science*, written by John Redford, Master of Choristers at St Paul's from around 1534 until his death in 1547.[20] Redford used *Wit and Science* to illustrate how the boys' education could lead to social advancement, to demonstrate through speeches their skills of memorization and oratory while the songs and dances displayed the choristers' musical ability and physical agility. The allegorical narrative suggested such an appropriate course of study could lead to 'viertue' in the many senses of that word.[21] Records of performance are lost but Redford, who died in the same year as Henry VIII, wanted to make St Paul's boys Henry VIII's first choice of entertainment.[22] (The surviving manuscript containing *Wit and Science*, GB-Lbl Add. MS 15233, is now thought to have been compiled and bound with extra material in the mid-1550s.[23] This does not change the dating of the original play to around 1540.) Within the stage directions of *Wit and Science*, there is one of the first references to the use of viols on stage being played by choristers; at the end is stated 'Here cometh in four with viols'.[24] There is also a galliard earlier in the play, presumably also played by the viols. Redford's successor, Sebastian Westcote (1524–1582), developed the scope of the chorister actors even further. Evidence of choristers playing viols is found consistently from the 1540s, initially by choristers of the Chapel Royal and then by St Paul's boys.[25]

A surviving number of songs and ballads from this period are found in a collection made by Richard Edwards (1525–1566), entitled *The Paradise of Dainty Devices*. Published posthumously in 1576, it also includes Edwards's own poems.[26] The preface by the publisher, Henry Disle, states that the poems are to be sung. Edwards was Master of Choristers at the Chapel Royal from 1561 to 1566 and continued the play writing tradition begun by Cornysh.

The growth of viol playing in sixteenth century England

Viols first appeared in England at the Tudor Court at the beginning of the sixteenth century. A simple Spanish form of the viol may have come to England in 1501 with a musician in the retinue of Catherine of Aragon.[27] In 1506, Philip I of Castile (brother-in-law to Catherine of Aragon) was shipwrecked off the Dorset coast and subsequently entertained by Henry VII. Among his retinue were three musicians, identified as string players. Two of these players were later employed at the Tudor court, Bertrand Brouart from 1509 and Matthew van Wilder from around 1515. The record for Court revel accounts for 6 January 1515 contains a reference to viols.[28] Matthew van Wilder's name appears in royal accounts dated 7 January 1516/17 recording his appointment warrant as a lute and viol player.[29] Peter van Wilder, thought to be his son, was also probably employed around the same time. A third member of the family, Philip van Wilder (1500–1554), arrived early in the 1520s; like the rest of his family, his origins are thought to have been in the French-speaking part of the Netherlands and he probably spent time in northern Italy.[30] Thus Philip van Wilder's expertise could have been acquired directly from the area in which viols were first used as a consort instrument. The Italian courts at Ferrara and Mantua were of particular significance for the development of the viol and the emergence of instrumental ensemble music. In Mantua, Isabella d'Este established a viol consort in 1495.[31] In Ferrara, viol playing also emerged at the court of Isabella's brother, Alfonso. The D'Este family were the first aristocrats known to play consort instruments, the first amateur musicians to do so.

Philip Van Wilder became one of the most important musicians at Henry VIII's court from around 1528. He was prominent at court from 1540, and became tutor to the royal children. He was involved in the transmission of the chanson to England and the composer of at least 30 chansons. The chanson had significant influence on English vocal music and in the development of textless music for consort instruments. Van Wilder influenced the establishment of an English tradition of abstract polyphonic composition. He was one of a small number of composers in England who had music published on the continent. His chansons are found in two collections published by Tielman Susato (1500–1561) in Antwerp in 1544 and 1545. Two of Byrd's motets *Aspice Domine* and *Ne irascaris* display the direct influence of Wilder, including material drawn from Wilder's own five and six-part versions of *Aspice Domine* and his most famous chanson, *O doux regard*.[32]

By the 1520s the references to viols at the English court increase. The names of two more viol players of Flemish extraction, Hans Hossenet and Hans Highorne, appear in lists of court musicians from 1526.[33] It is assumed that they formed a trio with Philip van Wilder to play written music.[34] Six further viol players arrived from Italy in 1540, followed by a further two in 1545 thus establishing a significant number of players at the English court (mainly of Jewish extraction). At the time of Henry VIII's death in 1547, twenty-five viols were listed in the court inventory. The earliest known payment made in Britain for viols was recorded in Scotland, made in 1535 by the Scottish court to Richard Hume.[35]

By 1540, viol players began to appear outside the Royal Court. The Earls of Essex, Hertford and Rutland had all purchased viols for their musicians by 1538.[36] By the mid-1540s, viol playing had spread from the Royal Court to the choir schools and to musicians of the aristocracy. This was the beginning of the popularity of the viol consort in Tudor England, but until the latter part of the sixteenth century, the playing of viols was the domain of professional musicians. Significantly, during the 1540s, as the boy choristers began to learn to play viols, so the first English names appeared among the list of court musicians.

Choristers playing viols were first recorded performing in plays but by the end of the decade, viol consorts made up of choirboys were giving freestanding performances. In 1549, the choristers of St Paul's performed at the annual dinner of the Merchant Taylors' Company. Records show that following this, they were invited to provide musical entertainment for other eminent bodies. Around 1551/2 they performed before Princess Elizabeth at Hatfield House. The Master of St Paul's Choristers, Sebastian Westcott, had his own chest of viols played by his choristers. On his death in 1582, he left the instruments to the cathedral for following generations of choirboys to play.[37] The inclusion of viol-playing choristers would also mean that the choir boys could be accompanied without the necessity of adult singers being present. Performances by viol-playing choristers from the Chapel Royal and St Paul's became common between 1550 and the early 1560s, when they played (and sang) at a variety of celebrations and festivities including public pageants, weddings and at ceremonial dinners during the annual elections of City companies.[38] These performances meant that viols were heard by a much wider audience than if they had just been played at court or in aristocratic households.

Byrd would have received the main part of his chorister education during a period in which choristers learnt to play the viol. Playing viols could serve two important purposes for choristers. As fretted instruments, they provided an excellent way for boys to gain instrumental skills and learn to read music. It also provided the performers for plays and entertainment. It is no coincidence that composers began to write a significant amount of textless music for viol consorts (or voices). Much of this was based on a cantus firmus, and included the specifically English composition, the In Nomine, most of which appeared between the mid-1550s and mid-1560s, the period during which Byrd began composing.

The composition of In Nomines is of interest because it is peculiarly English and directly linked to chorister education. It is based around the cantus firmus of the Benedictus in the *Missa Gloria Tibi Trinitas* by John Taverner (1490–1545), found at the words 'in nomine Domini'. In Nomines provided a vehicle, through the repeating cantus firmus, for choristers to learn to read music and for them to play (or sing) with more advanced musicians playing the other parts. In Nomines would have also provided a framework for compositional studies and suitable solemn music for viol playing choristers to perform at important functions.

Byrd's earliest surviving consort piece would seem to be two settings, in three parts, of *Sermone blando*, also based on a cantus firmus. Presumably written in Byrd's chorister days, the wide range of the two lower parts would suggest it was written for viols. Oliver Neighbour suggests that it is typical of the type of music required of music students to compose as a technical exercise.[39] In the second setting, Byrd makes significant use of canon, a device he could have learnt from Tallis. In both he shows his understanding and experience of chant that he would have learnt as a chorister.

It is difficult to discover to what extent choristers outside London were playing viols. Choristers were playing the viol at Ely by 1567 and in Newark and possibly Lincoln (where Byrd had arrived by 1563). Payment for viol players is recorded at Lincoln in 1594 in the cathedral accounts. Choristers from St George's Chapel in Windsor Castle were known to perform playing viols, though on a smaller scale than the London choristers. Chorister performances started to decline from the mid-1560s.[40] This coincides with the setting up of adult theatre companies and the growth of the number of musicians, such as the Waits, who could now play viols. The London Waits began to play viols in the 1560s, placing themselves in direct competition with the choristers for work.[41] (The spread of the plague may also have contributed to the decline.[42]) However, viol playing still continued to play an important role in chorister education and in private houses, as amateur viol playing emerged towards the end of the century. Ex-choristers became professional musicians, taking up posts in aristocratic households.

The skill and technical expertise of viol players developed during the span of years Byrd was composing his consort music. Viols were initially imported from Italy and the Bassano family brought viol-making skills to Britain,[43] By the end of Elizabeth I's reign, English makers, including the most famous, father and son, both named John Rose (d.1562? and d.1611), were making significant numbers of viols. English viols developed their own particular character and came to be highly valued outside England.[44] The developing skill of viol players and the technical capabilities of their instruments are important when considering the richness and technical demands of Byrd's compositions, both in the range of notes and complexity of rhythmic patterns.

The emergence of music for viols and its influence on Byrd

The growth of ensemble performance from the 1540s by instruments encouraged the composition of suitable music. Appropriate musical forms needed to be found to support music without words. A significant amount of textless music was probably sung to solmization syllables as much as it was played. Certainly, mid-sixteenth-century music copied in the 1570s was being used both ways. The largest surviving source of sixteenth-century ensemble music, GB-Lbl Add. MS 31390, is entitled *A booke of In nomines & other solfainge songs.*

Continental musical practices had strongly influenced English music in the first part of the sixteenth century; after the Reformation, English composers looked to new ways of composing, although many were still obviously aware of continental developments. English composers did not use the canzona or ricercare as their continental contemporaries did. Instead, music based on hymns, or a cantus firmus (that might have a sacred origin or be based on a popular song) or on a ground began to appear, as did a small number of fantasias and music based on dances. This included a significant number of the uniquely English In Nomine.[45] Taverner's In Nomine provided a central point for composition for both experienced composers such as Tye and by young composers, such as Byrd, embarking on their careers. Perhaps their composition also gave Catholic composers in a Protestant world the opportunity to compose in style reminiscent of music based on plainsong, or even for them to subversively and safely allude to their faith.[46] By the time Byrd left London for Lincoln in 1563, it is likely that he had composed all his Latin-titled consort works and most of his In Nomines. The earliest of these will have been student works such as the first three-part *Sermone blando* (BE 17/23). Byrd's consort works began to appear in manuscripts from around 1570.

As well as studying with Thomas Tallis, who served the Tudor monarchs from Henry VIII to Elizabeth I through the changes of the Reformation, Byrd learnt compositional skills from those composers with whose work his earliest compositions were found, such as Sheppard and William Mundy, and from other influential composers such as Philip van Wilder. He also became familiar with the works of English composers writing consort music during the sixteenth century, in particular, Tye, Robert White (*c.*1538–1574), Robert Parsons (1530–1572) and Alfonso Ferrabosco I (1543–1588). None of these sixteenth century contemporaries explored consort music to the same extent as Byrd.

Byrd was one of the first generation of musicians for whom instrumental performance on viols was an important part of his musical education. Instrumental music was beginning no longer to be considered of significantly less value than vocal music although it took time for it to acquire equal status. He was writing at a time when musical literacy was becoming increasingly important, particularly for ensemble playing.

The sixteenth century saw an extraordinary flowering of music in England. This was partly due to the musicality of the Tudors, the importance they placed on music and their patronage throughout the sixteenth century, which spread from the court into the aristocracy.[47] Byrd experienced musical life under four monarchs, Edward VI, Mary Tudor, Elizabeth I and James I & VI. Through his education, membership of the Chapel Royal and his patrons, he was ideally situated to explore the new concept of art music for consort playing.

1 See Harley, *William Byrd Gentleman of the Chapel Royal*, p. 14.

2 Tallis's signature is found on the manuscript, BL MS Lansdowne 763 f. 124v; see John Milsom, 'Tallis, Thomas', in Brian Harrison (ed.), *Oxford Dictionary of National Biography* (Oxford, 2004), 53, p. 746.

3 Alan Mould, *The English Chorister* (London, 2007), p. 81; quoted from Henry VIII's Canterbury statutes, as amended 1636, in English translation as found in *The Statutes of the Cathedral and Metropolitical Church of Christ,* Canterbury (Canterbury, 1926).

4 See Roger Bowers, 'To Chorus from Quartet', in John Morehen (ed.), *English Choral Practice 1400–1650* (Cambridge, 1996), pp. 1–47, p.32 and Alan Mould, *The English Chorister*, p. 77.

5 Jane Flynn, 'The Education of Choristers in England during the Sixteenth Century', in Morehen (ed.), *English Choral Practice 1400–1650*, pp. 180–200, at pp. 182–3.

6 Hyun-Ah Kim, *Humanism and the Reform of Sacred Music in Early Modern England* (Aldershot, 2008), pp. 118 and 124.

7 Arthur Francis Leach, *A History of Winchester College* (London, 1899; reprint 2013), p. 260.

8 Mould, *The English Chorister*, p. 90.

9 David Mateer, 'The Gyffard Partbooks: Composers, Owners, Dates and Provenance', *Royal Musical Research Chronicle,* 26 (1995), pp.19–43, at p. 38.

10 Kerry McCarthy, 'Evidence of Things Past', *Journal of the Royal Musical Association*, 135/2 (2010), pp. 405-411, p. 407.

11 Mateer, 'The 'Gyffard Partbooks: Composers, Owners, Dates and Provenance', p. 41.

12 John Harley, *The World of William Byrd*, (Farnham 2010), p. 46.

13 Ibid., p. 47.

14 Richard Turbet, 'Wings of Faith', *Musical Times,* 138 (December1997), pp. 5–10, p. 5;

15 Andrew Carwood, CD notes for *William Byrd The Great Service & Other Works*, The Cardinall's Musick, Andrew Carwood, (Recorded Arundel 2011, Hyperion CDA67937, Released 2012), pp. 4–5.

16 Mould, *The English Chorister* p. 96–7.

17 Flynn, 'The Education of Choristers in England during the Sixteenth Century', p. 194.

18 Mould, *The English Chorister*, p. 66.

19 Ibid., p. 113;

20 Victor I. Scherb, 'Playing at Maturity in John Redford's *Wit and Science*' in *SEL Studies in English Literature 1500–1900*, 45/2 (2005), pp. 271–97, at p. 271.

21 Ibid., p. 272.

22 Reavley Gair, *The Children of St Paul's: the story of a theatre company, 1553–1608* (Cambridge, 1982), p. 76.

23 Louise Rayment, 'A New Context for the Manuscript of *Wit and Science*' in *Early Theatre*, 17/1 (2014), pp. 49–73, at p. 50.

24 John Redford, *Wit and Science,* ed. Ben Byram-Wigfield (London, 2013), p. 43.

25 Ian Woodfield, *The Early History of the Viol* (Cambridge, 1984), pp. 208–9 and 213.

26 Richard Edwards, *The Paradise of Dainty Devices 1576–1606*, ed. Hyder Edward Rollins (Cambridge Mass., 1927), pp. 55–8.

27 Woodfield, *The Early History of the Viol*, pp. 206–7 and Peter Holman, *Four and Twenty Fiddlers* (Oxford, 1993), p. 70.

28 Ibid. Woodfield, p. 207.

29 Document E101/417/2; see Holman, *Four and Twenty Fiddlers*, p. 71.

30 Ibid. Holman, p. 73.

31 Ibid., p. 15; Woodfield, *The Early History of the Viol*, p. 94.

32 Richard Turbet, 'A Note on Philip van Wilder and Byrd', *Early Music Review*, 155 (August 2013), p. 19; David Humphreys, 'Wilder and Byrd; Wilder's *Aspice Domine* a 6', *Annual Byrd Newsletter*, 10 (May 2004), p. 26.

33 Woodfield, *The Early History of the Viol*; Holman, *Four and Twenty Fiddlers*, p. 70.

34 Holman, *Four and Twenty Fiddlers*, p. 75.

35 Michael Fleming, '"Such As Do Lawfully Exercise Any Art, Mistery, or Manual Occupation": Viol Making As a Trade or Occupation' in *Early English Viols* (Abingdon, 2016), p. 178.

36 Woodfield, *The Early History of the Viol*, p. 210.

37 Flynn, 'The Education of Choristers in England during the Sixteenth Century', p. 196.

38 Woodfield, *The Early History of the Viol*, p. 214.

39 Neighbour, *The Consort and Keyboard Music of William Byrd*, p. 52.

40 Mould, *The English Chorister*, p. 120.

41 Woodfield, *The Early History of the Viol*, pp. 214 and 222.

42 Robert White, *III Ritual Music and Lamentations*, ed. David Mateer, EECM 32 (London, Stainer and Bell, 1986), p.xi.

43 Holman, *Four and Twenty Fiddlers*, p. 80.

44 Annette Otterstedt, *The Viol: History of an Instrument* (Kassel, 2002), p. 158.

45 John Harper gives the total of 122 found in sources copied or printed after 1560. Harper, 'Ensemble and Lute Music', in Roger Bray (ed.), *Music in Britain The Sixteenth Century* (Oxford, 1995), p. 266.

46 John Bryan, '"Not Unlike a Confused Singing of Birds in a Grove": An Introduction to the In Nomine', *The Viol*, 6 (Spring 2007), pp. 15–19, at p. 15; Virginia Brookes, 'In Nomine: An Obscure Designation', *The Viol*, 6 (Spring 2007), pp. 22–25, at p. 22.

47 John Milsom, 'Music' in Boris Ford (ed.), *Sixteenth Century Britain*: The Cambridge Cultural History of Britain, 3 (Cambridge, 1992), pp. 168–207, at p. 170.

Chapter 2

The question of mode in Byrd's consort works

Looking at Byrd's consort music it becomes clear that he was living and working in a transitional period in which the use of modes was gradually superseded by a tonal approach to music. Finding the appropriate language for Byrd's use of chords and their relationship to each other presents a challenge. Before examining Byrd's music in detail, it is necessary to establish what is relevant to the structure of Byrd's instrumental consort music and find the musical language to describe it.

Identifying what is modal and what is the 'tonal' structure of the music of Byrd and his contemporaries has been a perennial problem for musicologists. In the first half of the twentieth century, scholars such as Edmund Fellowes described Byrd's music in terms of tonal harmony;[1] from the 1950s, modal theory has formed the basis of analysis of sixteenth-century music. The modal theory that has had the greatest influence on musicologists has been that labelled by the American academic Jessie Ann Owens as 'neo-modal'; in this theory, the twelve modes described by the Swiss theorist Heinrich Glarean in *Dodecachordan* (1547) are reduced to five transposable 'modes' (Dorian, Phrygian, Mixolydian, Aeolian and Ionian).[2] It was applied by H. K. Andrews in *The Technique of Byrd's Vocal Polyphony* (1966),[3] and most musicologists analysing Byrd's music have continued to follow this approach.

There are two problems facing analysis of sixteenth-century English music. Firstly, as Owens writes, 'English music *sounds* tonal and English music theory uses concepts associated with tonality well before either happens on the continent'.[4] Secondly, musicologists have to try to ascertain to what extent English composers were aware of and applied continental modal theory to their compositions. Both these questions obviously need to be asked in relation to Byrd's music.

In adapting forms of vocal music for instrumental performance and searching for new forms for textless instrumental music, sixteenth-century composers must have considered how their music was 'tonally' structured, i.e. the relationship between chords. Where particular chords are positioned became significant as did the degree of the scale on which they are found and the relationship between major and minor. This is still a much-discussed subject. In the examination of Byrd's music in this study, any reference to 'tonal' refers to the relationship between chords.

As Owens has stated, English sixteenth-century music may sound tonal in modern terms but as Margaret Bent points out, the presence of a triad in music (i.e. a chord of three tones) 'does not guarantee that the laws governing its succession will be those we have come to expect'.[5] In a footnote to *From Psalmody to Tonality*, Harold Powers comments on early English writers' apparent ignorance of continental theory.[6] Owens quotes Carl Dalhaus arguing against analysing Byrd's music from either a tonal or modal point of view.[7] Candace Bailey writes that '"Mode" was of little concern to English composers during most of the seventeenth century'.[8] John Harley has done significant work on Byrd's use of mode and key. In his book on Byrd's modal practice, he writes:

> How far modal theory was accepted in England is a matter which is difficult to determine. A few English sources mention the modes, but none deals with them at length. On the other hand, foreign treatises were available in England, and it would be hard to believe that they had no effect on the thinking of English musicians. In any case, since Byrd's music has much in common with music that was known to theorists, his works are bound to exhibit some of the characteristics they thought of as modal.[9]

It is likely that Byrd passed on his knowledge of theoretical concepts to his pupil, Thomas Morley (1557–1603), who dedicated his *Plaine and Easie Introduction to Practicall Musicke* to Byrd. Morley appears to be recording what he learnt from his teacher and makes little mention of mode. However, Byrd's instrumental compositions include works based on a cantus firmus, which necessitates some consideration of mode since the chants used may be classified by mode; similarly, he makes use of popular tunes in some of his compositions which are modal.

Owens considers both the modal and neo-modal approaches to analysis to be unsatisfactory:

> The problem, as I see it, is that none of these approaches employs concepts derived from theoretical writings that originated at approximately the same time and in the same geographical area as the music itself. Byrd surely did not employ the kind of modality we associate with Lasso or Palestrina, and still less either the modern version – "neo-modality"– or tonality. I believe that close reading of contemporary English theory can provide some of the elements on which a historically grounded approach

could be based.[10]

English treatises on music theory began to appear from 1561. These were not aimed at professional musicians. From the 1550s, music was also becoming part of an aristocratic education, where skilled musicians were being employed to teach musical skills and literacy to children in wealthy households. In the latter part of the century aristocratic amateurs were playing music for pleasure, including viol music.[11] The surviving English treatises on music from 1561 to the beginning of the seventeenth century were aimed at educating and teaching beginners. They were intended to provide the skills for practical music making, to teach notation of pitch and rhythm, solmization and elementary counterpoint. They can be divided into three types: treatises about how to make music; psalm books, some of which contained instruction for singers; and instrumental tutors.

In the first category, seven major treatises survive dating from 1584 to 1636: William Bathe, *A Briefe Introduction to the True Art of Music* (1584); the anonymous *The Pathway to Musicke* (1596); Thomas Morley, *A Plaine and Easie Introduction to Practicall Musicke* (1597); Thomas Ravenscroft, *Treatise of Musicke* (GB-Lbl MS Add 19758 of *c.*1610); Thomas Campion, *A New Way of Making Fowre Parts in Counterpoint* (*c.*1613); Elway Bevin, *A Briefe and Short Instruction of the Art of Musicke* (1631) and Charles Butler, *The Principles of Musick* (1636).[12] Only three of the authors, Thomas Morley, Thomas Ravenscroft and Elway Bevin, were professional musicians. The treatises were primarily concerned with teaching an understanding of music and practical music-making, rather than teaching composition skills, but they do give us an understanding of how music was perceived.[13]

In contrast, theoretical writing on music began to develop in Italy in the late fifteenth and early sixteenth centuries as part of a wider debate on theoretical issues.[14] The modal system originated out of classifying chant melodies. This was then applied to polyphonic composition. However, as academics researching this have discovered, there is not any single aspect about which all the sources are in agreement.[15] Henrich Glarean (1488–1563), a Swiss monk, expounded his theories in *Dodecachordon* (1547) and defined twelve modes. Gioseffo Zarlino (1517–1590), strongly influenced by number theory, also adopted twelve modes in *Insitutioni harmoniche* (1558). In *Dimostrationi harmoniche* (1571), he renumbered the modes of his original classification. Other theorists, such as the German Gallus Dressler (1533–*c.*1585) in *Praecepta musicae poeticae* (1563), attempted to link the principles of modality coherently with the rules applied to contrapuntal composition. Whether modal theory was actually used by composers when writing music is debatable. Harley suggests that 'it was perhaps inevitable that attempts to discover a system underlying musical procedures should lead to the formulation of principles which, to a greater or lesser degree, were interpreted as governing them'.[16]

Common to both English and Continental theorists is the use of the Gamut, combining the seven note names with the six hexachord syllables (ut, re, mi, fa, sol, la).[17] In continental music the Gamut was seen as being made up of three hexachords built into a universal scale containing both B♭ and B♮. There were rules for moving between the hexachords that define the notes in the scale. Normal practice was to work with 2 scales, with or without a B♭. The English writers, with one exception, set down three scales for the writing of music and applying solmization rules, one with no flats, one with one flat and one with two flats.[18] In his treatise, *A Plaine and Easie Introduction to Practical Musicke* (1597), Thomas Morley is reluctant to use a two-flat scale but acknowledges its existence. Each scale is solmized in a different way by each writer but the principles of application remain the same. They are ways of naming pitches (but which do not fix the final or mode of a composition). Scales in this context 'tell us the names of the pitches but not how to think about their use in a musical composition. But knowing their names will help us understand the concepts associated with the actual pitches of musical compositions'.[19] The anonymous author of *The Pathway to Musicke* (1596) is the only writer who makes references to modes.[20] Instead of referring to mode, the other writers use the terms 'key', 'tone' and 'air'. Owens summarizes this, grouping them together under 'tonalities', meaning the combining of key (the final), 6 'tones' or 'airs' (an ordered pitch collection) and the three scales. Further rules for composition included what notes were allowed in a particular key and where cadences should be placed.

The English theorists of the late sixteenth century were apparently recording what happened in practice. Starting from this approach helps us look at the music of Byrd and his contemporaries in a new light. Owens compares the tonalities of Byrd's music in *Cantiones sacrae* with those described by Charles Butler (*c.*1560–1647) in *The Principles of Musick*, published 1636,[21] and notes in *Concepts of Pitch in English Music Theory* that she believes Byrd composes in eleven of the twelve tonalities described as frequent by Butler.[22]

English music, both vocal and instrumental, developed its own peculiar characteristics during the latter part of the sixteenth century; composers were selective in what they adopted from Continental music. Harley concludes that 'there is only limited evidence external to their music that English composers thought of composition in modal terms.'[23] Three signature accidentals (no accidental, one flat and two flats) relating to the three scales are commonly found in English sixteenth-century consort music, as recorded by the English theorists but just because Byrd's compositional methods parallel those described by the theorists, they are not necessarily based on these theories. Byrd's chorister background means he could not have avoided being influenced by mode, but that his music does not reflect its ordered application. The use of hexachord theory may have been more important than the use of modes.[24] However, research by Rebecca Herissone suggests that late sixteenth century, English theorists were rather poorly informed about the hexachord system.[25] By the end of the sixteenth century, there was movement away from hexachords.[26] Bathe, in his treatise of 1584, fails to clearly explain hexachord rules and his work is significant for encouraging the adoption of the seven-note scale.

Byrd's use of mode and key

John Harley identifies 14 keys used by Byrd in 284 works, nine of which are found in his consort works.[27] He defines the key of a piece as the last note of piece combined with the number of flats notated as signature accidentals. The nine keys are the key of A with no accidental, G and C using all three scales (i.e. no accidental, one flat and two flats) and F and D with one flat. Harley remarks on the tonal tendency of Byrd's keys, defining tonality as the 'relationship between pitches'.[28] He states that in Byrd's music, it is clear that chordal patterns are based on the relationship of a fifth and not determined by mode, and that neighbouring areas of tonality centred on notes a minor third apart are commonly found.[29] Harley writes that it is difficult to define the point at which a mode becomes a key. It is impossible to separate pieces which seem most clearly to be modal from the notion of key, and Byrd's keys retain elements of modality.[30] The use of chords, both major and minor, is of great importance. Byrd also recognised the difference between flat and sharp keys and the contrast they achieved.[31]

As Harley also stresses, the gradual increase of the importance of the bass during the sixteenth century is of significance.[32] This is already apparent in Byrd's comparatively early motets.[33] Harley attributes Byrd's development of strong bass lines to experience gained from the composer's familiarity with keyboard and dance music.[34] In *A Plaine and Easie Introduction to Practicall Musicke*, Byrd's pupil Morley writes that in certain circumstances, the bass can provide the basis of harmony.[35] Herissone suggests that it was a lack of attachment by sixteenth-century English composers to modal theory that led to a development of harmonic tonality almost a hundred years before it became widely accepted on the continent.[36] She also observes that many European composers related major and minor to the modes, whereas English composers separated the two concepts, which led to a different approach.[37]

Byrd uses a bass line to support the tonal organisation of his music and define the key of a work; it often supports cadences with strong intervals of a fifth or fourth. His compositions reflect the transition from the modal to tonal systems.[38] As Harley writes, 'Byrd's music lies partly within and partly without two theoretical systems, neither of which is wholly relevant to it.'[39]

Harley's definition of tonality in Byrd's music as being a 'relationship between pitches' is probably the most helpful approach examining the chordal structure in his instrumental consort music In particular, the relationship of a fifth and Byrd's use of major and minor in 'keys' a minor third apart are likely indicators in identifying the progression of – and the tonal relationship between – chords in his music. Campion, in his 1613 treatise, recognises the importance of the fifth in major and minor harmony.[40]

Candace Bailey has made the link between the style of the Baroque and that of English music of the early years of the (17th) century'.[41] She sees the new style of the Baroque as the adoption of a different tonal language that can be found in early 17th century English music. She believes that the keyboard music of Orlando Gibbons (1583–1625) played a pivotal role, in the development of this new language, particularly his fantasias.[42] Gibbons was not a pupil of Byrd but they were colleagues at the Chapel Royal and collaborated with John Bull (1563–1628) in the production of *Parthenia*, the first printed collection of keyboard music in England published in 1612/13. Rebecca Herissone also concludes that seventeenth-century English theorists were at the 'forefront' of the modernization of music theory.[43] Byrd's music would seem to be part of the progression towards this new tonal language and his consort fantasias will be of particular interest when assessing this.

How Byrd constructed his consort music is relevant to the emergence and development of his personal instrumental style. His fantasias are identified by the number of parts and the basic tonality.[44] For example, his first six-part fantasia is known as Fantasia 6/F, it has a signature accidental of one flat and the final chord is a major chord on F. This works well with Owens's definition of 'tonalities' combining the final and the three scales. The second six-part fantasia, Fantasia 6/g1, has a signature accidental of two flats and a final on G; Byrd raises the third in the final chord of both sections in the fantasia to a b♮, but minor chords on G form the basis of its structure.

Modal influence on Byrd's music cannot be ignored, as seen in his In Nomines and in use of popular song, but the development of his individual instrumental style reflects the juxtaposition of the modal and polyphonic music of the Renaissance with the movement towards the development of modern harmony in the Baroque. Comprehending this is essential to understanding the structures Byrd found to support music without words.

1 Jessie Ann Owens, 'Concepts of Pitch in English Music Theory', in Cristle Collins Judd (ed.), *Tonal Structures in Early Music* (New York, 1998), pp. 183–246, at p. 184.

2 Ibid., p. 186

3 H.K. Andrews, *The Technique of Byrd's Vocal Polyphony* (London, 1966).

4 Owens, 'Concepts of Pitch in English Music Theory', p. 183.

5 Margaret Bent, 'The Grammar of Early Music: Preconditions for Analysis', in Cristle Collins Judd (ed.), *Tonal Structures in Early Music*, pp.15–60, at p. 31.

6 Harold Powers, 'From Psalmody to Tonality', in Cristle Collins Judd (ed.), *Tonal Structures in Early Music*, pp. 275–340, at p. 334.

7 Owens, 'Concepts of Pitch in English Music Theory', p. 188.

8 Candace Bailey, 'Concepts of Key in Seventeenth-Century English Keyboard Music', in Cristle Collins Judd (ed.), *Tonal Structures in Early Music*, pp. 247–274, at p. 250.

9 John Harley, *William Byrd's Modal Practice* (Aldershot, 2004), p. ix.

10 Owens, 'Concepts of Pitch in English Music Theory', p. 188.

11 Harper, 'Ensemble and Lute Music', p. 270; Woodfield, *The Early History of the Viol*, p. 227. Michael Fleming also suggests that viols were found in non-aristocratic homes; see Michael Fleming, 'An "Old Old Violl" and "Other Lumber": Musical Remains in Provincial, Non-Noble England *c*.1580–1660', *The Galpin* ♭ *Society Journal*, 58 (May 2005), pp. 89–99.

12 Detailed information of the treatises can be found in Owens, 'Concepts of Pitch in English Music Theory', pp. 190–230 and Rebecca Herissone, *Music Theory in Seventeenth-Century England* (Oxford, 2000).

13 Elway Bevin, *A Briefe and Short Instruction of the Art of Musicke*, ed. Denis Collins (Aldershot , 2007).

14 Iain Fenlon, 'Music and Society', in Iain Fenlon (ed.), *The Renaissance* (London, 1989), pp. 1–62, at p. 3.

15 Frans Wiering, 'Internal and External Views of the Modes, in Cristle Collins Judd (ed.), *Tonal Structures in Early Music*, pp. 87–107, at p. 88.

16 Harley, *William Byrd's Modal Practice*, p. 14.

17 The six notes of the hexachord follow the pattern of tone, tone, semitone, tone, tone.

18 Owens, 'Concepts of Pitch in English Music Theory', p. 192.

19 Ibid., p. 215.

20 Morley accuses the writer of lifting his information from continental treatises; Owens, 'Concepts of Pitch in English Music Theory', p. 212.

21 Jessie Ann Owens, *Charles Butler's Principles of Musick (1636)* (Aldershot, 2009).

22 Owens, 'Concepts of Pitch in English Music Theory', p. 232.

23 Harley, *William Byrd's Modal Practice*, p. 130.

24 Ibid., p. 32.

25 Herissone, *Music Theory in Seventeenth-Century England*, p. 78.

26 Ibid., p. 77.

27 Harley excludes Byrd's *Gradualia* and Masses and Services; Harley, *William Byrd's Modal Practice*, p. 29. He counts pieces such as the Pavan and Galliard 6/C as one work.

28 Ibid., p. 25.

29 Ibid., p. 37.

30 Ibid., for example in the Aeolian/Dorian, on A, D (♭) and G (♭♭).

31 Ibid., p. 29.

32 Ibid., p. 21 and 74.

33 Ibid., p.74.

34 Ibid., pp. 74–75.

35 Herissone, *Music Theory in Seventeenth-Century England*, p. 122.

36 Ibid., p. 113.

37 Ibid., p. 174.

38 Anne Martin, 'The Consort Music of William Byrd and its relationship to preceding and contemporary sixteenth century consort music' (MMus Dissertation, University of Surrey, 1998)., p. 65.

39 Harley, *William Byrd's Modal Practice*, p. 133.

40 Herissone, *Music Theory in Seventeenth-Century England*, n. 41 p. 122; reference to Thomas Morley, *A Plain & Easy Introduction to Practical Music*, ed. Alec Harman, (New York, 1963, rev. 1973), pp. 227–8 and 242–3.

41 Candace Bailey, 'Orlando Gibbons, Keyboard Music and the Beginnings of the Baroque; New Considerations of a Musical Style' in the *International Review of the Aesthetics and Sociology of Music (IRASM)*, 37/2 (2006), pp.136–7.

42 Ibid., p. 139.

43 Herissone, *Music Theory in Seventeenth-Century England*, p. 224.

44 As used by Neighbour, *The Consort and Keyboard Music of William Byrd*.

Chapter 3

The use of compass, range, clefs and signature accidentals in the music of Byrd and his contemporaries

As instrumental music began to develop post-Reformation, subtle differences between vocal and instrumental music could be seen emerging in the notated parts. Of particular note is the effect the Reformation had on voice ranges in English liturgical choral music and its notation. Over the last few years it has been realised there is a significant amount of information that can be learnt about sixteenth-century music by looking at its notation and at the pitch range of the parts. Considerable research has been carried out in examining the use of voice or instrumental ranges, clefs and signature accidentals in sixteenth-century music. As instrumental consort music developed during the sixteenth century, it began to acquire its own characteristics, separating it from vocal music. Looking at how and what is notated can help to identify whether the music was written for voices or instruments or intended for both singing and playing and in identifying particular traits and developments in instrumental music. Examining notation can help identify the original function of textless sixteenth-century music, particularly where there is some doubt as to its original purpose, as well as illustrating how instrumental music was becoming distinctive and separate from vocal music. It can enhance our understanding of the way in which liturgical and domestic repertoires can be distinguished from one another. This chapter looks at whether Byrd's use of compass, range, clefs and signature accidentals in his consort music reflects the differences appearing commonly between vocal and instrumental music and whether his usage is the same as that of his contemporaries.

In 2014, Roger Bowers published research into the effect of the Reformation on the compass (overall range), part ranges and clefs of English post-Reformation liturgical vocal music.[1] This showed that by *c.*1570 the most common pre-Reformation compass of liturgical vocal music of 23 notes across all the parts had been reduced to 20 notes, and that the range of each part was reduced from 11 notes to 9 or 10.[2] (An exception to this is the music written during the reign of Mary Tudor 1553–1558.[3]) Bowers suggests the reduction was due to the greater austerity in Reformation liturgical music and to the change from the melismatic setting of Latin to the one syllable per note of settings in English. In contrast, the wider compass and ranges found in pre-Reformation vocal liturgical music can be found in consort music after 1547.

Post-Reformation, the four ranges of English voices (boy treble, falsetto alto, tenor and bass) were each truncated by the removal of up to three semitones, resulted in the compressing of the compass of vocal pieces.[4] Parts continued to be notated as before, the bottom note of the bass line being notated as F, in spite of the three lowest notes being lost. Treble parts lost notes from the top of their range; tenor parts lost notes from either end. To make best use of the timbre of each voice, the music was raised so that singers could sing in the normal comfortable range of each part. The sounding compass became approximately G/A♭ in the bass to f'' in the treble but notated from F to d''.[5] Opinions differ as to what exactly was 'lost' from the top of note ranges. Simon Ravens and Andrew Parrott argue that Tudor performing pitch was at least a semitone above modern pitch.[6] David Wulfstan argued for a minor third.[7] This argument is not relevant to consort music; what is relevant are the differences between how voice and viol parts were notated, in particular any apparent difference in the use of clefs and pitch.

Bowers's research was specifically concerned with post-Reformation liturgical music. It did not include Latin motets written after 1547. These are important in considering how Byrd and his contemporaries used ranges and notation. Two distinct types of vocal music with sacred texts were composed after 1547, these being liturgical music written in English for the reformed church and post-Reformation Latin-texted music with sacred texts, which was destined for private performance in aristocratic homes and universities.[8]

If after 1547 liturgical vocal music had a narrower compass, then a wider compass of 23 notes or more in textless music is likely to be an indication that it is instrumental consort music. There is also the issue of music intended for both singing and playing– textless music is not necessarily instrumental music; it is not always clear whether some music was conceived to be performed vocally or instrumentally or had a dual purpose. (Vocal music was also commonly performed on viols and other instruments.) A consort of viols consisting of treble, tenor and bass instruments normally had a compass of at least 23 notes, with a possible extension to 26 or 28 notes.[9] Viols with six strings had a potential range of 19 notes from the lowest open string to the top fret of the top string.[10]

There is also a change in the clef combinations in English liturgical vocal music before and after 1547. Before the Reformation, the clef combination for four-part English choral music was G2, C2, C4 and F4. After the Reformation the norm became C1, C3, C4 and F4.[11] By 1570, the common pattern for vocal music with sacred texts was five voices: treble or meane, two altos, tenor and bass, with a predominant clef combination of C1, C3, C3, C4 and F4.[12]

To investigate for this chapter any differences between the compass, ranges and notation found in instrumental and in vocal music by Byrd and his contemporaries, all working in England between 1550 and *c.*1590, data was collected from a sample of 72 vocal works with sacred texts (both English liturgical music and motets with Latin texts) in four to seven parts by five English composers (John Sheppard, Christopher Tye, Thomas Tallis, Robert White (*c.*1538–1574) and Robert Parsons (1530–1572) and 77 consort pieces in four to seven parts by 13 composers working in England (Tye, William Whytebroke (1501–1569), Henry Stonings (*fl.c.*1600), Tallis, Osbert Parsley (1511–1585), Thomas Preston (d.1563), Nicholas Strogers (d.1575), White, Parsons, William Mundy, Clement Woodcock (*c.*1540–1590), William Daman (c.1540–1591) and Alfonso Ferrabosco I (1543–1588)).[13] Data from 86 pavans and galliards in four or five parts was also included. For Byrd's music, the data examined came from ninety-two vocal works with sacred texts (both English liturgical music and Latin motets) in four to seven parts and from his 29 surviving consort works in four to six parts, including his pavans and galliard. (The overall compass of notes is known in only 23 of Byrd's consort works in four to six-parts from surviving manuscripts or print source; six are missing a treble part.) A small amount of liturgical music with Latin texts was also included. The sample of dance music was specifically restricted to pavans and galliards, both music written for dancing and music intended for instrumental performance. These were the two most common forms of dance music used in consort music and are the only two dance forms found in Byrd's consort music.

A narrow compass is defined as a piece with an overall range of 21 or less and a wide compass of 23 notes or more. Music with a compass of 22 notes falls in the middle. A compass of 21 notes or less was chosen as the contraction to a compass of 20 notes in vocal music only became the norm by *c.*1570.[14] These numbers are arrived at by counting the pitches from the lowest note of a piece to the highest counting a note name as one pitch regardless of accidentals.

Note compass in vocal music with sacred texts and consort music

An examination of the data showed a distinct difference in compass between a significant amount of vocal and instrumental music. Only 8% of 72 vocal compositions with sacred texts in four to seven parts by the 13 English contemporaries of Byrd were found to have a compass of 23 notes or more; a further ten have a compass of 22 notes making a total of 16 works (22%) with a compass of 22 notes or more (Figure 1). Among these are found six liturgical works with a compass of 23 notes or more by Sheppard, Tye and White identified as having been composed at the end of Henry VIII's reign or during that of Mary Tudor. For example, Sheppard's *Missa Cantate*, likely written during the reign of Mary Tudor has a compass of 23 notes.[15]

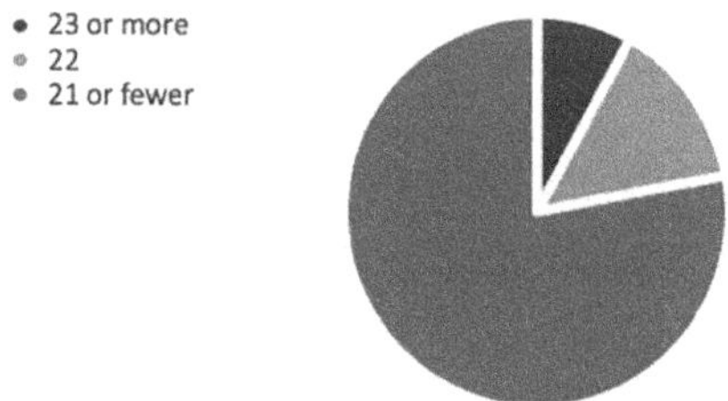

Figure 1 Compass in vocal music with sacred texts excluding Byrd (72)[16]

In 77 consort compositions by Byrd's contemporaries (excluding dances) in four to seven parts, 70% contain a compass of 23 notes or more; 14% have 21 notes or less (Figure 2). Fifty-two of the consort compositions are In Nomines, of which only two had a compass

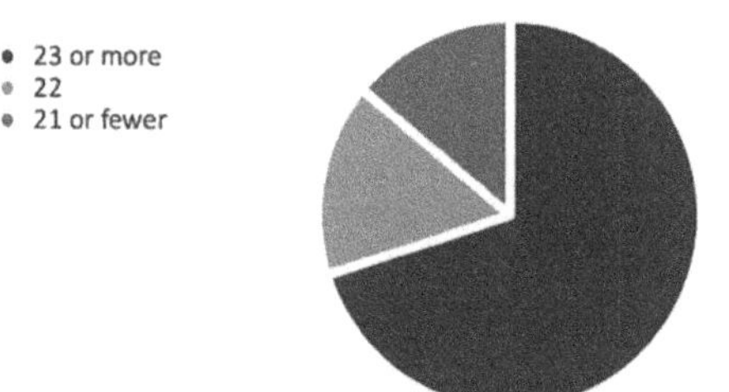

Figure 2 Compass in consort music excluding dances and Byrd (77)

of less than 22 notes and 81% are found to contain 23 notes or more including those by Tye, who made the largest contribution to English consort music in the mid-sixteenth century. Twenty seven of his 30 pieces of consort music in four to six parts have a compass of 23 notes or more; 16 have a compass of 26 notes and one has 28 notes.[17] Just 13 works were found to have a range of 19 to 22 notes. Most music with a compass of 21 or 22 notes was probably written to be sung or played but two of Woodcock's consort pieces, his *Browning* Fantasy and *Hackney*, have a compass of just 20 notes, but all the hallmarks of instrumental music. *Hackney* is full of fast repeated notes suggesting it might have been written for wind instruments, which would have had a narrower range than viols.[18] Music with a wide compass can clearly be linked to instrumental music but that with a narrower compass is not necessarily for voices.

Far fewer pavans and galliards with a compass of 23 notes or more are found compared with the other consort music. Dances were more likely to have been played on a range of instruments, including wind instruments, Out of 86 pavans and galliards in four or five parts, only 26% have a compass of 23 notes or more. A significant number have a compass of 22 notes (Figure 3).

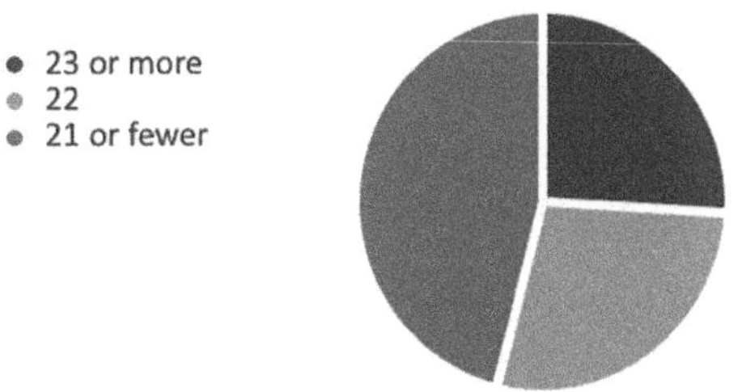

Figure 3 Compass in pavans and galliards excluding Byrd (86)

The narrow compass found in pavans and galliards could also have been because some notated dance music may have been intended for players of moderate ability or to provide a basis for improvisation by professional musicians. Popular melodies were commonly used when improvising to provide dance music.[19] There are still a greater number of pieces with a compass of 22 notes or more than are found in vocal music with sacred texts. The music sampled consisted of pavans and galliards from the Lumley part-books dating from the 1540s, to which simpler dance music was added later in the century (MSS Royal Appendix 74–6),[20] *Pavans, Galliards, Almains, and other short Aeirs* by Anthony Holborne (*c.*1545–1602) published in 1599, three pavans by Joseph Lupo (d.1616), Ferrabosco I, and the earliest surviving pavan by Peter Philips (1560/61–1628),[21] plus two pairs of pavans and galliards by Augustine Bassano (d. 1604).[22]

There is a clear difference in the compass found in the dance music of the Lumley collection, where the majority of pavans had a compass of 20 notes or less, and stylised works written for instrumental performance such as those found in Holborne's collection where six pavans and 15 galliards have a compass of 23 notes or more. Only one galliard from the Lumley collection has a compass of more than 21 notes. Some of Holborne's dances have a narrower compass of 21 notes or less (four galliards and 13 pavans), which can be explained by the fact that Holborne states at the beginning of his collection that it is suitable for viols, violins and wind instruments, the latter likely to have a narrower range. However, a range of 22 notes or less became common for stylised pavans and galliards.

Compass in Byrd's music.

The compass found in Byrd's vocal music with sacred texts is very similar to those of his contemporaries; there is a slightly higher incidence of works with a compass of 21 notes or less. The percentage (14%) of works with a compass of 22 notes is identical. In 92 vocal works by Byrd contained in the three volumes of Latin motets, *Cantiones Sacrae,* his English Anthems and his service music for the Anglican liturgy, 83% has a compass of 21 notes or less.[23] Only three works have a compass of 23 notes. All are found in *Cantiones Sacrae*: for example, the six-part *Tribue Domine* (EECM56/29) of 1575 is a large three-section motet, in which, John Milsom writes, Byrd 'gazes back into the Tudor past'.[24] All of Byrd's English anthems and services have a compass of 21 notes or less. His Latin-texted motets contain a slightly higher incidence of works with a compass of 22 notes (25%) but still have a small percentage of works with 23 notes or more (6%) and a large percentage of those with 21 notes or less (69%; Figure 4).

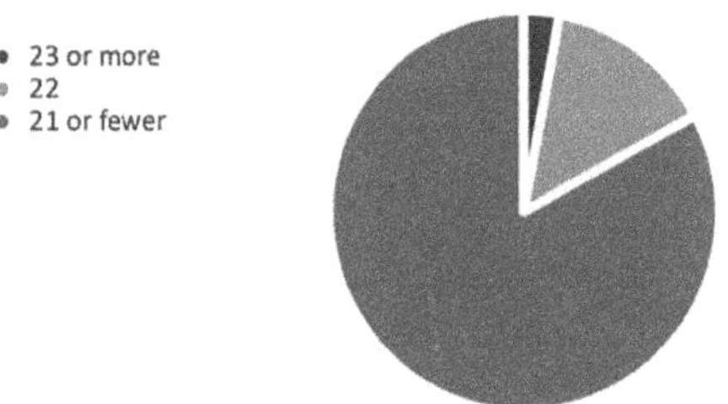

Figure 4 Compass in Byrd's vocal music with sacred texts

When comparing similar genres, the compass found in Byrd's consort music is very similar to that of his contemporaries. Two of his fantasias have an unusually small compass of 20 notes but so do a four-part work, *A fancy*, by Ferrabosco I and Parsons's six-part *The Song called trumpets*, both of which influenced Byrd, again illustrating that some textless instrumental works do have a small compass.[25] Complete parts survive for 20 of Byrd's consort works in four to six parts (excluding dances). On initial examination, a higher percentage of Byrd's consort music than that of his contemporaries would seem to have a narrower range. However if his textless Latin-titled works are removed, only two of Byrd's consort pieces have a compass of 21 notes or less (Fantasias 6/F and 4/g). Byrd's Latin-titled textless works may not have been written for any specific medium but to be either played by viols or sung to solfa syllables. Excluding the Latin-titled textless works (and dances), Byrd's consort music and that of his contemporaries have the same percentage (86%) of works with a compass of 22 notes or more (Figure 5). A smaller percentage have 23 notes or more (50%), but of course the sample is very small. Byrd's two pavans and one galliard have a compass of 22, 21 and 19 notes, all reflecting the compass and apparent convention found elsewhere.

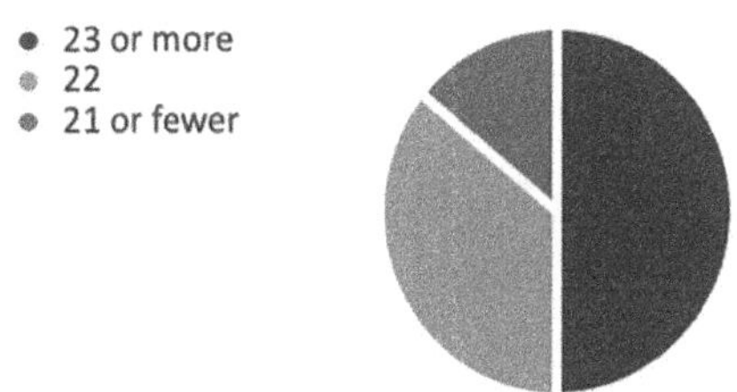

Figure 5 Compass in Byrd's consort music excluding Latin-titled works (14)

Commonly, a clear difference can be seen between the compass found in vocal liturgical music with English texts and Latin motets, and that found in consort music composed after 1547 by Byrd and his contemporaries. A wide compass of 23 notes or more is much more common in consort music. A compass of 21 notes or less is not as common, but is found in pavans and galliards and a small number of fantasias.

Voice and part ranges in vocal music with sacred texts and consort music

In vocal compositions with sacred texts by Byrd's contemporaries, the data showed that individual note ranges in both treble and bass vocal parts also tend to be narrower than those found in consort music. Only 21% of upper parts out of 70 from 66 vocal pieces with sacred texts have a range of 11 notes or more. No indication of instrumentation is given in manuscripts, but most consort music was clearly for viols. In contrast to the vocal upper parts, 40% of treble viol parts from 77 consort works (excluding Byrd) have a range of 11 notes or more. If upper parts containing the In Nomine cantus firmus taken from Taverner's *Missa Gloria tibi Trinitas* are excluded from the consort sample of treble parts, this figure rises to 62%.[26]

At first sight, only a slight difference can be seen between bass vocal parts and bass parts from the consort music. 52% of vocal bass parts have a range of 11 notes or more compared with 55% of the instrumental bass parts. But this is slightly deceptive as only 2.5% of bass vocal parts have a range of 12 notes or more compared with 29% of the bass parts found in the consort music, showing that a large wide range is more commonly found in bass viol parts. The ranges of inner parts are much closer between vocal and consort music. In both cases, around half of the inner parts have a range of 11 notes or more. Note ranges in all parts were found generally to be smaller in pavans and galliards. This probably partly reflects their suitability for various instruments with differing ranges.

In the music of Byrd's contemporaries, ranges of a large number of treble and bass parts can be shown to reflect the differences between post-Reformation vocal and instrumental music and in some instances help to identify instrumental music. There are a small number of exceptions, such as Tye's *Quaesumus omnipotens*,[27] which has both a compass of 23 notes and wide voice ranges.[28] There is also a significant number of vocal works with wide individual ranges but a compass of less than 22 notes, resulting in a greater overlap between voices, as in Tallis's *Derelinquit impius* in *Cantiones Sacrae* of 1575.[29] The consort music with wide individual parts usually has less overlap between the parts and a wide compass.

Voice and part ranges in Byrd's music

Looking at Byrd's music, we find that differences in range between his vocal and consort music are less evident than those found in his contemporaries' music. Parts with narrower note ranges are found in Byrd's English-texted sacred vocal music but are not as common in the Latin-texted works, illustrating a distinction between liturgical music and music with sacred texts for domestic use. Thirty percent of top vocal lines from 92 vocal works with sacred texts by Byrd, have a range of 11 notes or more as do 36% of known treble parts from

21 consort pieces by Byrd, excluding his pavans and galliard. This rises to 53% if cantus firmus parts are excluded. However, 15% of Byrd's top vocal parts are found to have 12 notes or more compared with just two treble viol parts. Nearly all of these are found in the Latin-texted motets in the *Cantiones Sacrae* of 1575 and 1591. It is clear that Byrd probably had higher expectations of his treble voices than of most of his treble viol players; this could be related to the limitations of his players or, as is more likely, the limitations of available viols.

As in the music of his contemporaries, the ranges of inner parts are found to be close in Byrd's vocal and consort music. There is however a noticeable difference in the percentage of wide ranging inner parts between Byrd's Latin-texted motets and his English-texted liturgical music, the Latin works having a much higher number of parts with a range of 11 notes or more (72% compared with 25%). Thirty-nine percent of inner parts from the Latin-texted music have a range of 12 notes or more as do 41.5% of those in Byrd's consort music.

The use of tenor parts in consort music is interesting. An overlap of inner parts is found consistently in both vocal and sixteenth-century consort music. In vocal music, where there are two inner parts, the higher part normally has the clef C3 and the lower is notated in C4. In writing inner parts for tenor viol, composers seem to have often followed a similar principle, with one higher and one lower part. The question needs to be asked as to whether dividing the music between two tenor viols using different ranges was for purely practical reasons, and if so, what implications that has for the technical capabilities of viols at this time. In the mid-sixteenth century, Tye was apparently already exploring a wide range in tenor parts in his consort music. In the vocal music surveyed, only two combined tenor parts, going down to A, were found to have a range of 14 notes; two, containing a B♭, had a range of 12 and 13 notes. In Tye's twenty-one In Nomines, seven tenor parts contained the low B♭; three of these have combined tenor parts of 13 notes and four have combined tenor pars of 14 notes up to a'.

In Byrd's fifteen Latin motets contained in *Cantiones Sacrae* of 1575, all of the combined tenor parts (with the clefs C3 and C4) have a c or B♭ as their lowest notes. Two have a combined range of 15 notes from B♭–b♭' and two a combined range of 14 notes from B♭/B–a'.) In some consort works, Byrd uses tenor viols in a similar way. In the In Nomine 5/4 the combined tenor parts have a range of 15 notes, from c to c". The Prelude and Ground also contains this combined tenor range and in Byrd's *Browning* Fantasy, the combined tenor parts range down to B♭ and up 15 notes to b♭'. Only one other surviving consort work by Byrd uses this low tenor note, Fantasia 4/g.

Where Byrd does differ from most of his contemporaries is in his use of wide bass parts. These are found in his consort music but also in his Latin motets. In the Latin-titled motets, 74% of 54 bass parts have a range of 11 notes or more and 30% have a range of 12 notes or more, compared with the 2.5% found in the vocal music of his contemporaries. This relates partly to the differences between vocal music for the liturgy and Latin motets for domestic use, but none of Tallis's motets in the *Cantiones Sacrae* of 1575 have a range of more than 11 notes, whereas six of Byrd's do. In Byrd's consort music (excluding his dances), 82% of 28 bass parts have a range of 11 notes or more. Twelve (43%) have a range of 12–13 notes. If the Latin-titled textless consort works are excluded, this rises to 55%, a larger number than that found in his contemporaries reflecting Byrd's interest in the bass line. The percentage of bass parts in the consort music with a really wide range is high but Byrd, as with his treble parts, also expected basses singing his Latin motets to have a wide range.

An F is the most common lowest note in Byrd's bass voice parts. From the composition of his In Nomines onwards, Byrd also commonly uses an F or sometimes a G as his lowest note for bass viol parts. The majority of his surviving bass viol parts fall in the range of F to c′. Excluding the Latin-titled consort works and the three dances, Byrd rarely writes a bass viol part of less than 11 notes. Of his remaining 18 consort works, where ranges are known, just Fantasias 4/g and 3/C1 have a bass part of less than 11 notes. (There are a number of Latin motets that have a bass part of ten notes or less.) Three of Byrd's In Nomines and all of his five- and six-part fantasias – including his *Browning* Fantasy – have a bass part of 12 or 13 notes, as do two of his Latin-titled textless works. Extending the use of the bass viol was something Byrd was doing from early on in his composing career.

Three of the motets by Byrd in the *Cantiones Sacrae* of 1575 with a range of 12 or 13 notes have a bass part notated down to a low E or E♭, low for a bass voice. However, we do not know exactly what pitch these were sung at. *Aspice Domine quia facta est*, for example, could easily have been sung at a higher pitch than the notation suggests. Byrd obviously sometimes expects bass voices to have a wide range, but he does not notate any bass vocal part down to D as he does in the bass lines in Fantasias 6/g1 and 6/g2. One bass part in Fantasia 6/g2 has a range of 13 notes, reaching from low D to b♭. Fantasia 6/g1 also has a bass part with a low D, which contains 11 notes reaching to g.

In *Early English Viols*, John Bryan remarks how rare it is to find bass viol parts in sixteenth-century consort music extending down to a low D on the open bottom string, suggesting that this indicates that this was little used before soundposts were common.[30]

The upper open string of the bass viol was also similarly rarely used.[31] Viols with six strings had a potential individual range of 19 notes from the lowest open string to the top fret of the highest string.[32] Very few viol pieces from before the early 1600s utilize the extremes of the viol registers and low notes were avoided.[33] Bryan suggests two possible reasons for the avoidance of notes at the extremes of ranges. It could be related to conventions of vocal tessitura and limitations of the Gamut or, as is more likely, instruments were limited in tonal quality at the extremes of ranges.

Non-standardisation of sounding pitch would seem to have been taken for granted before soundposts were added to viols; Ganassi recommended in 1542 that players should move the bridges of their instruments if it helped to achieve different pitch levels.[34] He considered this action appropriate, in order to correct badly designed viols.[35] This would have presumably meant that, if the bridge was moved downwards, low D would no longer be played on an open string. This cannot, however, explain how Tye, who died in 1572, was able to regularly use low D in his consort works, as his viol bass parts commonly have a range of 12–14 notes. Moving the bridge would affect the upper register. In twenty-three of his five-part In Nomines and Latin-titled works, written in the mid-sixteenth-century, Tye demands a low D of his bass players, which raises the question as to whether some players had access to particularly advanced instruments or strings.[36] In his vocal music Tye wrote no bass part wider than 11 notes and only one anthem, *I will exalt Thee O Lord*, had a bass part notated down to D, but it does not necessarily mean the bass voice was singing this note. It is very possible that clefs and pitch were only given for the convenience of notating the music without ledger lines.

In all except two[37] of 23 of Tye's consort works, any bass D could be transposed up an octave if necessary. However, the bass part for *Dum transisset sabbatum II*, contains a range of 14 notes and an astonishing number of nine Ds, including in two passages with running crotchets, and finishes on an E. The bass part would cross above the tenor part if transposed up. So although it was unusual, Tye probably had access to a bass viol with a reliable open D string, perhaps played by himself.

In the two bass parts in Fantasia 6/g1, Byrd explores a wide combined range from D to d'; the bass one part reaches the high d' and the second bass goes down to the D, playing it four times. The bridge could have possibly been moved for both of these parts if necessary, but equally, three of the low Ds could be transposed up an octave. If the fourth were transposed, then it would result in the two bass lines crossing, although the music would not be significantly affected. In Fantasia 6/g2 the first bass part has the conventional range of F to c'; the second bass reaches from D to b♭ and contains seven Ds. Transposing the D up an octave is feasible for all except one, found in a running crotchet passage, which also includes an E. If transposed up an octave, the part would cross above the tenor line. This bass part has a range of 13 notes. (With the exception of an early, Latin-titled work, *Te lucis* a 4 (I), which survives only in lute tablature, the only consort work by Byrd containing a bass part with a high e' is the six-part Galliard, probably written after 1600.)

No source containing the bass parts of these two six-part fantasias survive from before 1600 so we cannot be sure that Byrd originally wrote low Ds in the bass parts or added them later. However, if they were original, then probably bass viols and strings were improving in tonal quality by the late 1580s. It seems likely that by the time he wrote these two fantasias, Byrd had access to technically improved instruments and wished to exploit a wider range of sound and the full range of the bass viol.

John Bryan suggests that Byrd's decision to publish Fantasia 6/g2 in 1611 reflects the composer's awareness that bass instruments could now be safely played across this wider range.[38] In four of the six-part works in *Psalmes, Songs and Sonnets (1611)* containing untexted parts for viols, Byrd exploited the full compass of the 23 notes available to him 'confirming that Byrd regarded instrumental lines as being suitable for wider-ranging parts'.[39] Bryan points out that in *Psalmes, Sonets, & Songs of sadness and pietie* published in 1588, the bass viol parts in the 1588 music never go down below F or above d', which probably indicates that the open D string and the low E were often unsatisfactory when played and thus avoided in the middle years of the sixteenth century.[40] Bryan notes that by 1600 Weelkes considered that viols had workable ranges in excess of those of voices; the more frequent appearance of the lowest notes of the bass viol after 1600 suggests greater reliability in the low register.[41] Bass parts were regularly extended down to D and treble parts above a''. Tenor parts also began to be regularly extended down to b♭ and a pair of tenors used in different ranges. This is likely to be due to technological developments in instrument design, such as the addition of soundposts, changed body shape and improvement in quality in the manufacture of strings.

Wide bass parts are a feature of most of Byrd's consort music, but they need to be looked at in relation to compass and pitch to distinguish them from some parts found in his Latin motets. The distinction in ranges between vocal and consort music is not as clear as that found in his contemporaries' music. However John Bryan identifies Byrd's distinction between what were vocal and instrumental lines in *Psalmes, Sonets, & songs of sadness and pietie* of 1588.[42] The part songs contained in this are Byrd's adaptation of earlier consort songs, for solo voice and viols. In particular, Bryan notes the difference between the treble voice parts and treble viol part. In the majority of the singing parts, the vocal range is eight or nine notes, whereas the average range for the untexted *superius* parts is wider, typically covering a tenth or eleventh.[43]

In common with his contemporaries, Byrd's vocal music with wide individual ranges, there is greater overlap between the parts, and a narrower compass than found in the consort music, with a small number of exceptions. The ranges found in all parts in his pavans and galliards are similar to those of his contemporaries.

Clef combinations

The clef combinations in sixteenth-century English consort music appear to have a greater similarity with those found in pre-Reformation music than with those found in the vocal music with sacred texts dating from after 1547. These may not, of course, have been the clefs used by the composers at the point of composition, but reflect a convention used by the scribes copying the music, reflecting the tessitura of each part. We obviously know the clefs used by Tallis and Byrd in their published Latin motets and those Byrd used for his published Fantasias 4/g and 6/g2.

Of 72 vocal works with sacred texts by Tallis, Sheppard, Tye, Parsons and White, 47 pieces are recorded as containing only C and F clefs, which Bowers believes is typical of post-Reformation vocal music. Twenty-five works contain G clefs, but most of these can be identified as having been written before 1547 or during the reign of Mary Tudor, with the temporary return of Catholicism. In 77 consort pieces (excluding dances and music by Byrd), 63 have been copied using G clefs; 14 contain only C and F clefs. In five-part music, the combination of a G clef, three C clefs and F4 is very common, particularly in In Nomines. The most frequent combination is that of G2, C1, C3, C4, F4. G clefs are less common in pavans and galliard. Only four are found in the Lumley dances but in Holborne's dances, only five pavans out of 59 dances do not contain a G clef. The other pavans examined divided equally between those with or without a G clef. There is a simple explanation for this.

Although Bowers is right about post-Reformation liturgical vocal music commonly using the clef C1 in preference to G2, closer examination reveals that this is closely linked to the pitch of treble parts. In the vocal music, a G clef is found to have been used for any treble part going up to high g" or a". Sheppard, Tallis and Tye also all seem to have used a G clef for any treble part up to high f". Tye sometimes used a G clef for treble parts reaching d". White made use of a G clef for treble parts reaching g" or a", while he used the clef C1 for parts reaching f". Clefs were used in a similar manner in consort music. All the composers of instrumental music made use of a G clef for any treble viol part up to g" or a". All except four of Tye's thirty consort works have treble parts going up to g" or a". Just three reaching e" and d" are notated with C1.[44] Tallis, Preston and Woodcock also used a G clef for f" in consort music. Parsons was not as consistent; his consort music includes the use of a G clef for a treble part reaching up to high e" and C1 for two parts going up to f".[45] In the pavans and galliards found in the Lumley partbooks, with the exception of three pieces, C1 is used for any treble part reaching f" or below. One galliard with a G clef has a treble part going up to g" and three with G clefs reach d", f" or e". All of Holborne's pavans and galliards with treble parts reaching f", g" or a" use a G clef as do some with e", d" and c". Only five dances out of 59 contain the clef C1.

G clefs are much more common in works with a wide compass as the upper part is likely to reach g" or a" and, in some cases, f". They are found in the vocal pieces with sacred texts that have a compass of 22 notes or more. Most of the consort music by Byrd's contemporaries has a compass of 23 notes, contain G clefs and can be identified as instrumental music mainly for viols. No G clefs and a narrow compass does not, however, exclude the possibility that a piece of music is instrumental. For example Woodcock's *Hackney*, with its narrow compass of 20 notes, has the clef combination of C1, C3, C3, C4 and F4, as a d" is the highest note, but of course it is probably for wind instrument rather than voices. As one might expect, G clefs appear more frequently in the pavans and galliards that contain more challenging parts.

The link between clefs and the ranges of individual parts again reflects the pitch of the highest note. In vocal treble parts there is greater use of C1 due to the smaller number of parts of 11 notes or more, with fewer parts reaching up to g" or a". In contrast, there are a significant number of wide treble parts found in consort works with a range of 12 or 13 notes and all of these are notated with a G clef and, with one exception, reach g" or a". The clef C1 is consistently used for the part carrying the chant in the treble parts in In Nomines, which normally goes up to D. The only exception is where the In Nomine is at higher pitch in the treble part, travelling up to g", when it is noted using a G clef. G clefs are less common in post-Reformation vocal music with sacred texts because the reduction in the overall compass and range reflected the fact that treble parts were no longer commonly reaching g" and a". As the sixteenth century progressed, composers and scribes began using C1 for all parts reaching f". Treble parts reaching g" and a" were much more common in instrumental music and thus the use of a G clef is much more prevalent.

Byrd's vocal music with sacred texts and his consort music mainly display the same characteristic clef combination of post-Reformation English music. Like his contemporaries, Byrd uses a G clef for treble parts that reach g" or a" in his vocal music with sacred texts. G clefs are found in only 12 out of 92 of his vocal works with sacred texts; all are non-liturgical Latin motets, found in the three *Cantiones Sacrae* collections of Latin motets from 1575, 1589 and 1591, and have a treble voice part reaching to f" or g". In the *Cantiones Sacrae* of 1575 and 1591, for parts up to f", with one exception in each collection, the clef C1 is used. In the *Cantiones Sacrae* of 1589, Byrd used a G clef for all the six pieces with treble parts reaching f" or g". Two of these have a compass of 23 notes. There is completely consistent use of G and C clefs for treble parts in Byrd's consort music. All of the treble parts reaching a" or g" are notated with a G2 clef; those reaching f" are notated with the clef C1. His two published fantasias, Fantasia 4/g and Fantasia 6/g2 and Fantasias 6/F and 6/g1 and the *Browning* Fantasy therefore do not contain G clefs. Fantasia 5C contains parts in both G2 and C1 as one treble part reaches a", the other e".

In Byrd's consort music, 12 out of 23 works with a complete record of parts, including three dances, have a clef combination containing a G clef. All of his In Nomines contain a G clef and a compass of 22 notes or more, with a treble part reaching g" or a". Five of the seven of Byrd's consort pieces with 23 notes or more are notated with a G clef with the treble parts reaching g" or a". His six Latin-titled textless pieces where parts have survived have a compass of 20 notes or less, treble parts reaching only c' or d' and therefore no G clefs. This is an indication they were probably intended for singing or playing. His two pavans and one galliard contain G clefs as all have treble parts reaching up to g" or a", although the compass of the Pavan and Galliard 6/C is 21 and 19 notes respectively. Byrd's consort music is similar to other contemporary consort music in terms of the relationship between clefs and wide compass with the exception of two six-part fantasias, Fantasia 6/g1 and Fantasia 6/g2 (the second of which Byrd published), which have a wide compass of 23 and 24 notes but no G clefs because the highest note in the treble parts are f" and e♭".

The use of C clefs by Byrd in his vocal treble parts combined with a wide note range of 11 to 13 notes is more pronounced than in his contemporaries' music because almost all reach only as high as f". Fourteen parts out of 33 treble parts from Byrd's consort music including his two pavans and galliard contain the clef G2 but only eight have a range of 11 or 12 notes. The remaining six reach g" or a" but have a range of eight to ten notes. Four further treble parts found in the *Browning* Fantasy, Fantasias 6/g1 and 6/g2 and Fantasia 5C contain a range of 11 or 12 notes but only reach f" and therefore have the clef C1. Fantasia 5C also one wide part reaching up to a" and the clef G2, illustrating Byrd's consistency in his clef use.

Looking at bass vocal parts in the music of Byrd's contemporaries, five clefs are used, although F4 predominates. In the consort music, bass parts nearly all use F4. In both the vocal music with sacred texts and consort works by Byrd's contemporaries, F was the most commonly recorded lowest note in the bass parts, making F4 the most convenient clef. There is a similar use of clefs in both the vocal and the consort music in the inner voices. Both contain parts with wide ranges reflecting the use of highly accomplished singers in vocal music. The wider vocal parts make most use of C4 whereas in the instrumental inner parts, parts with wider ranges are evenly spread between C3 and C4.

Almost all of the clefs found in Byrd's bass parts are F4 or F3, both in his published music and as notated in manuscripts. Only five bass parts from both his vocal and consort music do not use these two clefs. Byrd's use of clefs for bass parts is similar to that of his contemporaries. Byrd's bass parts also predominantly have F notated as their lowest note in parts with a range of 11 notes or more, again making F4 the most convenient clef.

Signature accidentals

Either no accidentals or a signature accidental of one or two flats are found in sixteenth-century English music. This matches the three scales acknowledged by English theorists and Morley.[46] In a total number of 241 works,[47] both vocal music with sacred texts and consort music (including dances) in four to seven parts, by Byrd's contemporaries, one hundred and forty-eight had a signature of one flat, 71 had no signature accidental and just 22 had two flats. The incidence of one flat was higher in the consort compositions (78.3%, excluding dances) compared with the vocal music with sacred texts (54%); a signature of two flats was rare and only found in 13 out of 72 vocal works with sacred texts and six out of 83 consort works.

In Byrd's compositions there appears to be a more even spread in his use of each of the three signatures. This is only slight when comparing the entire sample of Byrd's vocal compositions with sacred texts with those of his contemporaries but becomes more pronounced if his Latin-texted motets (52) are isolated. Within these, an equal number of 20 works have no accidental or one flat (38.5% each) and 12 have a signature of two flats (23%).

Unlike the consort works of his contemporaries, in the total sample (29) of Byrd's consort pieces (including dances) in four to six parts, 13 (45%) contain no signature accidental. If his textless Latin-titled works are removed from the sample, leaving 19 works, then, as with his contemporaries, one flat becomes the most common signature, being found in ten pieces. The remaining nine works divide between four with no signature accidental and five with two flats.

The use of signature accidentals does not have any bearing on whether a work was vocally or instrumentally conceived although the use of one flat is very common in consort music. However Byrd makes greater use than his contemporaries of a signature of two flats, for example in his two six-part Fantasias 6/g1 and 6/g2, indicative perhaps of his interest in exploring new possibilities in his consort music.

A high percentage of sixteenth-century English consort music (excluding dances) has a compass of 23 notes or more, which can be an indicator that it was instrumentally conceived. If Byrd's textless Latin-titled works and Miserere settings are excluded, all except two of his consort works contain a compass of 22 notes or more. In his *Psalmes, Songs and Sonnets (1611)*, only four out of 32 items have a compass of 23 notes, and all involve untexted parts for viols.[48] Regarding the range of individual parts in Byrd's consort music, it is that of his bass parts that is of particular significance and the number of these with 12 or 13 notes combined with a wide compass of the music.

Although pitch varied during the sixteenth-century, for consort music consistency in notating music was clearly developing, which is reflected in Byrd's use of clefs. Particular genres of consort music, such as In Nomines and pavans and galliards, have certain characteristics apparent in their notation. Music for dancing commonly has the narrowest compass and few pieces of dance music contain a G clef, including those going up to f''. Narrow compass is also found in stylised dances; few pavans have more than 22 notes but are none the less stylistic textless instrumental music. A compass of 22 notes or less became common for consort pavans and galliards, as can be seen in Byrd's Pavan 5/c and in the six-part Pavan and Galliard 6/C.

The use of a G clef for notating wide-ranging treble lines in consort music clearly continued after the Reformation because of the continued use of higher notes than were commonly found in vocal music. In Nomine parts have the clef C1 because they rarely go above d". The convention of using C clefs in treble vocal music is directly linked to the reduction of the upper range. Post-Reformation, as choirboys began singing music commonly notated in C1, they were beginning to play viols. In Nomines were the first known pieces to be directly written for them, with composers such as Tye writing them after 1547. The In Nomine part, commonly notated in the clef C1, with its restricted range of nine notes, usually up to d", would have been ideal for teaching purposes. Learning to read and play in other clefs would be helped by the In Nomine tune being placed in different clefs, which occurs in some pieces. G clefs continued as the norm for notating more advanced treble viol parts reaching g" and a" (and in some cases f"), as they did for high treble parts in vocal music with sacred texts.

While compass, individual ranges, and possibly clef use, can help to identify whether the music of Byrd and his contemporaries is of instrumental or vocal origin, factors such as texture, tonalities, phrases, rests, basic note values, interval leaps, tempo, rhythmic complexity and relationships between parts are of course of great importance. Through looking at all these factors in Byrd's music, we can see how he explored and developed textless music for viol consort.

1 Roger Bowers, 'Chains of (Rehabilitated) Gold', *Early Music* Review, 159 (April, 2014), pp. 10–17. Like Byrd, Bowers uses the term 'compass' to describe the overall range of a piece, and 'range' applies to individual parts.

2 Ibid., p. 13.

3 During the reign of Mary Tudor, the re-introduction of Roman Catholicism resulted in a return to pre-Reformation forms of music and worship.

4 Bowers, 'Chains of (Rehabilitated) Gold', p. 12.

5 Ibid., p. 14.

6 See Simon Ravens, "A Sweet Shrill Voice': The Countertenor and Vocal Scoring in Tudor England', *Early Music*, 26/1 (February, 1998), pp. 122–134 and 'Countertenor counterblast', *Early Music*, 28/3 (August, 2000) p. 507; Andrew Parrott, 'Performing pitch', *Early Music*, 32/2 (May, 2004).

7 David Wulfstan, *Tudor Music* (London, 1985), p. 202.

8 Kerry McCarthy, *Byrd* (New York, 2013), p. 39.

9 See John Bryan in '"Choice Consorts....(Rare Chests of Viols)": The Evidence of the Repertory', pp. 13–64.

10 Ibid., p. 60.

11 Bowers, 'Chains of (Rehabilitated) Gold', p.13.

12 Ibid., p. 14.

13 The music may be found in Early English Church Music (EECM), volumes 18, 19, 24, 32, 33, 40 and 56 (London, Stainer and Bell, 1976–2014); Musica Britannica (MB) volumes 44, 45 and 101 (London, Stainer and Bell, 1979 and 1988); The Byrd Edition (BE), volumes 2, 3, 10a, 11, 12, 14 and 17 (London, Stainer and Bell, 1971–1988); Christopher Tye, *Complete Consort Music*, ed. Bernard Thomas (Brighton, London Pro Musica, 1991); Anthony Holborne, *Pavans, Galliards, Almains 1599*, ed. Bernard Thomas (London, London Pro Musica, 1980); publications by the Viola da Gamba Society of Great Britain and online in IMSLP (International Music Score Library Project: https://imslp.org/wiki/Main_Page,

14 Bowers, 'Chains of (Rehabilitated) Gold', p.14.

15 John Sheppard, *Masses*, ed. Nicholas Sandon, EECM 18 (London, Stainer and Bell, 1976), p. ix; see also Jeremy Summerly, CD notes for *Christopher Tye, Missa Euge bone and Western Wynde Mass*, Westminster Abbey Choir, James O'Donnell (Recorded London 2011, Hyperion CDA67928, released 2012) and EECM 32.

16 The figures displayed in this chapter contain information collected as part of academic research into Byrd's consort music completed in 2020; Anne Martin, 'Idiomatic instrumental style in the textless consort music of William Byrd', (unpublished PhD dissertation, University of Aberdeen, 2020), pp. 26–48.

17 Bernard Thomas in Christopher Tye, *Complete Consort Music*, (Brighton, London Pro Musica, 1991), p. iii, shows Tye's 4-part *In Nomine* as having a compass of 26 notes; Paul Doe believes that Tye intended that the top line should be an octave lower, thus reducing the compass. See *Elizabethan Consort Music II*, ed. Paul Doe, MB 45 (London, Stainer and Bell, 1988), p. 28.

18 MB 44/32 and 38. Paul Doe suggests *Hackney* might be wind or vocal music. See MB 44, p.188. He also suggests (p. xv) that it might be a representation of one or more London street cries. The narrow range, large number of repeated notes and fast moving quavers does suggest wind music.

19 See John Harper, 'Ensemble and Lute Music', in Roger Bray (ed.), *Music in Britain The Sixteenth Century* (Oxford, 1995), p. 299.

20 Ibid. Harper, p. 279; Doe, MB 44, pp. 153–7; Peter Holman, *Four and Twenty Fiddlers* (Oxford, 1993), p. 90.

21 Warwick Edwards in 'The Sources of Elizabethan Consort Music', (unpublished PhD dissertation, University of Cambridge, 1974), p.18, writes that this pavan of Philips 'seemed to have been the most popular for there are numerous arrangements'. For a discussion of this piece, see David J. Smith, The Instrumental Music of Peter Philips: its Sources, Dissemination and Style, (DPhil dissertation, University of Oxford, 1994), vol. 2, pp. 303–27.

22 Robert Johnson and Joseph Lupo, *A Knell of Johnson* and *Pavan*, ed. Virginia Brookes, VdGS 199 (Viola

da Gamba Society of Great Britain, no location stated, 2005 and 2013); Alfonso Ferrabosco I, *Pavan*, ed. Richard Charteris, VdGS 159 (Viola da Gamba Society of Great Britain, no location stated, 1990 and 2004); Peter Philips, *1580 Pavan* in *Peter Philips and Richard Dering: Consort Music*, ed. David J. Smith, Musica Britannica 101/1, (London: Stainer and Bell, 2016; Augustine Bassano, *Pavans* and *Galliards*, ed. Albert Folop, IMSLP Petrucci Music Library 164722, 164733, 164745 and 164765, https://imslp.org/wiki/Pavans_and_Galliards_for_5_Viols_(Bassano%2C_Augustine)

(Authored 2011). See also Frank D'Accone (ed.), *London British Library MS Egerton 3665, The Tregian Manuscript* (New York, Garland, 1988).

23 EECM 56; William Byrd, *Cantiones Sacrae I* (1589), ed. Alan Brown, BE 2 (London, Stainer and Bell, 1988); William Byrd, *Cantiones Sacrae II* (1591), ed. Alan Brown, BE 3 (London, Stainer and Bell, 1981); William Byrd, *The English Services*, ed. Craig Monson, BE 10a (London, Stainer and Bell, 1983); *The English Anthems*, ed. Craig Monson, BE 11 (London, Stainer and Bell, 1983).

24 John Milsom in Thomas Tallis and William Byrd, *Cantiones Sacrae 1575*, ed. John Milsom,, EECM 56 (London, Stainer and Bell, 2014). p. 385.

25 Paul Doe writes that the consort origin of Ferrabosco's *Fancy* is suggested 'by the single-voice concordance' and 'omissions in the lower voices of the keyboard source'; MB 45/127, p.145. John V. Cockshoot and Christopher D. S. Field describe one of Ferrabosco I's two keyboard fantasies as a short score of fantasy for four viols; 'Ferrabosco family, *The New Grove Dictionary of Music & Musicians*, online 2001; https://doi-org.nls.idm.oclc.org/10.1093/gmo/9781561592630.article.09507

26 The In Nomine chant, *Gloria tibi Trinitas*, has a prescribed note range in long note values.

27 Christopher Tye, *III Ritual Music and Motets*, ed. Nigel Davison, EECM 33/9 (London, 1987).

28 These being works thought to have been written before 1547 or during Mary's reign.

29 EECM 56/13.

30 He mentions Thomas Middleton's description in a *Mad World, My Masters* (1608) of an annoying husband as being like a 'grumbling bass viol'; John Bryan, '"Choice Consorts….(Rare Chests of Viols)": The Evidence of the Repertory', in Michael Fleming and John Bryan (ed.), *Early English Viols* (Abingdon, 2016), pp. 60–61.

31 Ibid. Bryan, p. 60.

32 Viols with six strings are most commonly documented as being tuned in 4ths with a third in the middle.

33 Bryan, '"Choice Consorts….(Rare Chests of Viols)": The Evidence of the Repertory', p. 60.

34 Ibid., p. 16.

35 Philip Thorby, 'A question of status', *The Viol*, 54 (Spring 2019), p. 8.

36 Bryan, '"Choice Consorts….(Rare Chests of Viols)": The Evidence of the Repertory', p. 47.

37 *Dum transisset Sabbatum II*, MB 45/146, GB-Lbl MS 31390, f. 68v and *Howld fast*, MB 45/169, GB-Lbl MS 31390, f. 73.v.

38 Bryan, '"Choice Consorts….(Rare Chests of Viols)": The Evidence of the Repertory', p. 22.

39 Ibid., p. 21.

40 Ibid., p. 19.

41 Ibid., p. 23.

42 Ibid., p. 18.

43 Ibid., p. 16.

44 A fourth has the clef G1 and is notated to c" but was probably played an octave lower; Doe in MB 45/135, p. 146.

45 *Ut re mi* and *De la court.*

46 See Jessie Ann Owens, 'Concepts of Pitch in English Music Theory', in Cristle Collins Judd (ed.), *Tonal Structures in Early Music* (New York, 1998), pp. 183–246, at p. 192

47 Including six Fantasias by White.

48 William Byrd, *Psalmes, Songs and Sonnets (1611)*, ed. John Morehen, BE 14 (London, Stainer and Bell, 1987).

Chapter 4

Manuscript sources of Byrd's consort music

Forty manuscripts and one printed publication, dating from the late 1560s to around 1660–70, contain one or more of Byrd's consort pieces. A further two printed sources (the *Cantiones Sacrae* of 1575 and *Gradualia* of 1605) each contain a motet believed to have been adapted from a consort work by Byrd. In this chapter, each of these sources is numbered from 1 to 41. The following tables list all the sources of Byrd's consort works in probable chronological order. Greater detail for each source can be found in Appendix Two. Both consort music, referring to works conceived without a text that would have been performed by viols, and vocal music copied without text are found in many of the sources. Textless vocal music was commonly played by consorts of viols.

Exploring the probable chronology of the 41 sources containing Byrd's consort works helps identify the order in which they were probably written. It is impossible to definitively date most manuscripts, but an idea of chronology may be determined from the information available. What else is contained in each manuscript and the placing of Byrd's music within it also provides clues about a source's provenance. In in the tables 4.1–4.3, the manuscripts are sorted by decades up to 1600; the remaining three tables consist of sources compiled after the turn of the century. This categorisation is partly for convenience, but is also linked to the fact that Byrd had written almost all his surviving consort pieces by the 1590s, when he began to retire from life at the Chapel Royal.

Three consort pieces by Robert Parsons and three by Alfonso Ferrabosco I are indicated in the following tables. The works by Parsons are among the most copied pieces of Elizabethan consort music and they influenced Byrd. They are Parsons's five-part In Nomine, the only one of his three five-part In Nomines to survive complete, *De la court* and the six-part *The song called trumpets*. The three listed works by Ferrabosco I are his In Nomine I, his four-part *Fancy* and a six-part textless work without a title.

Parsons's five-part In Nomine is found in 14 of the manuscripts containing Byrd's consort music, including three manuscripts from the Paston collection, and in over 20 sources altogether.[1] *De la court* is found in 11 of the manuscripts containing consort music by Byrd and in 13 sources altogether.[2] *The song called trumpets* is found in six sources, four of which contain consort works by Byrd. The three works by Alfonso Ferrabosco I also had a significant influence on Byrd. Ferrabosco's In Nomine I appears in 13 sources, nine of which contain consort works by Byrd.[3] His four-part *Fancy* appears in two sources and the six-part textless work in just one.[4] The links to these works will be explored in later chapters.

Tables showing manuscript sources for Byrd's consort music

+	items only found in one MS
*	MS contains all or part of Parsons, *De la court*
#	MS contains Parsons, Five-part In Nomine
~	MS contains Parsons, *The song called trumpets*
$	MS contains Ferrabosco I, In Nomine I
^	MS contains Ferrabosco I, *Fancy*
x	MS contains Ferrabosco I, un-named six-part textless work

Table 4.1 Sources up to 1580

MS		Date	Place of Origin	Pieces	Folios	Notes
1. GB-Lbl Add. MSS 30480–84	*	*c.*1570– after 1610 Hamond partbooks	Suffolk?	*Christe qui lux* (II)	f. 70, 74v, 69v, 71v	5 partbooks
2. GB-Lbl Add. MS 31390	*# ~x	compiled from *c.*1570. Corrected 1578	Chichester?	+In Nomine 5/1 In Nomine 5/4 In Nomine 5/5 *Browning* Fantasy	ff. 43v–44r ff. 58v–59r ff. 120v–121r ff. 124v–125r	Table book
3. GB-Ob MS Tenbury 1464		1570–1575	Norwich	In Nomine 5/2	f8	Bass part only

Table 4.2 Sources 1580–1590						
MS		**Date**	**Place of Origin**	**Pieces**	**Folios**	**Notes**
4. GB-Och MSS 979–83	~	*c.* 1575–1581	Windsor	+Fantasia a 6/F (also found adapted as a motet *Laudate pueri* in *Cantiones Sacrae* 1575, No.17)	No. 157	5 of 6 partbooks; one part missing
5. GB-Och MSS 984–8	*#	1581–1588 Dow partbooks	Oxford	*Browning* Fantasy In Nomine 5/5	No. 73 No. 85/6	5 partbooks
6. GB-Ob MS Mus. Sch. e. 423	*#	after 1577 to around 1589	Essex	*Browning* Fantasy In Nomine 5/5 Fantasia a 6/g1 Fantasia a 6/g2	No. 29 p.149 No. 50 p.182 No. 28 p.303a No. 30 p.307	1 partbook contratenor
7. GB-Lbl Add. MS 22597	*#	1580s?		In Nomine 5/5	f.35v	One partbook
8. GB-Lbl Add. MS 32377	*# ^$	1585–1590	Exeter/Dorset?	*Browning* Fantasy Prelude & Ground In Nomine 5/2 In Nomine 5/5	f.2r f.2r f.9v f.8v	One partbook,mainly treble

Table 4.3 Sources *c.*1590–1600						
MS		**Date**	**Place of Origin**	**Pieces**	**Folios**	**Notes**
9. US-Ws MS V.a. 408	$	*c.* 1590	Wells?	*Browning* Fantasy	f.1	One partbook; cantus
10. *My Ladye Nevell's Booke* GB-Lbl MS Mus 1591 (Keyb.)		1591	Windsor	Fantasia 5/C in keyboard version, *A lesson of Voluntarie* Keyboard version of Ground: *The Second Grownde* Pavan 5/c	No. 29 No. 30 No. 10	
11. GB-Ob MS Tenbury 389	*# ~$	*c.*1595– *c.*1613		In Nomine 5/5 In Nomine 5/2 *Browning* Fantasy	f.71 f.72 ff.86–88	One partbook altus; also 2nd partbook, cantus, 'James ms' in private hands, now known as GB-Lmcghie s.s

Table 4.4 Sources *c.*1600–1640s Paston manuscripts *c.*1590 into early 1600s						
MS		**Date**	**Place of Origin**	**Pieces**	**Folios**	**Notes**
12. GB-Ob MSS Tenbury 379–84		started1590s	Norfolk	Fantasia a 6/g1 (no galliard or coda)	f.42v	6 partbooks
13. GB-Ob MSS Tenbury 341–4		early 17th century	Norfolk	Fantasia a 6/g/ (5 parts complete)	ff.55v, 68, 67v, 57v, 58v	5 of 6 partbooks; bass part missing
14. GB-Lbl Add. MS 29246	#	early 17th century	Norfolk	*Sermone blando* a 3 +*Sermone blando* a 4 (I) Fantasias 3/C1, 3/C2 & 3/C3 Fantasia 4/a Fantasia 4/g +*Te lucis* (I) *Christe qui lux* (I) *Te Lucis* (II) +*Salvator mundi* *Christe redemptor* *Miserere*	f.14v f.15v f.22r, 22v, 27v f.39r f.41v f.44v f.46r f.41v f.47v f.48v f.48v	for lute (no top line)
15. GB-Ob MSS Tenbury 354–8	#	early 17th century	Norfolk	In Nomine 4/1 *Christe redemptor* *Miserere* +*Christe qui lux* (III) +*Sermone blando* (II) *Christe qui lux* (I) *Christe qui lux* (II) *Te lucis* (II) In Nomine 5/5	f.17v f.22 f.23 f.23 f.23r f.24v f.24 f.24v f.43v	5 partbooks
16. GB-Lbl Add. MSS 29401–5	#	*c.*1613	Norfolk	In Nomine 5/5	f.55v	5 partbooks
17. GB-Lbl Add. MSS 41156–8		early 17th century	Norfolk	Fantasia 3/C2 Fantasia 3/C3	f.11v f.9v	3 of 4 partbooks
18. GB-Lbl Add. MS 34049		early 17th century	Norfolk	In Nomine 5/5	f.47v	One partbook, cantus
19. GB-Lcm MS 2036 (music transposed)		early 17th century	Norfolk	Fantasia 3/C1 Fantasia 3/C2	f.4v f.5v	3 partbooks
20. GB-Lbl Add. MSS 18936–9 (connected with Paston household)		*c.* 1615	Norfolk	*Sermone blando* a 3 *Miserere*	f.6v ff.20v & 3v	4 of 5 partbooks

Table 4.5 Manuscripts *c.*1600–1640s from sources other than Paston						
MS		**Date**	**Place of Origin**	**Pieces**	**Folios**	**Notes**
21. GB-Lbl Add. MSS 37402–6	*	completed after 1606		Fantasia a 6/g2 Pavan 5/c	ff.50, 49v, 53, 70, 51v ff.98v, 89v, 91v, 86v	5 partbooks part 4 missing
22.D-Kl MS mus. 125	#	*c.*1600	Kassel?	Pavan 5/c		5 partbooks
23. GB-Lbl Add. MSS 34800A–C		after 1600 to *c.*1618 +later additions		Fantasia 3/C1	f.15v, 17v	3 partbooks
24. GB-Lbl Add. MSS 17786–91	*	before 1610–1620s first part completed by 1610	Oxford	Fantasia 5/C Fantasia 6/g1 (coda added added later) *Behold now praise the Lord* (no text)	f.2v f.3v f.33v	6 of 7 partbooks
25. GB-Ob MSS Mus. Sch. d.212–6	#$	mainly completed by 1610	Oxford	In Nomine 4/1 + In Nomine 4/2 In Nomine 5/2 In Nomine 5/3 In Nomine 5/4 In Nomine 5/5	f.14v f.17 f.7 (bassus f. 33) ff.36, 10 ff.40, 14 f.53	2 x 5 partbooks
26. Print; *Psalmes, Songs and Sonnets*		1611	London	Fantasia 4/g Fantasia 6g/2	No. 15 No. 26	6 partbooks
27. GB-Lbl Add. MS 29427	$	*c.* 1612–1618	Cambridge? & London	Fantasia 4/a + Fantasia 4/G	f.45 f.45v	One partbook; altus & contratenor only *In manus tuas* in *Gradualia* 1605
28. GB-Lcm MS 2049	*$	early 17th century		In Nomine 5/5	ff.15v, 12v, 13v	4 of 6 partbooks; cantus & contratenor missing
29. GB-Lbl Egerton 3665	#$	*c.*1613–19 (Tregian)	London	In Nomine 5/5	f.156v	Score

Table 4.5 continued						
30. NYp MSS Drexel 4180–5	*# ~$	*c.* 1615–1625 (Merro)	Gloucester	In Nomine 5/5 Fantasia 6g/2 Fantasia 4/g	ff.71v, 71r, 73v, 67v, 48v ff.168v, 179v, 183v, 165v, 150v, 71v ff.180v, 184v, 166v 151v	6 partbooks
31. GB-Ob MSS Mus Sch D. 245–7		*c.* 1610–after 1634 (Merro)	Gloucester	Fantasia 4/g	pp. 104, 105, f.23v	3 partbooks, include tablature; part 3 missing
32. GB-Lbl Add. MSS 17792–96		1620s–30s (Merro)	Gloucester	Prelude & Ground *Browning* Fantasy	f. 58r in all except 17795, f.28r ff. 72v, 73r, 72v, 43r, 71r	5 of 6 partbooks
33. GB-Lbl Add. MSS 39550–4	$	1630s completed by 1644	Norfolk	In Nomine 5/3 In Nomine 5/4	p. 56 p. 60	5 of 6 partbooks
34. GB-Ob MSS Mus Sch. C 64–9		*c.* 1635–*c.*1640	Oxford & Gloucester shire	+Pavan 6/C +Galliard 6/C	ff.203v, 153v, 75v &140v, 212v, 4v ff.203v, 153v, 75v & 140v, 212v, 4v	6 partbooks

Table 4.6 Keyboard and Lute manuscripts completed in the 17th century						
MS		**Date**	**Place of Origin**	**Pieces**	**Folios**	**Notes**
35. GB-Lbl MS 29996 (Keyb.)	#	mid-16th–17th century	Winchester/London /Worcester?	In Nomine 5/5	f.68v–69	
				Browning Fantasy	f.153v	
				Fantasia 5/C	f.210–210v	beginning missing
				Fantasia 6/g1	f..211–213v	
				Fantasia 6/g2	f. 213v–216	
36. Hirsch Lute Book GB-Lbl MS Hirsch M.1353		Early 17th century after 1620-1	Sussex?	Fantasia 4/g	f.21v	
37. D-Bds MS Lynar A2 (Keyb.)		after 1620 to before 1630	Northern Germany	Fantasia 5/C as in *My Ladye Nevell's Booke*	f.60	
38. NYp MS Drexel 5612 (Keyb).		1630s	Salisbury?	Pavan 5/c	p.132	
39. F-Pc MS Rés. 1122 (Keyb.)		1646–1654	Worcester	Fantasia 4/g Fantasia 5/C	f.16 f.38	
40. GB-Och MS 1113 (Keyb.)		after 1650	Oxford	Fantasia 5/C	p. 161	part only
41. GB-Lcm MS 2093 (Keyb.)		1660s–1670s		Fantasia 4/a	f.25	

The most detailed examination of manuscripts from between the 1560s and 1670s containing consort music was made by Warwick Edwards in 1974.[5] Most of the 41 sources containing Byrd's consort works are included in this study. Four online sources provide information about the sources. The Viola da Gamba Society's (VdGS) *Thematic Index of Music for Viols, William Byrd* lists all the known manuscripts containing Byrd's consort works.[6] The VdGS also provides an *Index of Manuscripts containing consort music.*[7] The Tudor Partbook Project and the Digital Image Archive of Medieval Music (DIAMM) also provide information about some manuscripts, as does the Early English Church Music (EECM) Primary Source Database for vocal music in the manuscripts.[8] In the second half of the sixteenth-century a significant number of copyists were using printed manuscript paper rather than ruling paper themselves. Information on watermarks and border patterns can help indicate the earliest a manuscript could have been copied. Iain Fenlon and John Milsom have completed significant work on this, as has Katherine Butler on printed borders.[9]

Of the 41 sources, 31 are partbooks or sets of partbooks, including one in lute tablature and one printed set; one is a table book; one is in scorebook form; one is for lute and seven are keyboard collections. Three of the keyboard manuscript collections were completed after 1650, well after Byrd's death. No music specifically composed for viol consort is found in print except for the two fantasias Byrd published in the 1611 edition of *Psalmes, Songs and Sonnets* (26) and three-part works by Orlando Gibbons (1583–1625) published in 1620.[10] Viols are specified as suitable for use in the performance of Holborne's *Pavans, Galliards, Almains, and other short Aeirs* (1599) and Dowland's *Lachrimae, or seaven Teares figured in Seaven Passionate Pavans* (1604) but otherwise are rarely mentioned by name. Individual parts are commonly given names used in vocal music to indicate their place within the texture (e.g. cantus (or canto), bassus (or basso)).

Some of Byrd's consort works appear in only one source, these being the Latin-titled works, *Christe qui lux* (III), *Sermone blando* a 4 (I) and (II), *Te lucis* (I) and *Salvator mundi*, his In Nomines 4/2 and 5/1, Fantasia 4/G and the Pavan and Galliard 6/C. A further five Latin-titled works and Fantasias 3/C2 and 3/C3 are found only in manuscripts collected by or associated with Edward Paston (1550–1630), who assembled the largest collection of surviving partbooks dating from the seventeenth century.[11] In 41 sources, the most commonly found consort work by Byrd is his In Nomine 5/5, which is contained in 14 manuscripts including three Paston manuscripts and a keyboard collection. The second most copied Byrd consort piece, the *Browning* Fantasy, is found in eight sources including a keyboard one.

Excluding the nine manuscripts attributed to the Paston household (or associated with it), many of the sources emanate from (or are connected with) cathedral cities and university colleges where there was a significant professional choir – Chichester, Windsor, Oxford, London, Gloucester, Winchester, Salisbury, Norwich, Exeter and Wells. As well as the Paston manuscripts from Norfolk, East Anglia was probably the home of several other manuscripts.

No manuscripts of consort music in Byrd's handwriting are known to survive. However a small number of manuscripts are particularly important for their probable direct link to Byrd. The original owner of GB-Ob MS Mus. Sch. e. 423 (6), a surviving single partbook compiled between 1577 and *c.*1589, was John, first Lord Petre, patron and friend of Byrd. It can be identified by the initials '·I·P·' on the front cover. The handwriting in the manuscript is that of Petre's steward, John Bentley (d. 1597); it has been identified through comparison of the account books kept by Bentley.[12] David Mateer believes that Byrd and the Petre family must have been acquainted around the time the manuscript was started, although the first documentary evidence of a relationship dates from 1581.[13] It is quite possible that Bentley was given access to the pieces as they were being written. The manuscript contains a large number of vocal pieces by Byrd. He was visiting Petre in London by 1581 and in Essex at Thorndon Hall by 1586; in the latter, a room was referred to as 'Mr Birdes Chamber' in 1608.[14] Petre was Catholic but careful in his practice. He knew his fellow Catholic, Edward Paston, who collected so much of Byrd's music and who may also have known Byrd from the 1570s.[15]

My Ladye Nevell's Booke, GB-Lbl MS Mus. 1591 (10), dating from 1591, is a collection of Byrd's keyboard music that includes intabulations of two of Byrd's consort works and a third work based on the ground used by Byrd in his consort Prelude and Ground. The manuscript was copied by John Baldwin (before 1560–1615), a lay clerk at St George's Chapel Windsor.[16] It is thought that Baldwin worked from holograph manuscripts. John Harley writes that it is likely that Byrd supplied Baldwin with copies and that Byrd could also have planned the compilation. The corrections and alterations appear to have been made by Byrd himself.[17] Baldwin was the scribe of an earlier manuscript, GB-Och 979–983 (4), dating from the latter part of the 1570s, which contains Fantasia 6/F. John Milsom in his commentary on Byrd's remarks on Baldwin's accuracy as a copyist and agrees that Baldwin may have received music directly from Byrd.[18]

Eleven manuscripts containing consort music by Byrd survive from before 1600. Three of these have been dated as being from before 1580 and five from the period 1580–1590. The number falls to three again for the period 1590–1600, when performances by viol-playing choristers had begun to decline. Five of the eight manuscript sources of Byrd's consort music dating from before 1590 contain In Nomines and have an association with places where choristers were found.

From 1600 until the 1640s, there is an increase in the number of surviving manuscripts containing consort music by Byrd, which reflects the growth of amateur viol-playing. Of 30 sources surviving from after 1600, 21 are manuscript partbooks and one is a published set of partbooks. The remainder consist of one manuscript collection in score, six keyboard manuscript collections and one for lute.

The Manuscripts

(Further evidence for their dating can be found in Appendix 2)

Manuscripts dating from before 1580

Six of Byrd's consort works are found in three manuscript collections, likely to have been copied before 1580: *Christe qui lux* (II), In Nomines 5/1, 5/2, 5/4, 5/5 and the *Browning* Fantasy. Two of these three manuscripts contain only a small number of consort works within large vocal collections. Both contain Latin motets. *Christe qui lux* (II) is the only one of Byrd's Latin-titled textless works found outside the seventeenth-century manuscripts collected by or associated with Edward Paston. The two earliest manuscripts, GB-Lbl Add. MSS 30480–4 (1) and GB-Lbl Add. MS 31390 (2), are thought to have been begun by 1570, contemporary with a growth in viol playing. The third manuscript, GB-Ob MS Tenbury 1464 (3), contains music from the 1560s and was probably compiled between 1570 and 1575.[19]

The first book of *Cantiones Sacrae* published by Tallis and Byrd in 1575 contains the Fantasia 6/F adapted as a six-part motet, *Laudate pueri*. The argument for the fantasia being written first and then adapted for the 1575 publication is strong. In his 2014 edition of the1575 *Cantiones Sacrae*, John Milsom writes of *Laudate pueri*, that 'the metamorphosis of this work can be charted with confidence; the adaptation is clearly a compromise, since one musical section carries different words when repeated'.[20] There are also other small changes to the polyphony. This will be explored further in Chapter Six. Fantasia 6/F appears in its original form in the manuscript GB-Och MSS 979–83 (4), which was begun in the latter part of the 1570s and completed around 1581.

Just eight textless pieces written or arranged for viols are found in the five partbooks of GB-Lbl Add. MSS 30480–4 (1), a collection of 87 vocal works with and without text. Among these are Byrd's *Christe qui lux* (II). Evidence suggests it was collected over a long time with Byrd's Latin-titled work being added around 1570. GB-Lbl Add. MS 31390 (2), the first known English collection of consort music, is the most significant manuscript of the sources dating from before 1580. It is a table book containing 127 works, 66 of which have been identified as having been composed without words by a wide range of composers working in England. These include young, contemporary composers such as Byrd, Woodcock and Ferrbosco I as well as those from the older generation such as Tye, illustrating that there was an interest in consort music. The manuscript contains almost all of Tye's consort works (28 pieces). It is impossible to know whether it was collected primarily to sing or play.

The title 'A booke of In Nomines & other solfainge songes of v: vj: vji: and viij: parts for voyces or Instruments' would imply the collection was intended for both, but it would be impractical for six viol players to sit round a table and play. The contents suggest a resource for viol players but it could have been collected to be sung using sol-fa syllables.[21] One piece, *Hackney*, by Woodcock, is possibly a piece for wind instruments for which a performance would be far more practical sitting round a table. Some pieces in the collection would be almost impossible to sing, such as Byrd's *Browning* Fantasy.

GB-Lbl Add. MS31390 is the only source for Byrd's In Nomine 5/1 and also includes his In Nomines 5/4 and 5/5 and his *Browning* Fantasy, the latter likely to have been added at the end around 1578. *Browning* Fantasies by Woodcock and Henry Stonings (*fl. c.*1600) are found in the collection as are four works that influenced Byrd, these being Parsons's five-part In Nomine, *De la court* and *The song called trumpets* and the six-part textless 'fantasia' by Ferrabosco I. GB-Ob MS Tenbury 1464 (3), a surviving bass partbook, contains Byrd's In Nomine 5/2 among 15 textless works, mostly In Nomines, among a collection of 62 pieces.

The three earliest manuscripts confirm that Byrd's In Nomines were known and circulating before 1580 and that he had completed the *Browning* Fantasy in the late 1570s. As Fantasia 6/F was published as *Laudate pueri* in 1575, this shows that by 1580 Byrd had experimented with several kinds of consort works, these being Latin-titled works, In Nomines, a fantasia and variations.

Manuscripts from the 1580s

There are five manuscripts containing consort works by Byrd, which the evidence would suggest were completed in the decade up to 1590. They contain four works not found in the earlier manuscripts, plus further copies of three of the works circulating before 1580. The four works appearing for the first time are Byrd's three six-part fantasias and the Prelude and Ground. The first fantasia had, of course, already appeared in print in 1575, adapted as a motet but, as will be shown in Chapter Six, all the evidence suggests the motet came after the fantasia and not the other way round, as the sources might suggest. In Nomine 5/5 also reappears in four out of the five manuscripts from the 1580s, and the *Browning* Fantasy in three.

Of the five manuscripts dating from 1580 to 1590, only two contain a significant amount of music without text. Of the three other manuscripts, GB-Och 979–983 (4) is probably the earliest, dating from *c.* 1575–81 and copied by John Baldwin of St George's Chapel, Windsor. This collection of 172 works, almost exclusively Latin motets, contains just eight pieces without text, including Byrd's first six-part fantasia, Fantasia 6/F, for which it is the only known source. Only five of six partbooks survive. Fantasia 6/F is the first of four six-part consort works entered near the end of the manuscript, the other three being by Parsons, Daman and Taverner. Parsons's *The song called trumpets* is written for what became a common combination for a six-part viol consort – two trebles, two tenors and two basses – as probably was Daman's *Beati omnes.*[22] These two works could both have been sung, but the fact that they were entered together with Fantasia 6/F suggests all three were seen as instrumental music. Significantly, the fantasia has two bass parts. This, the identity of the scribe and the positioning in the manuscript are all significant in confirming that Fantasia 6F began life as a textless consort piece. The manuscript is bound together with a copy of the 1575 *Cantiones Sacrae,* thereby preserving Byrd's adaptation of the fantasia as a motet in the same volume.

The five partbooks, GB–Och 984–988 (5), copied mainly by Robert Dow (1553–88), are considered one of the most important surviving Elizabethan music manuscripts.[23] Dated 1581 at the beginning, they were probably completed by Dow's death in 1588.[24] Only 14 out of a collection of 127 pieces are textless consort pieces, including ten In Nomines and Byrd's and Woodcock's *Browning* fantasies, entered at the beginning of the group. A group of nine In Nomines opens with Parsons's five-part In Nomine, followed by Byrd's In Nomine 5/5. Fifty-six works by Byrd are found in the collection including consort songs.

The single partbook known as GB-Ob MS Mus. Sch. e. 423 (6) is one of the most significant manuscripts relating to Byrd because of its direct connection to his patron John, first Lord Petre. Among 11 consort pieces in a collection of 132 works, are the earliest known copies of Byrd's Fantasias 6/g1 and 6/g2, found at the end of the manuscript. John Bentley (d. 1597), the scribe was likely to have been a trained musician as well as being Petre's steward.[25] Copying of parts of the manuscript began after 1577.[26] The Fantasia 6/g1 appears to have been added to the manuscript by 1586 and the Fantasia 6/g2 just before the manuscript was bound in 1589. MS Mus. Sch. e. 423 also contains Byrd's *Browning* Fantasy and In Nomine 5/5 and Parsons's five-part In Nomine and *De la court.* [27] If Bentley did receive works from Byrd as soon as they were completed, it dates Fantasia 6/g1 as being composed by 1586 and Fantasia 6/g2 by 1589.

The two remaining manuscripts dating from the years up to 1590 contain significantly more music without text. Most of the consort music in the surviving partbook of GB-Lbl Add. MS 22597 (7) is found in Add. MS 31390 (2). Fourteen surviving textless works include eight In Nomines including Byrd's In Nomine 5/5 and Parsons's five-part In Nomine. Evidence suggests the manuscript was completed in the late 1580s.

Among the 80 works found in a treble partbook, GB-Lbl MS Add. 32377 (8) are 47 untexted pieces. Of these, 29 appear to have been instrumentally conceived of which 20 are In Nomines, mainly in five parts and include Byrd's In Nomines 5/5 and 5/2. Byrd's *Browning* Fantasy and the Prelude and Ground are the first two pieces in the manuscript followed by Ferrabosco I's four-part *Fantasy*. Ferrabosco I's In Nomines III and I. Parsons's five-part In Nomine and *De la court* are also found in the collection. The manuscript would seem to have been intended for viol players at Exeter Cathedral, collected by Hugh Geare, a vicar general at the cathedral from 1572.[28]

By 1590, ten of Byrd's consort works, *Christe qui lux* II, In Nomines 5/1, 5/2, 5/4, 5/5, the *Browning* Fantasy, three six-part fantasias, 6/F, 6/g1 and 6/g2, and the Prelude and Ground are known to have been in circulation. Byrd's In Nomine 5/5 appears in five and his *Browning* Fantasy in four sources. The other eight consort works by Byrd all appear once, with the exception of In Nomine 5/2, which appears twice. All the manuscripts up to 1590 suggest Byrd first wrote Latin-titled textless consort works, moved on to In Nomines and then to his first exploration into writing a fantasia and variations.

Manuscripts *c.* 1590–1600

Only three surviving sources of Byrd's consort music are thought to date from the period 1590 to 1600, these being two single partbooks and a manuscript of keyboard music. US-Ws V.a. 408 (9), is a single surviving cantus partbook containing 35 works. It was initially conceived as a collection of 27 works without text, of which 16 can be identified as instrumental consort music. Byrd's *Browning* Fantasy is the first work to be entered in the manuscript, followed by Ferrabosco I's In Nomine I. The Tudor Partbook Project dates it to *c.*1590; it may be associated with Wells Cathedral.[29]

A collection of 42 keyboard pieces by Byrd entitled *My Ladye Nevell's Booke* (10) is important because it includes a version of Byrd's Fantasia 5/C adapted for keyboard, entitled *A lesson of Voluntarie*, a keyboard piece (*The Second Grownde*), based on the same Ground used by Byrd in his consort Prelude and Ground, and the consort Pavan 5/c, adapted for keyboard. The manuscript was copied by Baldwin and signed by him as being 'ffinished & ended the leventh of september in the yeare of our lorde God 1591'.[30] Although the keyboard version of the Pavan 5/c is the earliest known, the consort version is presumed to pre-date it.

The third manuscript of this period, GB-Ob MS Tenbury 389 (11), a single partbook, was probably completed by 1613, but the bulk of the music likely added by the 1590s. Among 127 pieces, are 46 without text, of which 21 were seemingly instrumentally conceived.[31] These include a number of In Nomines, among them Byrd's In Nomine 5/5 and In Nomine 5/2. His Browning Fantasy is found towards the end of the manuscript, which also contains Parsons's five-part In Nomine and *De la court*. Altogether, thirty-six pieces identified as being by Byrd are found in Tenbury 389, including twenty-five Latin motets.

By 1600 a further two consort works by Byrd had been added to those already in circulation, these being the Fantasia 5/C and the Pavan 5/c. This makes a total of 12 consort works by Byrd known to be circulating in 11 manuscripts by 1600. Both In Nomine 5/5 and the *Browning* Fantasy appear in six of these sources, as does Parsons's five-part In Nomine. *De la court* appears in seven.

Manuscripts from after 1600

Thirty of the 41 sources containing Byrd's consort music are thought to have been completed or published after 1600. This reflects the growth of amateur viol playing *c.*1600. Twenty-two of these are sets or parts-sets of partbooks, (including a partbook in lute tablature, owned by Paston that obviously had a companion partbook to supply an upper part). By *c.*1615, when Byrd was aged around 75, all of his consort music other than the Pavan and Galliard in six parts (31works), had appeared in some form. This includes Fantasia 4/G, which was published as an anthem in 1605; as with Fantasia 6/F, it has been questioned as to whether this was in fact first an anthem, which Byrd or a scribe adapted as a fantasia.

Four partbook collections from after 1600 are instrumental collections for viols to play. The earliest of these, D-Kl MS mus. 125 (22), is a collection of dances. GB-Ob MSS Mus Sch D. 245–7 (31) is an extraordinary manuscript of 450 one to three-part works, almost all of which were instrumentally conceived. GB-Lbl Add. MSS 39550–4 (33) and GB-Ob MSS Mus Sch. C 64–9 (34) contain only textless consort works. Three sets of partbooks, GB-Ob MSS Mus. Sch. d. 212–6 (25), GB-Lbl Add. MS 29427 (27) and GB-Lbl Add. MSS 17792–96 (32), started out as instrumental collections to which vocal works were added later. A further four manuscripts from after 1600 are orientated towards music for viols; they include music for voices and viols, arrangements of songs plus other music. The earliest, GB-Lbl Add. MSS 37402–6 (21), contains 75 untexted madrigals as well as consort songs. Another two partbook collections reflect the growth of instrumental music and performance after 1600. Byrd decided to include two of his fantasias in his publication of 1611, *Psalmes, Songs and Sonnets* (26), Fantasias 4/g and 6/g2. He undoubtedly recognised the market for viol music as well as music for voices and viols. Another manuscript, NYp MSS Drexel 4180–5, completed in the 1620s by John Merro (d.1639), a singing master at Gloucester Cathedral, began life as a serious vocal collection to which was added over 80 textless works for viols, 33 of which were instrumentally conceived.

The Paston manuscripts (*c.*1590 to the early 1600s)

Eight manuscripts belonging to the collection made by Edward Paston in the early years of the seventeenth century contain consort music by Byrd. A ninth manuscript, containing consort music by Byrd, GB-Lbl Add. MSS 18936–9, has been identified as coming from Paston's household.[32] The vast Paston collection contains a wide range of music contained in over 40 manuscripts. Five lute books, containing over 500 arrangements of vocal and instrumental works by English and continental composers, are among the collection. The large amount of vocal music included in the collection, both with and without text, would suggest that vocal music was played instrumentally by the lute and consorts of viols. Edward Paston is believed to have been a lute player, which would account for his large collection of music.[33] Paston probably possessed six sizes of lute, which would account for the repetition of some pieces of music at different pitches, and for the sheer quantity of music.[34]

The manuscripts contain very little music dating from after Tallis's death in 1585. The collection includes a significant number of vocal and consort works by Byrd. Nineteen of Byrd's consort pieces are found in eight of the Paston manuscripts and the collection is particularly important because it includes 12 pieces by Byrd that are not found in any other sources.

Paston's scribes began copying music from 1590 but most of the manuscripts from the collection date from the early seventeenth century. What may be the earliest completed, GB-Ob MSS Tenbury 379–84 (12) and GB-Ob MSS Tenbury 341–4 (13), contain only one consort piece, Fantasia 6/g1. GB-Ob MSS Tenbury 379–84 contains only the first 89 breves of the fantasia, found among 43 Latin motets, suggesting that it was copied from a version circulating before the fantasia's inclusion in GB-Ob MS Mus. Sch. e. 423 (6) in the mid-1580s. The fantasia is found complete in GB-Ob MSS Tenbury 341–4 (13) among 100 Latin motets and liturgical settings.

The bulk of the music in the two manuscripts, GB-Lbl Add. MS 29246 (14) and GB-Ob MSS Tenbury 354–8 (15), consists of a large number of Latin motets, Magnificats and mass settings by English composers. Between them, these two manuscripts contain 18 of Byrd's consort pieces, including the 12 works only found in the Paston manuscripts (ten Latin-titled works and Fantasias 3/C2 and 3/C3). All of his textless Latin-titled works are found in these two manuscripts. GB-Lbl Add. MS 29246 (14), containing 29 consort pieces (13 by Byrd) among over 120 works, is one of five books in lute tablature collected by Paston. The top voice is missing throughout, indicating that it would have been sung or played by another instrument. The thirteen consort works by Byrd comprise Fantasias 3/C1, 3/C2 and 3/C3, Fantasias 4/a and 4/g and seven of his Latin-titled works. Within the collection, pieces and sections of pieces, with either two, three or more voices, are arranged in an increasing degree of difficulty. This suggests Add. MS 29246 may have been designed for teaching purposes. This could also explain why a student work, Byrd's three-part *Sermone blando*, is included in this collection and other Latin-titled consort works. Add. MS 29246 is significant because it is the only manuscript which includes all three of Byrd's three-part Fantasias and the only source for three of his textless Latin-titled works. The manuscript is also the only source for White's four-part fantasias. GB-Ob MSS Tenbury 354–8 (15) is a set of five partbooks containing 82 pieces of which just 17 were conceived without text.[35] Nine of the consort works are by Byrd, these being seven Latin-titled pieces, two of which appear only in this manuscript, and In Nomines 4/1 and 5/5. Taverner's original four-part In Nomine is found before Byrd's Latin-titled consort works.

The remaining four Paston manuscripts contain a significant amount of music by Byrd but only a small number of his consort pieces. In Nomine 5/5 is found in two, GB-Lbl Add. MSS 29401–5 (16) and GB-Lbl Add. MS 34049 (18), among a small number of In Nomines, including Parsons's five-part in Add. MSS 29401–5. GB-Lbl Add. MSS 41156–8 (17) and GB-Lcm MS 2036 (19) each contain two of the three-part fantasias. One further manuscript, GB-Lbl Add. MSS 18936–9 (20), is identified as being connected with the Paston household and contains Byrd's three-part *Sermone blando* and his *Miserere*.[36]

The Paston manuscripts contain a very personal collection of music. Of the nineteen of Byrd's consort works found in them, eleven are Latin-titled works. The presence of these works may reflect Edward Paston's Catholicism and also be a result of his desire to collect music from an earlier period (i.e. from before 1585) and a wish for suitable music for teaching. Paston's collection does not include the *Browning* Fantasy which was circulating before 1580. Perhaps it was not serious enough for him. Only two In Nomines by Byrd are found in his collection. Of course, manuscripts containing other In Nomines could have been lost. Fantasia 6/g1 appears twice in the collection so it was quite clearly a valued piece of music, especially as it is found alongside Latin motets.

Manuscripts not in the Paston collection dating from *c.* 1600 to the 1640s

Excluding the Latin-titled works, 17 and part of an eighteenth out of 22 of Byrd's consort pieces are found in the 13 sets of partbooks and one scorebook dating from the first part of the seventeenth century that are not part of the Paston collection. All of Byrd's fantasias are found in these except for two of the three-part fantasias and the first six-part fantasia, Fantasia 6/F, although one source, GB-Lbl Add. MSS 17786–91 (24), contains a textless version of Byrd's motet based on the fantasia likely to have been be treated as an instrumental piece.[37]

All of Byrd's In Nomines are found in these seventeenth-century manuscripts, except for In Nomine 5/1. This appeared only in GB-Lbl Add. MS 31390, suggesting that it was not widely circulated. In Nomine 5/5 is the most common work, appearing in five manuscripts as well as in the three Paston manuscripts. Byrd's *Browning* Fantasy and the Prelude and Ground appear in one manuscript, GB-Lbl Add. MSS 17792–96. Only one of the 14 sources contains more than three consort pieces by Byrd: GB-Ob MSS Mus. Sch. d. 212–6 contains six of his seven In Nomines included among a collection of 70 In Nomines. Byrd's consort music is also found in seven seventeenth century manuscripts for lute and keyboard.

Seventeenth-century partbooks reflect the growing demand for music for viol consort or voices and viols. The rise of amateur playing appears to have begun in the Inns of Court and the universities and was apparent from the 1590s.[38] In private households children were taught the viol by professional musicians, who were commonly ex-choristers. Many of these pupils became keen amateur viol players in the early seventeenth century. Playing the viol and the Jacobean fantasia became the favourite form of domestic ensemble music-making. The seventeenth century collections often reflect particular aspects of musical life at this time.

Craig Monson describes what is thought to be the earliest of these sources from the first decades of the seventeenth century, GB-Lbl Add. MS 37402–6 (21), as an 'anthology for viol players' of 139 pieces, probably compiled after 1606.[39] The five partbooks are a diverse collection that contain the range of musical forms found in the early Jacobean period and encompass 75 Italian madrigals, motets, consort pieces, Elizabethan madrigals, consort songs and Anglican service music, a substantial amount of which is without text. The composers of this collection of music mainly come from the generation after Byrd, including John Dowland (1563–1626), Thomas Tomkins (1572–1656), John Wilbye (1574–1638), Thomas Weelkes (1576–1623), Orlando Gibbons (1583–1625) and Byrd's pupil, Thomas Morley (1557–1603). Just nine pieces found in the manuscript were actually conceived as instrumental consort music, among which are Byrd's Fantasia 6/g2 and four parts of his Pavan 5/c, the latter the only dance in the collection, and Parsons's *De la court.* All five part of Pavan 5/c are found in D-Kl MS mus. 125 (22), which is almost entirely devoted to pavans. The manuscript reflects the repertoire performed by itinerant troupes of English actor-musicians working at the court of Landgrave Moritz of Hesse-Kassel from 1592–1627.[40] A third manuscript from the early years of the seventeenth century, GB-Lbl Add. MSS 34800A–C (23), contains untexted vocal music and three-part fantasias, among them Byrd's Fantasia 3/C1.

One of two early seventeenth-century manuscripts associated with Oxford, GB-Lbl Add. MSS 17786–91 (24) is the largest and probably the earliest.[41] Begun some time before 1610, the majority of composers found in this collection matriculated or received degrees in Oxford between 1590 and 1635; several have a particular connection with New College and Magdalen, including William Wigthorpe (*c.*1570–*c.*1610), who may have been the scribe.[42] The music is split between textless consort music and music for voices and viols. It reflects musical life during the first part of the reign of James I. It is also the earliest set of manuscripts to contain both a six-part fantasia by Byrd and a significant amount of consort music in six parts by other composers. Of the 45 pieces identifiable as being written for viols, 17 are in six parts. Although there are a larger number of five-parts works (26) the increase in six-part works is symptomatic of the increased demand for six-part music after 1600.

Three parts of Fantasia 6/g1 are confusingly found among five-part music. It was initially copied without the coda, which was added at a later date. This raises the question of whether Byrd wrote all three parts of Fantasia 6/g1 at the same time, which will be discussed in Chapter Eight. An adaptation of Byrd's motet *Laudate pueri* to accommodate the English words 'Behold now praise the Lord' is also found in the manuscript without text and is the second work in the six-part pieces. Virtually all of this section is instrumental music. Fantasia 5/C and Parsons's *De la court* are also found in the manuscript.

The second source associated with Oxford, GB-Ob MSS Mus. Sch. d. 212–6 (25), contains the largest known collection of In Nomines, 70 in all including six of Byrd's seven In Nomines. Initially consisting of 64 In Nomines by Byrd and his contemporaries and slightly younger composers such as Gibbons, this collection was likely complete by 1610. Taverner's original In Nomine is the second entered in the manuscript. Sometime later, a further nine In Nomines by later composers were collected and added and bound in the manuscript, making 70 in all.[43] Mus. Sch. d. 212–6 was known to be part of the Oxford Music School collection which would seem to indicate that In Nomines still had a connection with choirboy education.

Byrd's publication of *Psalmes, Songs and Sonnets* (26) in 1611 as 'Fit for Voyces or Viols', indicates his awareness of the developing market for music for both voices and viols and viol consort. This collection is the most diverse of Byrd's publications and the only one in which he included textless consort pieces, these being Fantasia 4/g and Fantasia 6/g2. The music is in three to six voices, carefully organised into sections, and consists of a mixture of serious and lighter works, including English motets, consort songs and three- and four-part songs. It is suitable for performance solely by viols, or by a mixture of voices and viols. Byrd seems to have carefully chosen works to serve this dual purpose and felt it was right to include alongside them two completely instrumental works, although we can ponder as to why he chose these particular works. *Psalmes, Songs and Sonnets* is, of course, the definitive source for Byrd's final versions of the two fantasias, 4/g and 6/g2.

Single parts for Byrd's other two four-part fantasias, 4/a and 4/G are found in GB-Lbl Add. MS 29427 (27), a single surviving partbook which, like many other manuscripts, is associated with ecclesiastical foundations and choristers. It was collected by Thomas Myriell (*c.*1580–1625) between *c.*1612 and sometime after 1618. Myriell was a London cleric, who graduated from Cambridge in 1600 or 1601.[44] The music reflects the scribe's life in Cambridge and London, where Myriell joined the circle of musicians based round St Paul's.

Byrd's most popular consort work in manuscripts, In Nomine 5/5, was still being copied in the first decades of the seventeenth century. It is the only one of Byrd's consort works found in two manuscript collections, GB-Lcm MS 2049 (28) and GB-Lbl MS Egerton 3665 (29). GB-Lcm MS 2049 (28) consists of a miscellaneous collection of instrumental music and English part and consort songs, including music used in choirboy plays, suggesting it was used in education of choristers. MS Egerton 3665 (29) is unusual as it written in score; it was probably copied by Francis Tregian (1574?–1617).[45] It contains a staggering 1038 pieces of which 700 are Italian madrigals and 167 appear to be instrumental consort pieces, mainly fantasias.[46] Byrd's In Nomine 5/5 is entered between Parsons's and Mundy's five-part In Nomines.

Three large manuscript collections, completed between 1625 and 1639, were made by John Merro in Gloucester. The earliest to be completed, NY-MSS Drexel 4180–5 (30), was likely made by Merro for informal use by the Gloucester Cathedral choirmen and friends, its contents being recreational music.[47] Six partbooks contain over 250 anthems, motets, madrigals, consort songs and consort pieces in three to six parts dating from the time of Edward VI to 1625. A significant group of 21 consort pieces is found at the end of the partbooks. The first of these are Byrd's Fantasia 6/g2 and Fantasia 4/g, followed by fantasias in three or four parts, with one five-part piece, by contemporary composers including Orlando Gibbons. Byrd's *Laudate pueri* (texted) is also entered, the first of a group of Latin motets. Byrd's In Nomine 5/5 is found earlier in the manuscript in a group of five works in five parts; it is followed by Parsons's In Nomine and Ferrabosco I's In Nomine I. Only one of the Italian madrigals in NY-MSS Drexel 4180–5 is texted. Byrd's song, close to a madrigal, *This sweet and merry month*, appears with text; it is followed by Marenzio's madrigal *Every singing byrd*, which has an English text substituted as a compliment to Byrd.

Merro's two other collections of partbooks seem to have been for his own use.[48] GB-Ob MSS Mus. Sch. D. 245–247 (31) contains an inscription 'John Merro/his booke'. The collection contains 450 pieces for one to three viols, the majority of which were instrumentally conceived. It includes three parts of Byrd's Fantasia 4/g, probably copied from Byrd's *Psalmes, Songs and Sonnets* of 1611. Merro's third set of partbooks, GB-Lbl, Add. MSS 17792–6 (32), reveals his interest in instrumental and contemporary music. Craig Monson describes the collection as 'a repository for instrumental composition'.[49] Five out of six surviving partbooks contain 236 pieces in three to seven parts of which 156 are consort pieces mainly by composers composing in the seventeenth century, such as Gibbons and Thomas Tomkins, including fantasias and pavans, almains and airs. Four five-part Elizabethan consort works are found in the manuscripts, these being Byrd's Prelude and Ground[50] (*Praeludium*) and his *Browning* Fantasy, Holborne's *The Funeralls* and Mundy's *Sermone blando*. Merro had responsibility for teaching the viol to the choristers at Gloucester Cathedral and the collection in Add. MSS 17792–6 was probably to supply music for consort-playing choristers.

A further two small sets of partbooks, containing just consort music, date from the 1630s to around the early 1640s and include a small amount of music by Byrd. GB-Lbl Add. MSS 39550–4 (33), owned by Sir Nicholas Le Strange (1603–1655) of Hunstanton in Norfolk, was probably completed by 1644, when John Jenkins (1592–1678), composer and viol player, first arrived in Hunstanton and became Le Strange's copyist.[51] The five surviving partbooks contain 103 consort works, mainly fantasias ('Fancies') in five and six parts. Thirteen In Nomines are found among the fantasias. These include Byrd's In Nomine 5/3, which is followed by Ferrabsoco I's three five-part In Nomine, after which is found Byrd's In Nomine 5/4. The placing of these five works together may mean the scribe saw the relationship between them.

The second set of six partbooks completed after 1640, GB–Ob MSS Mus Sch. C 64–9 (34) is dated 1641 with the signature 'George Stratford', an Oxford student and resident of Gloucestershire. Copying dates from sometime in the mid to latter years of the 1630s. The set is important as it is the only source for Byrd's Pavan and Galliard 6/C. The collection consists of over 150 consort pieces, all by composers writing in the seventeenth century with the exception of Byrd's two dances. Neighbour observes that it is unlikely Byrd composed his six-part pavan and galliard before 1610 and that English composers do not seem to have written six-part dances before the seventeenth century.[52] The six-part works open with a paired pavan and galliard by Tomkins, followed by Byrd's Pavan and Galliard 6/C.

Keyboard and lute manuscripts completed in the seventeenth century

Six manuscripts of keyboard music and one of lute music copied between 1620 and *c.*1670, contain consort music by Byrd. Five of these collections contain just one of Byrd's consort works arranged for keyboard or lute. Both keyboard and lute were popular instruments in the sixteenth and seventeenth centuries among amateur and professional musicians. Although printed keyboard music appeared on the Continent before it did in England, British composers were adventurous in developing keyboard techniques. Until the printing of *Parthenia* in 1612–13, containing music by Byrd, John Bull (1568–1628) and Gibbons, English keyboard music, like viol music, had circulated only in manuscript.[53]

Printed tutors for lute appeared from the 1560s but music continued to circulate in manuscripts. The lute repertory found in England between 1570 and 1630 was larger than that for either keyboard or viol. In her research on lute manuscripts, Julia Craig-McFeely found that the majority were copied between 1580 and 1615.[54] The popularity of the lute throughout Europe coincided with the period that two lutenists, father and son John and Robert Johnson, held appointments at the English court; John Johnson (*c.*1545–1594) served Elizabeth I from 1579 until his death and Robert Johnson (*c.*1583–1633) served James I and Charles I from 1604 until his death.[55]

Two of the six keyboard manuscripts, both of which relate to Thomas Tomkins, are of particular interest. The first of these, GB-Lbl Add. MS 29996 (35), was completed over a considerable period of time from the mid-sixteenth to mid-seventeenth centuries and eventually came into the hands of Tomkins, probably during his time as organist (from 1621) at the Chapel Royal. It is a confusing, extraordinary manuscript containing over 200 works including five of Byrd's consort pieces. Parsons's five-part In Nomine and Byrd's In Nomine 5/5 are found in the first part, compiled in the mid-sixteenth century, in short score. The second part contains later music written or arranged for keyboard and music in open score including fancies (fantasias), Byrd songs, English madrigals and pavans. Some of the copying is in the hand of Tomkins, including his accurate copy of Byrd's *Browning* Fantasy in open score, which Tomkins describes as 'A most Excellent piece'. Byrd's Fantasia 5/C (from which the beginning is missing) and the two six-part Fantasias 6/g1 and 6/g2 in keyboard score are also found in the second part of the manuscript.

The second manuscript relating to Tomkins, F-PC MS Rés. 1122 (39), was copied by him in short score during his last years at Worcester from 1646 to 1654. Almost all of its 88 pieces were composed for keyboard by Tomkins.[56] The collection includes keyboard arrangements of Byrd's Fantasias 4/g and 5/C. Both of these arrangements are of interest. Tomkins's adaptation of Fantasia 4/g, as well as containing some mistakes, is different from Byrd's version published in 1611, suggesting that it was copied from an earlier version that Byrd revised for publication.[57] Tomkins's keyboard arrangement of Fantasia 5/C is from the version found in the manuscript of consort music GB-Lbl Add. MSS 17786–91 (24), not Byrd's own keyboard version.

The remaining four manuscripts each contain just one consort work by Byrd. Scholars disagree on the date of the only lutebook, GB-Lbl MS Hirsch M.1353 (36); the repertoire in the manuscript dates mainly from the late sixteenth century. It contains adaptations of consort music for lute, among which is found Byrd's Fantasia 4/g (the version from 1611, with some mistakes).

The presence of Fantasia 5/C, as found in *My Ladye Nevell's Booke*, at the end of a collection of 42 keyboard pieces in D-Bds Lübbenau MS Lynar A2 (37) links Byrd with the music of Sweelinck, whose music is found in the companion manuscript, D-Bds Lübbenau MS Lynar A1. Pieter Dirksen places MS Lynar A1 and A2 as originating in north Germany and associated with the keyboard school of Sweelinck.[58] Part of Fantasia 5/C is also found in another keyboard manuscript, GB-Och MS 1113 (40), a collection of 118 pieces, including toccatas, canzonas, fantasias, In Nomines and Almaines copied in Oxford. It contains the earliest known examples of Italian keyboard music found in England.[59]

Finally, Pavan 5c is found in its keyboard version in US-NYp MS Drexel 5612 (38)' a collection of 191 pieces, a substantial amount of which is English dance music, which was likely completed by1660, and thirteen bars of Fantasia 4/a are found in a keyboard manuscript GB-Lcm, MS 2093 (41) containing 30 pieces. Dating from the 1660s to the 1670s, it contains instruction material, notably a series of preludes and polyphonic music.

There is a notable increase towards music composed for viols or voices and viols in the partbooks dating from after 1600 and the music becomes much more diverse. There is also a move from collections containing music predominantly in up to five parts to collections that include six-part works, reflecting the establishing of the six-part viol consort. Of the ten sets of partbooks containing consort music by Byrd begun after 1610, seven are from sets of six (which include the occasional seven-part work). There is also the emergence of collections for viols containing music for one to three parts. After 1600, In Nomines become less common in collections of consort music, although Byrd's In Nomine 5/5 is found in three of the Paston manuscripts and five other sources dating from after 1600. Overall fantasias and dance-based music, especially pavans, are much more prominent as is music for voices and viols, reflecting seventeenth-century taste and contemporary compositions.

What the sources tell us

Although many of Byrd's consort works survive in manuscripts copied a significant time after they were written, the chronological order in which these sources appeared does mainly seem to reflect the order in which Byrd wrote the music. Only one of Byrd's Latin-titled textless consort works is found in a manuscript dating before 1600, but it appears in one of the two earliest manuscripts to contain a consort work by Byrd, pointing to it being an early work. The fact that all the others only appear in manuscripts belonging to or associated with Edward Paston, suggest they were specifically collected for a general use of singing and/or playing and teaching within his household and otherwise not widely circulated.

Byrd's In Nomines appear in the earliest manuscripts and in the two surviving large collections. His most popular In Nomine 5/5 is, on several occasions, one of a very small collection of the genre, often with Parsons's five-part In Nomine. In six sources this is placed before or after In Nomine 5/5. They are the only two In Nomines included in a late keyboard source, GB-Lbl MS 29996 (35), which would suggest they were considered the best examples of the genre. Ferrabosco I's five-part In Nomines are also found with Byrd's In Nomines; of particular significance is GB-Lbl Add. MSS 39550–4 (33), where they are placed with Byrd's In Nomine 5/3 and 5/4.

Laudate pueri was published by Byrd in 1575 and Fantasia 6/F is only found in a manuscript dating from between the late 1570s to *c.*1580, but if it is accepted the fantasia came first, then it must have been written *c.*1570. The *Browning* Fantasy is the next to appear in a manuscript, followed by Fantasia 6/g1, Fantasia 5/C and Fantasia 6/g2. Only the Prelude and Ground and the Pavan 5/c would seem to have appeared in a manuscript out of the order of composition.

In eight sources, Byrd's *Browning* Fantasy is found twice next to Latin motets. Fantasia 6/F is found between Latin motets and Parsons's *The song called trumpets* in GB-Och MSS 979–983 (4). Both Fantasias 6/g1 and 6/g2 are found with Latin motets. Fantasia 6/g1 is the only consort work in two of Paston's manuscript collections, placed with Latin motets and both the Fantasia 6/g1 and Fantasia 6/g2 are found entered at the end of GB-Ob MS Mus. Sch. e. 423 (6) after Latin motets. This would suggest this music was valued as much as the motets, illustrating the change in attitude towards instrumental music that was taking place towards the end of the sixteenth century. In later manuscripts, Byrd's fantasias are found with fantasias by seventeenth-century composers, as in, for example, NYp MSS Drexel 4180–5 (30). He, of course, finally published two fantasias in his *Psalmes, Songs and Sonnets* of 1611.

With one exception, Byrd's three-part fantasias are found only in three Paston manuscripts, in two cases being found alongside Latin motets. Fantasia 3/C1 is also found in a manuscript containing other three-part fantasias, GB-Lbl Add. MSS 34800A-C (23). Five of the sources for Fantasia 5/C are keyboard collections; it is found only in one collection of partbooks, GB-Lbl Add. MSS 17786–91 (24), a significant collection of music for viols and voices and viols. Here it is the second work entered, following Parsons's *De la court*, suggesting the scribe's recognition of its importance in the repertoire. Fantasia 4/a and Fantasia 4/g are found with fantasias by White in one of the Paston manuscripts copied for lute, GB-Lbl

Add. MS 29246 (14), after Latin motets. In later manuscripts they are both found with other fantasias. In three out of four sources, the Pavan 5/c is found with other dances.

Fantasia 4/g is found in six sources from after 1600. These include Byrd's own publication, *Psalmes, Songs and Sonnets* of 1611 (26) and one keyboard collection, in which it may have been copied from a pre-publication version. It is the only consort work by Byrd found in the Hirsch Lute Book (36) and GB-Ob MSS Mus Sch D. 245–7, copied by Merro.

Linking the sources to Byrd's life also helps establish the order in which his consort music was composed, though precise dating is not possible. We know that Byrd studied with Tallis, whom he named as his teacher, and that he acted as assistant organist and worked with singers at the Chapel Royal before he went to Lincoln in 1563. It is highly likely that his Latin-titled textless works were written in the environment of the Chapel Royal as part of his composition studies; they could have been sung or played. It is also likely that he wrote at least four of his In Nomines before he left for Lincoln in 1563. His In Nomine 5/5 is a very mature work for a young composer still in his twenties, and closer examination will suggest it was his last, composed in Lincoln. It displays many of the traits and ideas he later developed.

After completing the In Nomines, Byrd seems to have written very little viol consort music in Lincoln. Towards the end of his time there, Byrd became very dissatisfied with his position. He also was considering how he could find new forms to support instrumental music i.e. music without words or a cantus firmus. The publication of an arrangement of Fantasia 6/F as a motet, *Laudate pueri*, in 1575, suggests the original was composed shortly before Byrd left Lincoln in 1572. The author noticed many years ago that the third theme in Fantasia 6/F, appearing in the bass at breve 38, is a direct quotation from an anthem *Lord for thy tender mercy's sake*, composed by Richard Farrant after 1566, at the words 'That we may walk with a perfect heart'.[60] Richard Farrant (1525?–1580) was Master of the Choristers at St George's Chapel Windsor from 1564 and, from 1569, worked in a similar capacity at the Chapel Royal.[61] Byrd undoubtedly wanted to return to the Chapel Royal or find a similar position. It seems too much of a coincidence that Byrd should incorporate the quotation into a fantasia written around this time. The scribe of the only manuscript in which it is found, GB-OCh MSS 979–983 (4), was John Baldwin, a lay clerk at Windsor. Surely Byrd must have wished the Fantasia 6F would come to Farrant's attention? This supposition would date Fantasia 6/F to after *c.*1567 and support Milsom and others' views that the fantasia was written first. This will be explored further in Chapter Six.

Byrd's next excursion into consort music was his exploration of variation form. The

Prelude and Ground probably came first, written about the same time as Fantasia 6/F although it does not appear in a manuscript until after 1585. The addition of Byrd's *Browning* Fantasy to GB-Lbl Add. MS 31390 in a separate hand, after the manuscript was mainly completed in 1578, suggests it was probably written after his return to London in 1572.

Byrd returned to writing fantasias sometime after his return to the Chapel Royal. Most were composed by around 1590. The three six-part fantasias were in circulation by 1589 and a keyboard version of five-part fantasia and Pavan 5/c by 1591. By 1615, when Byrd was in his old age, almost all of his fantasias could be found in contemporary manuscripts at a time when the viol had increased in popularity. Although he had begun to withdraw from the Chapel Royal and public life around 1592, Byrd was still astute enough to be aware of the market for viol music at the beginning of the seventeenth century, deciding to publish two of his fantasias in 1611. Only two new consort pieces by Byrd survive from after this date, the Pavan and Galliard 6/C. These only appear in the last known set of partbooks containing consort music by Byrd, GB-Ob MSS Mus Sch. C 64–9 (34), and date from after 1635, well after his death.

The four sources linked directly to Byrd are of particular importance in working out the chronology of his consort works. In spite of Fantasia 6/F not appearing until before the late 1570s in GB-Och MSS 979–983 (4), copied by Baldwin, it is the first Byrd fantasia to appear in any source, suggesting it was the first he wrote, especially as the related motet, *Laudate pueri*, is found in the *Cantiones Sacrae* of 1575. GB-Ob MS Mus. Sch. e. 423 (6), copied from after 1587 to *c.*1589 and connected to Byrd through his patron, John Petre, is the earliest source for Fantasias 6/g1 and 6/g2. The keyboard collection, *My Ladye Nevell's Booke* (10), again copied by Baldwin in 1591, possibly under Byrd's direction, contains versions of Fantasia 5/C, the Ground and the Pavan 5/c. Byrd's Fantasia 4/g does not appear in any manuscript before 1600 and its publication by Byrd in 1611 in *Psalmes, Songs and Sonnets* (26) points to this being one of the last fantasias he wrote.

There is enough information in the 41sources containing Byrd's consort music to put them in an approximate order, which helps to place the works in a likely order of composition and suggest the order in which Byrd explored individual genre. In the following chapters, individual works are examined in the order it is thought they were composed, taking account of the information found in the sources, any known historical information, circumstantial evidence and the evidence of the music itself.

1 Gordon Dodds and Andrew Ashbee (eds), *The Viola da Gamba Society* (VdGS) *Thematic Index of Music for*

Viols, http://vdgs.org.uk/thematic; Doe in MB 44, p. 191.

2 Dodds and Ashbee (eds), http://vdgs.org.uk/thematic; Doe, MB 44, p. 186.

3 Byrd, of course, may have influenced Ferrabosco I, encouraging him to write In Nomines.

4 Ferrabosco also wrote an unusual six-part fantasia for bass instruments, *Di sei bassi* (MB44/68).

5 Warwick Edwards, 'The Sources of Elizabethan Consort Music' (unpublished Ph.D dissertation, University of Cambridge, 1974).

6 Dodds and Ashbee (eds), http://vdgs.org.uk/thematic.

7 Andrew Ashbee, Robert Thompson and Jonathan Wainwright, *The Viola da Gamba Society Index of Manuscripts containing consort music*, http://vdgs.org.uk/indexmss/.

8 Universities of Newcastle and Oxford, (Magnus Williamson, Julia Craig-McFeely and Katherine Butler) 'Tudor Partbook Project', http://www.tudorpartbooks.ac.uk/; 'Digital Image Archive of Medieval Music' (DIAMM); http://www.diamm.ac.uk; Trinity College, Dublin, 'Early English Church Music (EECM) Primary Source Data Base', http://eecm.tcd.ie/volumes/.

9 Iain Fenlon and John Milsom, '"Ruled Paper Imprinted": Music Paper and Patents in Sixteenth-Century England', *Journal of the American Musicological Society*, 37/1 (Spring 1984), pp. 139–63; Katherine Butler, 'Printed Borders for Sixteenth Century Music or Music Paper and the Early Career of Music Printer Thomas East (*c.* 1540–1608)', *The Library*, 19/2 (2018), pp. 124–202.

10 Bryan, '"Choice Consorts….(Rare Chests of Viols)": The Evidence of the Repertory', p. 14.

11 Philip William Taylor, 'Music and Recusant Culture: The Paston Manuscript Collection and William Byrd's Songs', (unpublished PhD dissertation, University of Lancaster, 2007).

12 David Mateer, 'William Byrd, John Petre and Oxford, Bodleian MS Mus. Sch. E. 423', *Royal Musical Association Research Chronicle*, 29 (1996), p. 21.

13 Ibid, p. 37.

14 Harley, *William Byrd Gentleman of the Chapel Royal*, p. 94; *The World of William Byrd*, p. 171.

15 Harley, *The World of William Byrd*, pp. 181–2.

16 John Harley, '"My Ladye Nevell" Revealed', *Music & Letters*, 86/1 (February 2005), p. 2.

17 Harley, *William Byrd Gentleman of the Chapel Royal*, p. 243. In his research, Tihomir Popović disagrees, as he argues that there is no documentary evidence to support Byrd's direct involvement but he does not provide any alternative suggestion as to who did edit the manuscript: Tihomir Popović, *Mäzene — Manuskripte — Modi: Untersuchungen zu My Ladye Nevells Booke* (Stuttgart, 2013), p. 132.

18 EECM 56, p. 258.

19 Edwards, 'The Sources of Elizabethan Consort Music', p. 99.

20 EECM 56, p. 258.

21 Tim Carter, 'Secular Vocal Music', in Roger Bray (ed.), *The Sixteenth Century*, pp. 147–209, at p. 163: Edwards, 'The Sources of Elizabethan Consort Music', p. 78.

22 Craig Monson, *Voices and Viols in England, 1600–1650* (Michigan, 1982), p. 170; one part of *Beati omnes* is missing, but five parts, including two bass parts, survive.

23 John Milsom (ed), *Christ Church Oxford Library Music Catalogue*, 'GB-Och Mus.984–988', http://library.chch.ox.ac.uk/music/.

24 With the exception of two works added by John Baldwin, these being No. 53 (Parsons, *O bone Iesu*) and No. 54 (Nathaniel Giles, *Vestigia mea*).

25 David Mateer, 'William Byrd, John Petre and Oxford, Bodleian MS Mus. Sch. E. 423', *Royal Musical Association Research Chronicle*, 29 (1996), p. 34.

26 Ibid., p. 37.

27 Ibid,, p. 41.

28 Edwards, 'The Sources of Elizabethan Consort Music', p. 136.

29 Ibid. Edwards, p. 160.

30 John Harley, '"My Ladye Nevell" Revealed', *Music and Letters*, 86/1 (2005), p. 2.

31 The Tudor Partbooks Project, Gb-Ob Tenbury 389, Discantus Inventory, http://www.tudorpartbooks.ac.uk/.

32 Edwards, 'The Sources of Elizabethan Consort Music', p. 189; DIAMM, http://www.diamm.ac.uk.

33 Philip Brett, 'Edward Paston (1550–1630): A Norfolk Gentleman and his Musical Collection', *Transactions of the Cambridge Bibliographical Society*, 1964, pp 51–69; Hector Sequera, 'House Music for Recusants in Elizabethan England: Performance Practice in the Music Collection of Edward Paston (1550–1630)', (unpublished PhD dissertation, University of Birmingham, 2010).

34 Ibid, Sequera, p. 161.

35 21 pieces are listed but four are sections of the same Latin-titled pieces by Byrd; Edwards, 'The Sources of Elizabethan Consort Music', pp. 173–4: Taylor, 'Music and Recusant Culture: The Paston Manuscript Collection and William Byrd's Songs', pp. 41–2.

36 Edwards points out it was owned by Stephen Aldhouse, who was a witness to Paston's will, and quotes Philip Brett as believing it was completed by a member of the Paston Family or household; 'The Sources of Elizabethan Consort Music', p. 189.

37 See Monson, *Voices and Viols in England, 1600–1650*, p. 174.

38 Woodfield, *The Early History of the* Viol, p. 227.

39 Monson, *Voices and Viols in England, 1600–1650*, p. 210.

40 MB 101, *Philips and Dering Consort Music*, p. 184.

41 Monson, *Voices and Viols in England, 1600–1650*, p. 159.

42 See Monson, p. 17 and Smith in MB 101, *Philips and Dering Consort Music*, p. 185.

43 Three are duplicates.

44 Monson, *Voices and Viols in England, 1600–1650*, p.7; Pamela J. Willetts, 'Musical Connections of Thomas

Myriell', *Music & Letters,* 49/1 (1968), p. 39; Pamela J. Willetts, 'The Identity of Thomas Myriell', *Music & Letters* 53/4 (1972), p. 432.

45 See David J. Smith, 'A Legend? Francis Tregian the Younger as Music Copyist', *Musical Times*, 143, (Summer, 2002), pp. 7–16; MB 101, p. xxiv. Ruby Reid Thompson argues that there is not sufficient evidence that Tregian copied Egerton 3665. See Ruby Reid Thompson, 'Francis Tregian the Younger as Music Copyist: a Legend and an Alternative View', *Music & Letters*, 82/1 (February 2001), pp.1–31. David Smith repudiates her claims in his article in the *Musical Times.*

46 Frank D'Accone (ed.), *London British Library MS Egerton 3665, The Tregian Manuscript* (New York, 1988).

47 Andrew Ashbee, 'John Merro's Manuscripts Revisited', *The Viol da Gamba Society Journal*, 7 (2013), p. 2.

48 Andrew Ashbee, 'John Merro's Manuscripts Revisited', p. 5.

49 Monson, *Voices and Viols in England, 1600–1650,* p. 144.

50 Unfortunately with errors.

51 Andrew Ashbee, 'A Further Look at Some of the Le Strange Manuscripts', *Chelys*, 5 (1973–4), p. 27.

52 Neighbour, *The Consort and Keyboard Music of William Byrd*, pp. 86–7.

53 Rachelle Taylor and Frauke Jürgensen, 'Politics, Religion, Style and the Pazzamezzo Galliards of Byrd and Philips', in David J. Smith and Rachelle Taylor (eds), *Networks of Music and Culture in the Late Sixteenth and Early Seventeenth Centuries* (Abingdon 2013), p. 72.

54 Julia Craig-McFeely, 'English Lute Manuscripts and Scribes 1530–1630' (DPhil dissertation, Oxford University 1993), https://www.cs.dartmouth.edu/~wbc/julia/;), Introduction, p. 5.

55 Matthew Spring, *The Lute in Britain: A History of the Instrument and Its Music* (Oxford, 2006), p. 98.

56 Candace Bailey, 'Orlando Gibbons, Keyboard Music and the Beginnings of the Baroque: New Considerations of a Musical Style', *International Review of the Aesthetics and Sociology of Music* (IRASM), 37/2 (2006), pp. 142 and 147; Keith Elcombe, 'Keyboard Music', in Roger Bray (ed.), *The Sixteenth Century*, pp. 210–262, at p. 251.

57 See Neighbour, *The Consort and Keyboard Music of William Byrd*, p. 93.

58 Pieter Dirksen, 'New Perspectives on Lynar A1', in (ed.) Christopher Hogwood, *The Keyboard in Baroque Europe* (Cambridge, 2003), p. 66.

59 Candace Bailey, 'William Ellis and the Transmission of Continental Keyboard Music in Restoration England', *Journal of Musicological Research*, 20 (2001), p. 211.

60 The text can be found in a collected edition of prayers entitled *Christian Praiers and Holy Meditacions* edited by Henry Bull (d. 1575?), published 1570. The prayers were part of an earlier publication, *Lidley's Prayers,* also from a collection by Bull, published in 1566. See *Christian Prayers and Holy Meditations, as Well for Private as Public Exercise.* Collected by Henry Bull (A.D. 1566). Reprinted for the Parker Society, (Cambridge, 1842).

61 It is not clear exactly what position Farrant held at the Chapel Royal. Alan Mould suggests he was probably initially under-master there; see Mould, *The English Chorister*, pp. 119 and 308, n.36.

Chapter 5

Byrd's In Nomines and other chant-based consort works

Byrd's earliest consort works were based on Latin chant, the most important of which are his In Nomines. In writing the latter, he was contributing to an established genre to which nearly all sixteenth-century English composers contributed. The earliest known date of a composition by Byrd is 1558 when, at the age of approximately eighteen, he collaborated with Sheppard and William Mundy in a psalm setting for four voices, *Similes illes fiant.* As part of his chorister training, Byrd would have been expected to write textless works based on chant. Eleven early works with Latin titles survive, these being ten consort hymns and his Miserere settings. The earliest is thought to be the three-part *Sermone Blando.* After writing his Latin-titled consort works, Byrd then turned to the In Nomine, based on a chant commonly used to structure instrumental compositions. Seven In Nomines by Byrd have come down to us, two in four parts and five in five parts. They are the earliest of his consort works to appear in manuscripts with the exception of one consort hymn, *Christe qui lux* (II).

As will become clear, stylistically, the majority of Byrd's consort works based on cantus firmi, including In Nomines, point to them being early works, composed between 1555 and early in 1563 before he left London for Lincoln aged twenty-three. This comprises of his Latin-titled works, Miserere settings and at least four of his seven In Nomines, these being the two four-part In Nomines and the five-part In Nomines 5/1 and 5/2. All are likely to have been written while Byrd was at the Chapel Royal, the earliest when he was a pupil of Tallis and the later works after he had become Tallis's assistant. In Nomine 5/1 was originally ascribed to (William) Mundy; the attribution, in the one source, GB-Lbl Add. MS 31390 (2), was then altered by the scribe and attributed to Byrd.[1] There are strong indications that Byrd was the composer.

In Nomine 5/3, In Nomine 5/4 and In Nomine 5/5 date from either just before Byrd left London or just after he arrived in Lincoln. In Nomines 5/3 and 5/4 display the influence of Alfonso Ferrabosco I; these two works could not have been composed before the latter part of 1562. Ferrabosco became one of Elizabeth I's musicians in March 1562; Byrd was in Lincoln by February 1563.[2] Byrd's In Nomine 5/5 is a mature work and probably the last of his seven In Nomines and must have been written in Lincoln. His next venture into the composition of consort music was to explore two new forms, the fantasia and variation form, resulting in Fantasia 6/F and his Prelude and Ground. The surviving evidence points to Fantasia 6/F also having been written while Byrd was in Lincoln; this will be explored in the next chapter but, as will become clear, there is also a relationship between it and Byrd's first In Nomine. There is no record of Byrd being involved with viol players at Lincoln and it is impossible to know exactly for whom he was writing consort works, including In Nomine 5/5, while he was there.[3] It is possible that Byrd was continuing to write for the Chapel Royal musicians. Harley points to evidence suggesting that Byrd occasionally visited London during his years in Lincoln.[4]

Around 150 settings of the In Nomine written for viol consort survive from a period of 150 years dating from immediately after the circulation of Taverner's original work, the In Nomine section of his festal mass *Gloria tibi Trinitas* (Example 5.1). This was probably composed while Taverner was in the service of Cardinal Wolsey between 1526 and 1530.[5] John Bryan describes Taverner's In Nomine as 'a beautifully crafted example of a compositional style' and points out that the individual parts are very closely related to each other.[6] The growth of interest in the In Nomine in the 1560s corresponds with the realisation by composers that the techniques of crafting church music round plainsong, no longer possible under Elizabeth I's Protestant regime, could be transferred to the composition of textless consort music.[7] Byrd was of course developing his compositional skills in the 1560s. The In Nomine offered compositional opportunities to both established and fledgling composers and a practical application in its suitability for beginner viol players, who could play the cantus firmus. The latter provided a way of teaching beginners to read music and the opportunity to play with experienced players, as happened in the choir schools. By the time Byrd was writing his In Nomines, the corpus of music included works by Tye, Tallis, Parsley, William Mundy, Parsons and White. In Nomines are centrally concerned with imitation; the cantus firmus is accompanied by imitative melodies exchanged between the other voices.[8] This imitation was termed *fuga* by sixteenth century composers.

Tye and Tallis were the earliest important composers of In Nomines. Twenty-one In Nomines by Tye survive,[9] the largest number by any composer, in which he explored different ideas and the individual ranges of viols and possible compass of a viol consort. Only two In Nomines by Tallis, Byrd's teacher, survive, both in four parts. Byrd must have known and indeed probably played these two works. The developmental steps and exploration taken by Byrd in his In Nomines reflect the start of his journey towards an individual instrumental style. In her book on Byrd, Kerry McCarthy writes that 'Byrd's group of In Nomines for five voices traces the broad outlines of his early development as a consort composer'.[10]

Example 5.1 John Taverner, In Nomine from Benedictus from *Missa Gloria Tibi Trinitas*

Sources

Except for one work, *Christe qui lux* (II), Byrd's Latin-titled consort works are only found in three manuscripts owned by Edward Paston and his family. All of the Latin-titled consort works are found in two manuscripts, GB-Lbl Add. MS 29246 (14) and GB-Ob MSS Tenbury 354–8 (15). Just the three-part *Sermone Blando* and Miserere are found in the third manuscript, GB-Lbl Add. MS 18936–9 (20). *Christe qui lux* (II) is found in GB-Lbl Add. MSS 30480–84 (1), a manuscript on which work started in *c.*1570 and probably the earliest source for any of Byrd's consort music.

In Nomines by Byrd are found in 16 of the 41 surviving sources of his consort music. The earliest source is GB-Lbl Add. MS 31390 (2), which contains In Nomine 5/1, In Nomine 5/4 and In Nomine 5/5 (and the *Browning* Fantasy) and was copied between *c.*1568 and *c.*1578. In Nomine 5/1 is found only in GB-Lbl Add. MS 31390 and is probably the first In Nomine Byrd wrote. It is the only one of his five-part In Nomines to appear in just one manuscript, with its altered attribution from Mundy to Byrd. It is found near the beginning of the five-part music, shortly after three of Tye's In Nomines.

Byrd's two four-part In Nomines survive only in manuscripts dating from the early seventeenth century, suggesting they did not circulate widely in his lifetime. Maybe this was because the majority of sixteenth-century viol music was written in five parts. Both are found in GB-Ob MSS Mus. Sch. d. 212–6 (25), completed around 1610 and In Nomine 4/1 is also found in a slightly different version in GB-Ob MSS Tenbury 354–8 (15), one of the Paston manuscripts.

In Nomine 5/2 is found in four manuscripts, spanning a period from the early 1570s to 1610. Only In Nomine 5/5 is found in a greater number of manuscripts; all of Byrd's other In Nomines, with the exception of the 5/4, found in three manuscripts, are found in just one or two manuscripts. The earliest manuscript containing In Nomine 5/2, GB-Ob MS Tenbury 1464 (3) dates from 1570–75; In Nomine 5/2 is the first of a group of eight In Nomines, five of which are by Tye. In Nomine 5/2 is the only one of Byrd's In Nomines included in the manuscript. It is found with In Nomine 5/5 in Add. GB-Lbl MS 32377 (8), a manuscript dating from the second half of the 1580s, among twenty In Nomines, the first two being by Ferrabosco I followed by Byrd's In Nomines 5/5 and 5/2. The collection would seem to have been all intended at least partly for viol players. It also includes Byrd's *Browning* Fantasy. In Nomine 5/2 is also found in GB-Ob MS Tenbury 389 (11), a manuscript started in the 1590s and in the largest known collection of In Nomines GB-Ob MSS Mus. School 212–6 (25), which was probably compiled in Oxford by 1610. This contains all of Byrd's In Nomines except for the In Nomine 5/1. Three of the manuscripts containing In Nomine 5/2 are associated with cathedral cities – Norwich, Exeter and Oxford – the latter two having well-documented evidence of viol playing.[11]

Byrd's In Nomine 5/3 was the last to appear in surviving manuscripts and is found with In Nomine 5/4 in two sources, GB-Ob MSS Mus. Sch. d. 212–6 (25) and GB-Lbl Add. MSS 39550–4 (33) both compiled in the seventeenth-century, well after the work's composition. GB-Lbl Add. MSS 39550–4 was completed in the 1640s and owned by Sir Nicholas Le Strange. In Nomines 5/3 and 5/4 are the only two works by Byrd in the manuscript. The In Nomine 5/3 precedes Ferrabosco's three In Nomines, which, in turn, are followed by Byrd's In Nomine 5/4, the relevance of which will be explored later in this chapter. In Nomine 5/4 is also one of the four of Byrd's works found in the early manuscript GB-Lbl Add. MS 31390 (2).

Byrd's In Nomine 5/5 is found in 14 manuscripts, making it the most frequently copied of all his consort works; all of these manuscripts are for viols except one (for keyboard). It is the only consort work by Byrd in five of these manuscripts and it was still appearing in collections up until *c.*1630. The earliest of the fourteen manuscripts was copied between *c.*1568 and 1578; the latest, for viols, is one of Merro's sets of manuscripts, GB-Lbl Add. MSS 17792–96 (30), dating from 1615–25. It is also found in the keyboard source, GB-Lbl MS 29996 (35), which spans the mid-sixteenth to the mid-seventeenth centuries. Parsons's surviving five-part In Nomine (III in MB 44 /56) is found in 12 of the sources containing Byrd's In Nomine 5/5. In six of these, the two works are placed together. The relationship between these two works is explored later in the chapter. Parsons was around ten years older than Byrd and an established composer when he wrote his highly successful consort pieces, including his surviving five-part and two seven-part In Nomines and *De la court*, before his untimely death in 1570. Parsons's five-part In Nomine was the most copied In Nomine in sixteenth and seventeenth-century sources. The VdGS *Thematic Index of Music for Viols* lists 20 manuscript sources in which it is found (plus an eighteenth century source); the sources include adaptions for lute and keyboard.[12]

Latin-titled works

Oliver Neighbour suggests that Byrd did not intend his Latin-titled consort pieces to be widely circulated, which would seem to be borne out by the fact the rest are known only from the Paston manuscripts dating from the seventeenth century.[13] Neighbour points to the influence of White on Byrd's textless Latin-titled works, in particular on *Christe qui lux* I and II. White set one hymn melody repeatedly as an exercise. Byrd followed his lead, making settings both for voices and instruments.[14] In his Latin-titled consort works, Byrd began to include traits that became characteristic of his instrumental consort works. This is apparent in his what is probably his earliest known textless composition, the three-part *Sermone Blando*, which includes a canon at the seventh in the second part (Example 5.2).

Example 5.2 *Sermone Blando* part two

By the time Byrd wrote *Christe qui lux* III, his instrumental style was beginning to emerge with his use of running crotchet movement and dotted crotchets and quavers, which appear in all the parts with the exception of the cantus firmus (Example 5.3a). This contrast with the small number of crotchet passages, no dotted crotchets and just two quavers found in *Christe qui lux* II (Example 5.3b). It is possible that Byrd intended three verses of *Christe qui lux* II to be played as even-numbered stanzas between three vocal verses, but the reverse may have been intended, with the even-numbered voices being sung.[15]

Example 5.3a Opening of *Christe qui lux* III

Example 5.3b Opening of *Christe qui lux* II*

* Found in BE 17/25, without text, as *Christe qui lux* (II).

In Nomines

In Nomine 5/1

John Milsom's belief that In Nomine 5/1 (Example 5.4) is one of Byrd's early compositions, written when he was a pupil of Tallis, seems highly plausible.[16] It is impossible to know why the scribe initially attributed it first to Mundy and then changed the attribution. GB-Lbl Add. MS 31390 (2) contains five works by Mundy, including one consort work, *O mater mundi*. A vocal work by Mundy, *In aeternum*, is the first piece entered in the manuscript, so the scribe was familiar with his compositions. William Mundy is believed to have written at least two In Nomines but, other than this initial misattribution, none are included in GB-Lbl Add. MS 31390. In Nomine 5/1 does not bear any resemblance to the two In Nomines attributed to Mundy.[17]

Example 5.4 Opening of In Nomine 5/1

There are a number of indications in In Nomine 5/1to suggest that it was composed by Byrd. It opens with a canzona-like theme of a repeated pitch on a semibreve and two minims followed by a leap of a fifth or a fourth played by all the parts, except that playing the In Nomine. Byrd's Fantasia 6/F, which will be examined in greater detail in the next chapter, also has a similar opening. At breve 8 in both In Nomine 5/1 and Fantasia 6/F, Byrd alters the three opening notes in the themes of both works to a rest followed by three repeated minims, as is commonly found as an alternative pattern in canzonas, in all the following entries of the first section (excluding the In Nomine part) of both works. Surely this must be the work of the same composer? Tallis's In Nomine 4/2 also begins with a canzona-like figure and a leap of a fifth down in each of the three parts;[18] this theme returns in breve six with three repeated minims, following a rest, again in all three parts (Example 5.5), suggesting that Byrd was influenced by his teacher when writing his first In Nomine 5/1. He also used the same bass range as Tallis, of 11 notes from F to b♭. The signature accidental of two flats, resulting from the cantus firmus being placed in a treble line starting on g′, may also be an indication that this In Nomine is by Byrd. Out of a survey of 34 five-part In Nomines from

Example 5.5 Opening of Thomas Tallis, In Nomine II

the sixteenth-century, only two other composers, Parsley and Woodcock, make the same transposition, leading to a signature accidental of two flats. A signature accidental of one flat is much more common in In Nomines. Leaving aside his Latin-titled works, Byrd uses a two-flat signature accidental in five of the remaining 23 consort works in four to six parts, including three fantasias – a much higher incidence than that found in his contemporaries' music.

Structurally, In Nomine 5/1 falls into four sections, the first being the longest. The opening theme appears five times and then a further eight times in the alternative canzona form beginning with three minims (Example 5.4). The second section lasts from breve 24 to the first minim of breve 39, the theme entering ten times (Example 5.6a). The final two sections are short. The third lasts for just seven breves (Example 5.6b). Its four-note theme enters eight times, followed by five modified entries, four of which are paired. In the final nine-breve section beginning at breve 46, the music changes metre; the pulse is mainly a dotted semibreve rather than a semibreve (Example 5.6b). The dotted five-note theme appears six times; the first entry in part three is repeated exactly an octave lower in the bass line. This pattern continues twice more, with repeating pairs an octave apart. Finally, in breves 51 to 53, Byrd takes the rhythm of the theme, shortens it and changes the direction of the notes to rise instead of fall, before the music comes to a close with a cadence on a G chord.

In placing the In Nomine chant to start on g′ in his In Nomine 5/1, Byrd transposes Taverner's original up a fourth. In the two other five-part In Nomines with the cantus firmus transposed to start on g by Parsley and Woodcock, the chant is found in a tenor part, sounding an octave lower than Byrd's placement in the treble. Byrd is likely to have known Parsley's In Nomine, which must have been in circulation in the mid-sixteenth century. Parsley was born in 1511 and belongs to the generation of composers before Byrd, but his only complete surviving five-part In Nomine (MB 44/55) is found in a manuscript dating from the first part of the seventeenth century, GB-Ob MSS Mus. Sch d. 212–6 (25), f. 65. Woodcock's first five-part In Nomine (MB 44/64) was probably written after Byrd's; it first appears in a manuscript dating from the 1580s, GB-Och MMS 984–8 (5), f. 92.

Example 5.6a Nomine 5/1, second theme

Example 5.6b Nomine 5/1, themes three and four

Parsley's In Nomine does not open with a typical canzona pattern but it does begin with a theme based on leaps of a fourth or a fifth with a similar rhythm (Example 5.7). Excluding the cantus firmus, the ranges of the parts are similar in Parsley's and Byrd's In Nomines, except for the fourth part in Parsley's work, which is one note wider than Byrd's (12 notes instead of 11). The parts overlap more in Parsley's In Nomine, resulting in a compass of just 20 notes, closer to that found in vocal music, whereas Byrd's In Nomine has a wider compass of 23 notes, suggesting that it was conceived primarily as instrumental music.

Example 5.7 Opening of Osbert Parsley, In Nomine III

In spite of the narrower compass in Parsley's work, the treble part reaches g′′ and is written in the G2 clef. As Byrd's transposition of the cantus firmus takes it up to g′′, he also used the clef G2. It would have been a useful way of teaching choirboys to read the treble clef as they would be playing the familiar In Nomine, but at a different pitch from most other settings. Many composers set their In Nomines round Taverner's original lower pitch using the clef C1, the clef most familiar to boy choristers.

From breve 39 in In Nomine 5/1, Byrd begins to explore rhythmic patterns, including cross rhythms, a feature that he developed significantly in his later consort works. The third theme, of just four notes, opens with a distinctive dotted rhythmic pattern that is found in every breve of this short section (Example 5.6b). In the final, fourth section of nine breves, where a dotted semibreve becomes the basic pulse, there are intimations of Byrd's dance-like second sections of his second and third six-part fantasias, Fantasia 6/g1 and Fantasia 6/g2.

The succession of tonalities in In Nomine 5/1 does not display the structure that became typical of Byrd's later works, but they are centred on C and G, producing minor chords a fifth apart, which did become typical of Byrd's tonalities. Contrast between minor and major is apparent, with movement to major chords on B♭, a minor third away from G, illustrating that neighbouring areas of major and minor centred on notes a minor third apart are found early on in Byrd's music. The bass part does not as yet play the major role found in Byrd's later consort works, but there are places where the bass is governing the tonalities, particularly in the last four breves where the sequences in the bass part draw the music to a close.

The imbalance between the sections in In Nomine 5/1, the relentless movement and the slightly pedestrian nature of the music point, as Milsom suggests, to an early composition by a young composer. There are still strong indications that In Nomine 5/1 is by Byrd and the music displays signs of his emerging distinctive instrumental style.

In Nomines 4/1 and 4/2

Byrd's two four-part In Nomines were probably the next to be composed and also display elements of what eventually became characteristics of Byrd's individual instrumental style, for example the suggestion of canon in In Nomine 4/1 and his use of a semitone. The two four-part In Nomines may have been written as a pair, since In Nomine 4/1 starts with a descending stepwise pattern (Example 5.8), and In Nomine 4/2 with an ascending pattern (Example 5.9).

Example 5.8 Opening of In Nomine 4/1

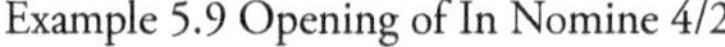

Example 5.9 Opening of In Nomine 4/2

In both In Nomines, the chant is at the same pitch as is found in Taverner's original In Nomine. Oliver Neighbour observes that the two four-part In Nomines are closer to Taverner's original than any other contemporary settings and that Byrd had clearly studied it in detail.[19]

In Nomine 5/2

The confidence Byrd displays in his In Nomine 5/2 makes it a very different work from In Nomine 5/1. In this second In Nomine, he transposes the chant up a fifth from Taverner's original and places it in part three (tenor). The music opens in a sonorous and gentle manner. Byrd lifts his material from the opening of Tye's In Nomine *Seldom sene* (Example 5.10a and b). It would have been strange if Byrd had not been acquainted with Tye's In Nomines. Records show that Tye was associated with the Chapel Royal at least in the 1550s, and circumstantial evidence suggests he acted as music tutor to Edward VI.[20] As the greatest contributor to English consort music in the middle of the sixteenth-century, Tye's music must have been circulated at court.

As in *Seldom sene*, Byrd's bass line enters half way through the first breve after the first note of the cantus firmus. Tye builds his entries up from the bass, with two entries on G, an octave apart, followed by two beginning on D an octave apart, the third entry being a fifth above the second. Part one (treble) is the last to enter in breve seven. In contrast, Byrd's initial bass entry is followed by part one in breve three, two octaves higher than the bass and at the same pitch as Tye's treble entry. The impact of a rising semitone notes in Tye's opening theme, must have attracted Byrd, as it is found again in the opening theme of his In Nomine 5/3.[21]

In Nomine 5/2 falls into three carefully structured and balanced sections and lasts for 58 breves. The calm opening consists mainly of semibreves and minims, extends to breve ten from where the music slowly begins to change in mood as running crotchets are gradually added. In the first section (Example 5.10b) which lasts for 22 breves, Byrd quickly develops the opening material, with the first theme already appearing at a different pitch in breve 7, by which time both a c# and f# have appeared, with G# following in breve 13 (Example 5.11).

Example 5.10a Opening of Christopher Tye, In Nomine *Seldom sene*

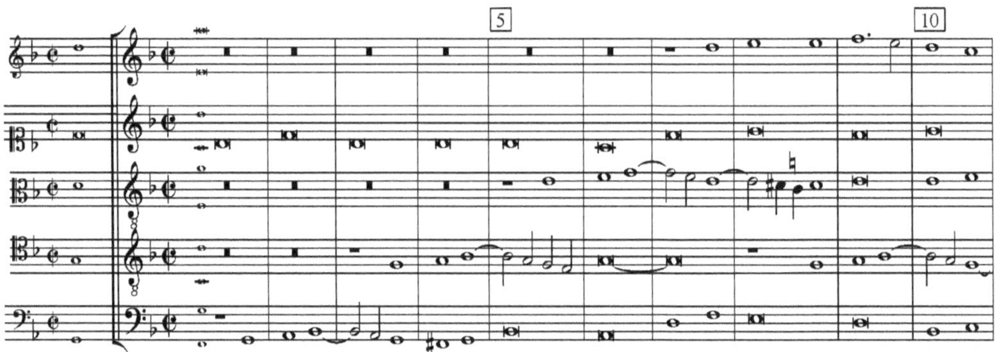

Example 5.10b Opening of Byrd, In Nomine 5/2

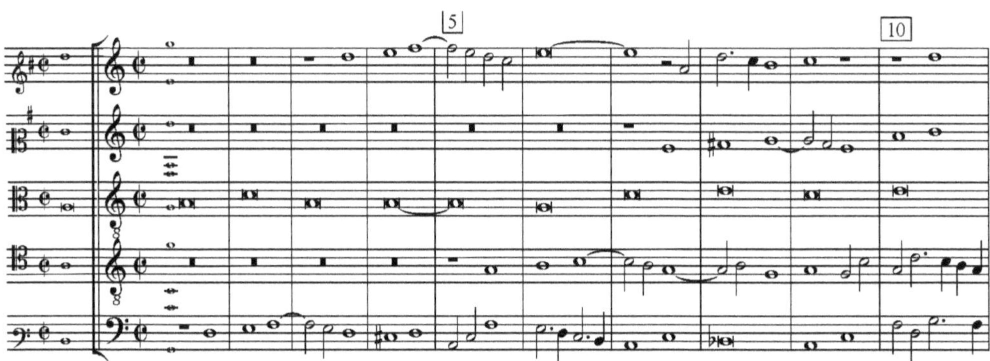

Example 5.11 In Nomine 5/2, first section breves 12 – 18

A short variant of the theme is added in breves 7–9 (in part one, Example 5.10b) and Byrd develops this from breve 14 into a phrase containing a dotted minim and descending crotchets. The original theme appears with a rhythmic alteration from breve 13. The music increases in intensity from breve 20, the first section ending with a cadence on E in breve 22 (Example 5.12).

Example 5.12 In Nomine 5/2, opening of the second section

The second section lasts from breves 22 to 40. Theme 2 develops out of the theme in breves 7–9 with the addition of two notes at the beginning, giving a falling fifth and rising octave between the first three notes. An intimation of this theme is found in the octave leap in part two in breve 20 and in part four leading into breve 22, which concludes onto the E cadence with two leaps of a fifth following a dotted descending pattern (Example 5.12). In effect Byrd cuts this motif in half and reverses the two halves in order to construct his new theme, replacing the second upward leap of a fifth with an interval of an octave. Part one introduces the theme starting on b′ followed two minims later by the bass on e. The momentum is carried through the second section with continuous close entries of the theme from breve 27 and contrasting ascending and descending crotchet patterns.

The bass line begins the final section in breve 40, the theme opening with a rising fifth followed by rising and falling semitones (Example 5.13). This concluding section lasts for almost 19 breves with Byrd extending the cantus firmus further than is found in In Nomine 5/1. The music becomes calmer and more sustained; there is much less crotchet movement. Byrd sometimes uses only part of the third theme, which adds to the sense of moving towards closure.

Example 5.13 In Nomine 5/2, opening of the third and final section

The second theme in In Nomine 5/2, with its octave leap, is distinctive and unusual (Example 5.12). Although octave leaps are common in In Nomines – only three of the 92 In Nomines in MB 44 and 45 do not contain at least one octave leap – they are not commonly found in such a prominent place in a theme that is repeated by every part. They are not found in Byrd's six other In Nomines. (Tye's *Seldom sene* is one of three In Nomines that do not contain any octave leap.[22]) Byrd's second theme in In Nomine 5/2, with its octave leap, occurs 20 times between breves 22 and 40 across all the parts. Such prominent use and repetition of an octave leap is found only in one other In Nomine, Tallis's second four-part In Nomine (Example 5.5). In Tallis's opening theme, a downward leap of a fifth is also followed by an octave leap up and a dotted downward pattern. There are 12 entries within 19 breves. Both Tallis and his pupil Byrd appear to have made the specific decision to exploit the impact of an octave leap. Neither composer incorporated an octave leap in the same way into any of the motets found in the Cantiones Sacrae of 1575 although, as in the In Nomines, octave leaps are common.[23] So, as well as Byrd turning to Tye for In Nomine 5/2, he also looked to Tallis's In Nomine II as he did in In Nomine 5/1. Byrd exploits a particular interval again in his last In Nomine, 5/5, when he makes use of a leap of a sixth, an interval used far more rarely than an octave.

As well as imaginative development of melodic phrases, the structure of In Nomine 5/2 is enhanced by Byrd's careful development of harmonic progression. Unusually for an In Nomine, he does not use a signature accidental, the result of his transposition up a fifth from Tye's *Seldom sene.* This requires the sharpening of notes in the upper two parts to maintain the semitone found in the opening of Tye's In Nomine. A relationship between fifths can be clearly seen in the music. In the opening breves the music is centred on D and A (Example 5.10b), then it moves between A and E (Example 5.11), finishing the first section with a major chord on E (Example 5.12). By breve 40 it has returned to A (Example 5.13), having passed through chords based on C, G back to C and then to A. The music concludes in the tonality of A, but there are one or two surprises on the way, such as at breve 48, where a D chord is followed by a sudden F natural and an inverted G minor chord on B♭ (Example 5.12). This is far more adventurous than the simpler tonality of In Nomine 5/1. The bass plays a significantly stronger role in In Nomine 5/2, setting the tonality with its opening phrase, and reinforcing cadence points, for example in breves 12 to 14.

Byrd is far more in control of the development of the music in In Nomine 5/2 than he was in In Nomine 5/1. He manages to develop his themes in spite of the restrictions of the cantus firmus. He carefully adds or removes crotchet movement in the music, affecting its mood and sense of speed. There is contrast between the sections and between the rising and falling crotchet patterns that pass between the parts. The first seven breves contain equal notes of a minim or longer; this heightens the impact of the first dotted rhythm in breve eight. In the final section, the number of dotted notes reduces substantially as does the use of crotchets, calming the music.

The clefs of In Nomine 5/2 are as might be expected for a mid-sixteenth century In Nomine: a G clef, three C clefs and an F clef (G2, C2, C3 (cantus firmus), C4 and F3). The compass of In Nomine 5/2 is 22 notes, slightly narrower than that of In Nomine 5/1, but this is the average compass for In Nomines of the period. The widest range for an individual part, of 12 notes, is found in part four (tenor). The bass has a range of 11 notes, as does part two; part one (treble) has a range of ten notes.

In In Nomine 5/1, Byrd creates little contrast of texture and does not exploit the range of the instruments available to him, apart from the regular entries in the first five breves and three breves without the bass (Example 5.4, breves 10–12). In Nomine 5/2 opens with the bass viol and the cantus firmus; they are joined in breve three by part one (Example 5.10b). This gives a sparse texture of sustained notes for almost five breves. All the parts are heard by breve eight. Byrd reduces the overall texture once more in breve 43, when part one is silent for just over a breve. He varies the texture by the use of running crotchets. He also displays his awareness of the overall compass; in breve 17, his bass part reaches its lowest note in the music; this is followed by part one (treble) reaching the highest note in the music in breve 18 (Example 5.11). This is reversed later in the music (at the end of breve 32 and beginning of 34), when the treble reaches its highest note followed by the lowest note of the bass part one breve later. The first use of these notes occurs approximately a third of the way through the music and the second, two-thirds. The bass also plays a distinctive role in supporting the harmonic structure of the music with falling fifths and rising fourths reinforcing the cadences.

In Nomine 5/2 is a much more highly developed and complex work than In Nomine 5/1. Although first found in a manuscript aimed primarily at singers,[24] it displays all the characteristics of a consort work that has been instrumentally conceived. There are long phrases, which sometimes move into the succeeding phrases without an obvious place to 'breathe', indicating that this is instrumental not vocal music. The development of the thematic material is typical of Byrd's later fantasias and indicative of his emerging instrumental style. John Harley suggests the compositional skill of In Nomine 5/2 illustrates why Byrd was appointed to his post in Lincoln at the age of 23. [25]

In Nomine 5/3 and 5/4

Byrd's In Nomine 5/3 and 5/4 reflect his acquaintance with Alfonso Ferrabosco I, who wrote three five-part In Nomines. Ferrabosco appears to have written these shortly after he arrived in England around 1562.[26] The genre obviously interested the Italian composer; John Bryan notes that Ferrabosco had truly studied Taverner's original In Nomine and took it as the inspiration for the opening of his In Nomine III.[27] (This is actually thought to be the first In

Nomine Ferrabosco wrote.[28]) In this In Nomine, Ferrabosco uses the same 22-note compass as Taverner's original, though the music is pitched a tone higher than Taverner's In Nomine. Byrd and Ferrabosco engaged in musical rivalry – in particular, a set of 80 canons written by each, based on the *Miserere* plainsong, was mentioned by Morley in 1597.[29] Sadly they do not survive. Byrd's opening of his In Nomine 5/3 is an adaption of Ferrabosco's opening in his In Nomine III (Example 5.14 a and b). Byrd emulates Ferrabosco in delaying the entry of the cantus firmus for three breves.

Example 5.14/a Opening of Alfonso Ferrabosco I, In Nomine III

Example 5.14b Opening of In Nomine 5/3

Ferrabosco's In Nomine I begins with a five-note stepwise theme (Example 5.15a) rising upwards from g′ to d″ followed by a fall of a fourth down and back from d″ to a′. The initial five notes consist of a dotted rhythm, three crotchets and a minim. In his In Nomine 5/4, Byrd uses this rhythmic pattern but his five note phrase steps downwards from an a′ to d′ (Example 5.15b). It ends with a leap of a fifth up to a′ followed by a leap of a fourth from a′ to d″ at the same position and pitch as is found in Ferrabosco's work. Byrd follows Ferrabosco in his use of quavers (from breve 42) and of dotted rhythms. Both Byrd's In Nomine 5/4 and Ferrabosco's In Nomine I have a compass of 22 notes (as do Byrd's 5/3 and Ferrabosco's In Nomine III). Byrd was influenced by Ferrabosco in his choice of clefs for both In Nomine 5/3 and In Nomine 5/4. Excluding the cantus firmus line, these two In Nomines and Ferrabosco's In Nomine I use the clefs G_2, C_2, C_3 and F_3. In his other three five-part InNomines Byrd uses C_4 for the fourth line. Both Byrd and Ferrabosco exploit wide ranges of 12 and 13 notes in the inner parts. In all three of his In Nomines, Ferrabosco takes the third part (tenor) up to c″, resulting in a high tessitura. Byrd does the same in the In Nomine 5/4, but the In Nomine 5/3, he goes one note higher, taking the part up to d″, as he did in In Nomine 5/2, but he also makes this part wider, taking it down to f. In Nomine 5/4, Byrd imitates Ferrabosco by taking the bass part up to a high d′.

Example 5.15a Opening of Ferrabosco I, In Nomine I

Example 5.15b Opening of Byrd, In Nomine 5/4

It is clear that Byrd learnt a great deal about instrumental style from Ferrabosco that he went on to apply in later consort works. The end of Ferrabosco's In Nomine I demands virtuosic viol playing of scale passages from all parts (other than the cantus firmus). Byrd follows suit at the end of In Nomine 5/4 (Example 5.16a and b). David Wulfstan writes in 'Byrd, Tallis and Ferrabosco' that 'it can safely said that Byrd would not sound like the Byrd we know had Ferrabosco not exerted a profound influence at a crucial stage in Byrd's development'.[30]

Example 5.16a Virtuosic parts in Ferrabosco I, In Nomine I

Example 5.16b Virtuosic parts in Byrd, In Nomine 5/4

In Nomine 5/5

It is in his In Nomine 5/5, probably composed by 1565, that Byrd really comes into his own. It displays ability and maturity, reflected in the fact it was his most copied consort work. Nevertheless, this In Nomine still shows the influence of other composers, in particular Robert Parsons, and his most popular In Nomine, in five parts, and one of his seven-part In Nomines. Parsons's surviving five-part In Nomine lasts for 53 breves and has a compass of 23 notes. It has a clef combination of G2, C1, C4, C5 and F4. The In Nomine cantus firmus is found in the second part, starting on d′, using the clef C1. Three parts have a range of 11 notes. The lowest part, for bass viol, has a range of nine notes, the same range as the cantus firmus. Byrd's Nomine 5/5 consists of 57 breves and has a slightly different clef combination, G2, C1, C3, C4 and F4. The In Nomine cantus firmus is also placed in part two using the clef C1. The compass is 24 notes. All of Byrd's parts (with the exception of the cantus firmus) have a range of 11 notes or more. Part one (treble) has a range of 12 notes and one inner part has a range of 13 notes (Example 5.17a). Byrd takes his music one note higher than Parsons and exploits a higher range in three of his parts. He takes ideas from Parsons, but the structure of In Nomine 5/5 is his own.

Example 5.17a Opening of In Nomine 5/5

Byrd's In Nomine 5/5 falls into five more-or-less equal sections: one of 13 breves, three of 11 breves and a final section of 12 breves. It opens with a gently falling step-wise melody, initially paired an octave and a third apart in parts one and four. The first entry in In Nomine 5/5, lasts for seven breves (Example 5.17a). Its calm opening theme resembles that of Parsons's In Nomine 7/1; both contain a distinctive upward leap of a sixth (Example 5.17a and b). Byrd's theme falls from the onset before the rising leap of a sixth while Parsons's theme rises before falling and reaching the rising sixth.

Example 5.17b Opening of Robert Parsons, In Nomine 7/1*

* Named In Nomine V in MB 44/75

Byrd also appears to pay homage to Taverner. In the opening breves of In Nomine 5/5, Byrd takes the first four notes of each part from the end of the first phrase of the Sanctus from Taverner's *Mean Mass* (Example 5.17c). (In the first two entries, Byrd exchanges Taverner's two parts, changing the pitch and interval between them, and he flattens the f sharp to f natural.) He returned to Taverner's *Mean Mass* again when writing the Sanctus for his Mass for four voices.

Example 5.17c Taverner, opening theme from Sanctus

Byrd's second theme rises stepwise after an initial step down (breve 13; Example 5.18).

Example 5.18 In Nomine 5/5, second theme

The first entry lasts for four breves, but Byrd takes the first five notes as the basis of all the other fourteen entries, which enter in quick succession over 11 breves. Unusually, the third entry is incorporated into the cantus firmus in breve 14. Theme three opens with three repeated minims (breve 24) and the music increases in density and intensity; these notes are followed by a pattern of descending crotchets starting with a dotted crotchet-quaver passage. The third theme enters seven times, but entries are spaced further apart than those of the previous section. Byrd doubles the theme at a third and a sixth at two of the entries. This theme has echoes of Ferrabosco's simpler but effective use of three minims in his first In Nomine (MB 44/50), which are then followed by a short downward pattern (Example 5.19a and b). Byrd emphasises the repeated notes by doubling them.

Example 5.19a In Nomine 5/5, third theme

Example 5.19b Ferrabosco I, In Nomine III

Byrd's fourth, much shorter motif, from breve 34, is based round three falling or rising crotchets in intervals of a third or variants of this pattern. It first appears in the bass in breve 34 (Example 5.20a) at the end of the third section, using a pattern found in breve 38 of Parsons's five-part In Nomine (Example 5.20b). It leads to a cadence, after which the fourth section begins in breve 35. This section is full of small rhythmic patterns adding urgency to the music. In breve 37, Byrd makes his first reference to a short two-note pattern, an upward leap of a fourth used by Parsons (Example 5.20a and b). This texture is found at breve 36 in Parsons's In Nomine; Parsons's use of a fourth refers back to earlier in his In Nomine, particularly the passage from breve 15 (Example 5.20c).

The fifth section, starting in breve 45, is based round two and three-note crotchet patterns. Byrd takes the homophonic section from the final section of Parsons's In Nomine, subtly changing it (Example 5.21a and b). The concluding section of In Nomine 5/5 contrasts greatly with the sustained, long opening with its leap of a sixth (Example 5.17a).

Example 5.20a In Nomine 5/5, fourth theme

Example 5.20b Parsons, In Nomine in 5 parts

Example 5.20c Parsons, five-part In Nomine (initial use of a leap of a fourth)

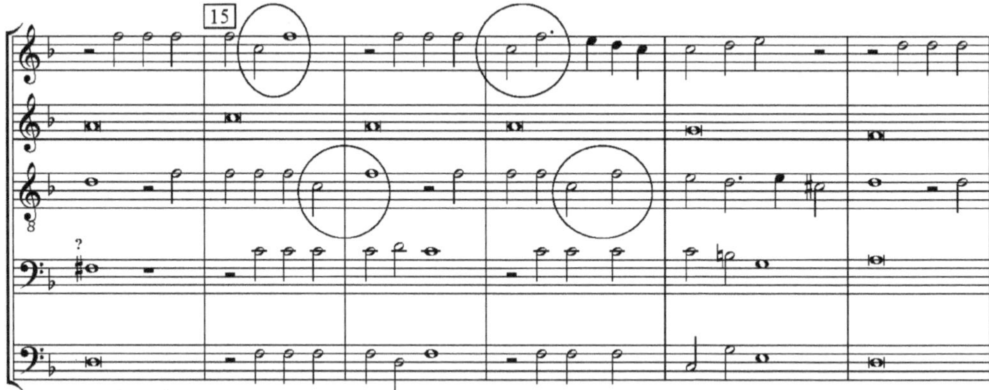

Example 5.21a Excerpt from final section of Byrd, In Nomine 5/5

Example 5.21b Excerpt from final section of Parsons, In Nomine in 5 parts

Unlike leaps of an octave, leaps of a sixth or seventh are much less common in sixteenth-century English music and composers appear to have avoided using them. Few of the 92 In Nomines collected in MB 44 and 45[31], contain more than one or two leaps of a sixth or seventh and some contain none at all. In Byrd's seven In Nomines, excluding In Nomine 5/5, only one other In Nomine (5/3) contains more than three leaps of a sixth. The majority of the 31 motets by Tallis and Byrd in the *Cantiones Sacrae* of 1575, contain no or just one leap of a sixth. In three motets, a small number of leaps of a sixth or seventh appear to have been specifically used to illustrate particular words. Tallis makes use of leaps of a sixth in the opening of his seven-part motet *Suscipe quaeso Domine* ('Receive from below, I ask Lord, the voice of one confessing'; MB 56/27).The leap is found in six of the parts as they enter, as the melody leaps from 'Domine' (Lord) to 'vocem' (voice; Example 5.22). A further leap is found at the word 'confitentus' (confessing), making seven leaps of a sixth in 21 breves.

Example 5.22 Tallis, opening of *Suscipe quaeso Domine*

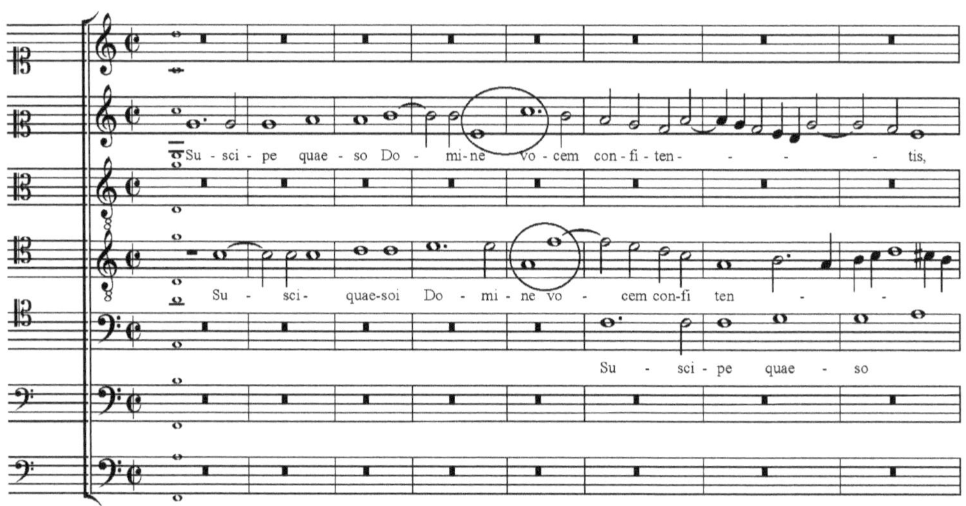

Byrd makes makes significant use of the interval of a sixth in two of his motets in the *Cantiones Sacrae* of 1575, particularly in the third section of his six-part *Tribue Domine* ('Grant, Lord'; MB 56/29). Here, he incorporates leaps of both a sixth and a seventh, found following the cadence in breve 207. The section is based on the words 'cuius opera inseparabilia sunt, cuius imperium sine fine manet' ('whose works are inseparable, whose command remains without end'). A leap of a sixth or seventh is found in every voice up to the end of the section (breve 236). A leap of a sixth is found at the words 'opera inseparabilia' (inseparable works) in voice 1 and 5 (Example 5.23). Following this, three voices sing a leap of a seventh for the same two words. Two further leaps of a seventh are found at the word 'imperium' (command). Like Tallis, Byrd has placed his leaps very carefully and with purpose. John Milsom suggests that Tallis's *Suscipe quaeso Domine* and Byrd's *Tribue Domine* may have been composed as a pair for the *Cantiones Sacrae* of 1575.[32] This is supported by their close proximity in *Cantiones Sacrae*, and their unusual texts taken from medieval books.[33] The calculated use of leaps of a sixth or seventh by both composers also suggest they are connected.

Example 5.23 *Tribue Domine*, third section

Although Tallis uses a leap of a sixth in the opening of *Suscipe quaeso Domine*, the seven entries are spread over 21 breves. The interval falls between the eighth and ninth notes. In the opening of Byrd's In Nomine 5/5, the impact of the leap of a sixth is much more immediate (Example 5.17a). The leaps from a to f (at different octaves) occur between the fourth and fifth notes of the theme. Altogether, there are six leaps in 12 breves, the last of which is transposed and leads to the cadence at the end of the first section (Example 5.18). Initially a leap of a sixth is found at two breve intervals, as three parts enter following the first note of the cantus firmus. The final leap of a sixth occurs just before the final cadence.

This feature of a leap of a sixth would have been an unusual sound for sixteenth century ears. In the small number of In Nomines that contain several leaps of a sixth, nearly all use a leap involving a and f. Three In Nomines would seem to be of particular relevance, Tye's *Crye* (MB 45/184), Parsons's In Nomine 7/1(MB 44/75) and a five-part In Nomine (MB 45/156) by a little-known composer, John Eglestone. In *Crye*, Tye introduces a prominent leap from a′ to f″ in part one (treble) in breve 5 and repeats it in breve 9 (Example 5.24. The frequent occurrence of a sixth being from a to f in other In Nomines would suggest homage to Tye.[34]

Example 5.24 Tye, opening, viol 1, of In Nomine *Crye*

Parsons incorporates three leaps of a sixth in the first two entries of his opening theme, giving three leaps in the first eight breves (Example 5.17b). The initial two occur between the eighth and ninth notes (as in Tallis's *Suscipe quaeso Domine*[35]), and the second part repeats the sixth. All except one of Parsons leaps of sixth are from d′ to b♭′; only the second leap is from a′ to f′′. He does not pursue using a leap of a sixth except for three more isolated entries. Unlike Byrd's In Nomine 5/5, Parsons's first three leaps of a sixth all occur before the entry of the cantus firmus at breve 17. However, it seems likely Byrd may have liked the impact of the close proximity of the sixths in Parsons' work as well as paying homage to Tye in using a to f in the first five leaps of In Nomine 5/5.

Eglestone's In Nomine I is only found in GB-Ob MSS Mus. Sch. d. 212– 6, the largest known collection of In Nomines.[36] No date is known for his In Nomine. Each of the four parts accompanying the In Nomine chant have, like Byrd's In Nomine 5/5, a leap of a sixth between the fourth and fifth notes of the opening theme, which the bass part repeats. All the leaps, from a to f (in different octaves) are found between the third and sixth breves. It appears that Eglestone was imitating Byrd. No other composers apparently followed suit, but there is no doubt about the popularity of Byrd's work.

As well as Byrd's unusual use of a sixth in the opening theme, what is immediately apparent in In Nomine 5/5, is the new way in which Byrd chooses to make his instrumental parts work together. He was obviously attracted to the homophonic writing in Parsons's In Nomine, which forms the basis of the fifth and final section of In Nomine 5/5. He also pairs instruments, playing in thirds and sixths together in six places in the music, three times in the first section (reminding us of the opening and Taverner), and four times in the third. Byrd previously experimented with pairing two instrumental lines together in his first five-part In Nomine in breves 42–43 and 43–45 (see Example 5.6b). He exploits this further in In Nomine 5/5. It opens with the pairing of parts one and three; this is followed by a short pairing between parts four and five at breve 5 (Example 5.17a). In breves 8–12, parts three and four are paired together. The third section opens with a pairing of parts one and four (breve 24, Example 5.19a); this pairing is repeated at breve 30; at breves 26 and 33, parts one and three are paired together Example 5.20a). Parsons puts his lower parts together to play homophonically right from the beginning of his In Nomine and pairs his two lower parts for a substantial part of the music (see Example 5.25). Byrd uses pairing between instruments much less frequently but to greater effect and impact.

Example 5.25 Parsons, opening of In Nomine in 5 parts

Byrd is clearly exploring instrumental tessitura and texture in In Nomine 5/5. It opens with three instruments; parts one and four play the first theme an octave and a third apart round the cantus firmus. (Example 5.17a). The fourth part enters in breve three; the bass finally enters in the fifth breve. In the second section (breve 13), the music gathers momentum with rising crotchets and the parts chasing each other (Example 5.18). The paired entry (breve 24) of the three repeated minims at the beginning of the third theme, followed by a lively downward crotchet pattern, contrasts with what has gone before (Example 5.19a). The treble part spans the majority of its range, descending from high f″ to d′; the bass enters in the third breve and descends in five breves across the whole of its range from b♭′ to F (breve 30). Following the repeat of the double entry at breve 30, the treble dances upwards in a lively dotted crotchet-quaver passage (breve 33) into the fourth section (Example 5.20a). The entry of short chordal patterns in the final section at breve 45 is in sharp contrast to the previous section (Example 5.21a). Short crotchet patterns in the treble viol are answered by the homophonic three lower parts. In the last six breves, the music rises in pitch, climaxing with highest note in the music, a″, three breves before the final chord (Example 5.26).

Example 5.26 Final six breves of In Nomine 5/5

In In Nomine 5/5, Byrd creates changing mood and contrast through his use of contrasting themes, the speed and number of notes, rhythmic patterns, texture and his use of instrumental ranges. The sections are well balanced in length, contrast and the use of tonal colour. In the opening breves, the music moves between minor chords on G and D. By breve eight, it has reached a major on C (Example 5.17a). The first section concludes on a major chord on D, preceded by a major chord on A (Example 5.18). The second section also ends similarly having passed through major chords on C and F (Example 5.27). The third and fourth sections end on an F chord (Examples 20a and 21a), the music in the third passing from a D chord through chords on G, A, F, D and C. In the fourth section the rate at which chords change increases as the music becomes more urgent. Following the cadence onto F, the final section opens moving between chords on B♭ and F; it moves to conclude with chords on G and D, passing through chords on C, ending on a major chord on D (Example 26).

What is noticeable in In Nomine 5/5 is the importance Byrd places on the bass line, illustrating the development of his instrumental style. He uses the bass line to support chord progressions. For example, at the end of the first section and beginning of the second (breve 13), the bass sustains a pedal D to enforce the tonality (Example 5.18). In the second section, the bass repeats the theme in sequence by moving it up a semitone (breves 20–23) bringing the music to the cadence in breve 24 (Example 5.27). In the last section, the bass pushes the music forward by sequentially repeating the crotchet patterns of the treble part. The bass line reinforces the cadences at the end of each section either by falling or rising fourths or fifths or

Example 5.27 In Nomine 5/5, conclusion of second section

by broken chords at the end of the third and fifth sections. The falling thirds in the bass at the end of the third section in breve 34 become the basis for the fourth section (Example 5.20a). The music concludes with the bass playing rising thirds based on a G chord (breve 55) resolving on D, which is reinforced by rising thirds based on D in part four (Example 5.26).

Byrd makes effective use of wide intervals in the melodic lines in this In Nomine. In the first three sections, octave leaps rarely appear; these are used for very specific reasons. In breve 9, the bass leaps down an octave, moving the music towards the end of the first section (Example 17a). In the second section, at breve 16, the octave leap found in parts one alter the tessitura of the music (Example 5.18). In the fourth and fifth sections, leaping crotchets and running quavers require instrumental dexterity. At the end of the fourth section, fast octave leaps can be found just before the cadence in to the fifth section (Example 5.21a). Finally five breves before the end, together part one (treble) leaps up an octave and part five (bass) down an octave, both on G, preparing the way for the highest note in breve 55 and the end of the music (Example 5.26). In Nomine 5/5 makes high technical demands on viol players.

Through his In Nomines Byrd established himself as a composer of instrumental consort music. This can be seen in his handling of his material and the demands he made on viol players. His In Nomines are a major contribution to a genre in a tradition established by composers such as Tye, Tallis and Parsons. Byrd learnt and took ideas from all three composers but extended them to develop his own distinctive style. In the last, In Nomine 5/5, he emerged as a confident composer of music for viols in command of his material.

None of Byrd's textless Latin-titled works with a known compass exceed a compass of 20 notes, giving them a similar compass to vocal music. They contain instrumental elements but nonetheless could have been sung. In contrast, all of his In Nomines have a compass of at least 22 notes, with two containing a compass of 23 notes (In Nomine 4/1 and In Nomine 5/1) and one, In Nomine 5/5, containing a compass of 24 notes. Individual parts in the In Nomines have consistently wider ranges than most of those found in the Latin-titled works, with one or two exceptions. Byrd began to use bass parts with a range of 11 and 12 notes in his Latin-titled works. All of his In Nomines have bass parts with a range of 11 or 12 notes. With the exception of In Nomines 5/1 and 5/2, all of Byrd's In Nomine viol parts, excluding the cantus firmus part, have ranges of 11 notes or more. In Nomine 5/3, In Nomine 5/4 and In Nomine 5/5 all have an inner part with a range of 13 notes, reflecting the increased range demanded of players. In Byrd's In Nomines 5/4 and 5/5, virtuosic playing is required reflecting Byrd's exchange of musical ideas with Ferrabosco I.

In In Nomine 5/5 it can be seen how far Byrd had come as a composer compared with his early Latin-titled consort works, and the emergence in his music of distinctive idiomatic instrumental characteristics. In Nomine 5/5 displays a command of ideas and material and an understanding of the capabilities of experienced viol players. Byrd carefully worked out, linked and grew his themes to achieve one of the finest In Nomines in the genre which, although influenced by other composers and following in their tradition, was unique in its melodic shape and development of homophonic patterns. As far as we know, In Nomine 5/5 is the last Byrd wrote. Possibly, he felt that the In Nomine form did not give him any further scope for development. He clearly wanted to find other ways of supporting music without words that did not rely on previously established structures, particularly those linked to words, and develop his own unique voice. His next explorations into instrumental form, before he left Lincoln, were into the fantasia, which had the potential to give him more freedom, and into variation form.

1 Neighbour, *The Consort and Keyboard Music of William Byrd*, p. 40; see also GB-Lbl Add MS 31390 online at www.diamm.ac.uk/sources/1888/#/

2 Harley, *The World of William Byrd*, p. 54.

3 There may, of course, have been viol playing in Lincoln of which no evidence survives.

4 Harley, *William Byrd Gentleman of the Chapel Royal* pp. 174 and 40.

5 Paul Doe and Roger Bowers, rev. Hugh Benham, 'John Taverner', *The New Grove Dictionary of Music and Musicians* online 2001, updated 2009; https://doi-org.nls.idm.oclc.org/10.1093/gmo/9781561592630.article.27571

6 John Bryan, '"Not unlike a Confused Singing of Birds in a Grove": An Introduction to the In Nomine', *The Viol*, l6 (Spring 2007), p. 15.

7 Ibid., p. 16.

8 See John Milsom, 'A Composer's-Eye View of the In Nomine', *The Viol*, 6 (Spring 2007), p. 26.

9 The bass part of another In Nomine, *The flats*, is found in GB-Ob Lbl MS Tenbury 1464.

10 McCarthy, *Byrd*, p. 48.

11 Ian Payne, 'The Provision of Teaching on the Viols at some English Cathedral Churches, *c.*1594–*c.*1645: Archival Evidence', *Chelys*, 19 (1990), pp. 3–15; Craig Monson, *Voices and Viols in England, 1600–1650*, pp. 159–208.

12 Dodds and Ashbee (eds), http://vdgs.org.uk/thematic.

13 Neighbour, *The Consort and Keyboard Music of William Byrd*, p.52.

14 Ibid., p. 53.

15 Harley, *William Byrd Gentleman of the Chapel Royal*, p. 163 and Warwick Edwards in William Byrd, *Latin Motets I*, BE 8 (London, Stainer and Bell, 1982), p. 215.

16 Milsom, 'A Composer's-Eye View of the In Nomine', p. 27.Oliver Neighbour questions whether In Nomine 5/1 is actually by Byrd, but says it looks more like a work by Byrd than anyone else; Neighbour, *The Consort and Keyboard Music of William Byrd*, p. 39.

17 MB 44/53 and 54.

18 A fifth part is found in one source, but this is believed to be a later addition; Doe in MB 44, p. 39.

19 Neighbour, *The Consort and Keyboard Music of William Byrd*, p. 35.

20 Paul Doe, rev. David Mateer, 'Tye, Christopher' in *The New Grove Dictionary of Music and Musicians* online 2001, updated 2009; https://doi-org.nls.idm.oclc.org/10.1093/gmo/9781561592630.article.28665.

21 In Nomine 5/2 is found in GB-Ob MS Tenbury 1464, followed by four of Tye's In Nomines. *My deathe bed, My farewell, Hold fast* and *The flatts. Seldom sene* is found only in GB-Lbl Add. MS 31390, which does not contain Byrd's In Nomine 5/2, although it does include three of his In Nomines, those numbered 5/1, 5/4 and 5/5.

22 The other two are Taverner's original In Nomine and In Nomine I by Woodcock, MB 44 /64; the latter has narrow part ranges and could be for wind instruments, like *Hackney*.

23 For example, Byrd's motet *Libera me Domine, et pone me* contains 27 octave leaps.

24 GB-Ob MS Tenbury 1464 (3).

25 Harley, *William Byrd Gentleman of the Chapel Royal*, p. 168.

26 Ibid., p. 172.

27 Bryan, '"Choice Consorts…(Rare Chests of Viols)": The Evidence of the Repertory', p. 46.

28 Neighbour, *The Consort and Keyboard Music of William Byrd* p. 43.

29 Ibid., p. 173 and McCarthy, *Byrd*, p. 58.

30 David Wulfstan, 'Byrd, Tallis and Ferrabosco', in Morehen (ed.) *English Choral Practice 1400–1650*, p. 126.

31 *Elizabethan Consort Music I* and *II*, *Musica Britannica* 44 and 45.

32 Milsom in EECM 56, p. 361.

33 Kerry McCarthy, 'Byrd, Augustine and Tribue Domine', *Early Music*, 32/4 (2004), pp. 569–76.

34 Tye's In Nomine *I comme* (MB 45/183) contains five leaps of a sixth; all except one involve a and f.

35 Was Tallis maybe referring to Tye's *Crye*?

36 Eglestone's In Nomine I is found at folio 29, Parsons's In Nomine 7/1 at folio 47 and Byrd's In Nomine 5/5 at folio 53.

Chapter 6

Byrd's first fantasia

Byrd's earliest surviving consort fantasia, the six-part work known as Fantasia 6/F (Example 6.1) exists in three guises: it is found as an instrumental consort work, as a Latin motet, *Laudate pueri* (Example 6.2), and in the form of an English anthem, *Behold now, praise the Lord.* Although it is the least demanding of his six-part fantasias to play, it is an interesting work because of its construction and background. Only five parts of the fantasia survive. Most commentators accept that it was originally conceived as an instrumental work and that Byrd adapted it as a motet for the *Cantiones Sacrae* of 1575 which he published with Thomas Tallis (1505–1585). There is strong evidence that the fantasia came first; the adaptation of this instrumental consort piece for voices informs our understanding of the relationship between Byrd's Latin motets and his consort music and whether the apparently instrumental idiom Byrd was developing in writing consort music applied to all his non-liturgical compositions for instruments or voices. He wrote very little consort music after 1590; the same is true of his composition of his sacred songs.[1] Around this time, Byrd retired from public life and turned his attention away from secular music to liturgical music.[2]

Sources

Fantasia 6/F is one of the very first six-part fantasias to be found in English manuscripts. The first significant English manuscript collection of consort music, GB-Lbl Add. MS 31390 (*c.*1570–1578) contains only one named fantasia or '*Phancy*' out of 66 works identified as consort music. This is a five-part work by Edward Blanks (c.1550–1633). There is also the untitled textless six-part work by Alfonso Ferrabosco I (1543–1588), which editors have treated as a fantasia, but it is found in another manuscript, GB-Cfm MU. MS 734, with the title *Sur la rossee* raising questions as to whether it may have started life as a chanson.[3] Fantasia 6/F and its two vocal versions are found in six sources. The five surviving parts of Fantasia 6/F are found in one source, GB-Och MSS 979–83 (4), copied between 1575 and 1581by John Baldwin (before 1560–1615), a lay clerk at Windsor, whose initials are stamped on the late sixteenth-century leather covers. The earliest known source of *Laudate pueri* is found in the *Cantiones Sacrae* of 1575, where it was published with fourteen other motets or 'sacred songs' by Byrd, thus predating the manuscript source of the fantasia. *Laudate pueri* is included with just its title and no words in a single partbook, GB-Lbl Add. MS 47844, a small collection of vocal works in five to seven parts, mainly motets, begun in 1581. It is also found texted in NYp MSS Drexel 4180–85 (30), dating from 1615–1625, a large collection of over 250 works made by Merro.

Example 6.1 Opening of Fantasia 6/F

Example 6.2 Opening of *Laudate pueri*

An adaptation for English words of *Laudate pueri*, entitled *Behold now, praise the Lord*, is found texted in GB-Och MSS Tenbury 1382,[4] and untexted in GB-Lbl Add. MSS 17786–91 (24), a collection of 80 works that contains both vocal and consort music. It is thought that the addition of English words was not made by Byrd.[5] It has been the practice to use the fourth part of Laudate pueri (tenor three) as the missing part of the fantasia.

Fantasia 6/F; circumstantial evidence

Fantasia 6/F (Example 6.1) is the earliest surviving example of Byrd's exploration of musical structure in consort music not constructed around a known melody or chant. As mentioned in Chapter Four, Byrd included a direct quotation from Richard Farrant's anthem, *Lord for thy tender mercy's sake* in the fantasia (Example 6.3a and b). Farrant's anthem must have been written sometime after 1566, when the words were first published. The incorporation of the quotation suggests that Byrd wrote Fantasia 6/F after *c.*1567 but before he left Lincoln Cathedral in 1572.

Example 6.3a Quotation from Richard Farrant's *Lord, for thy tender mercy's sake* found in the bass part of Fantasia 6/F

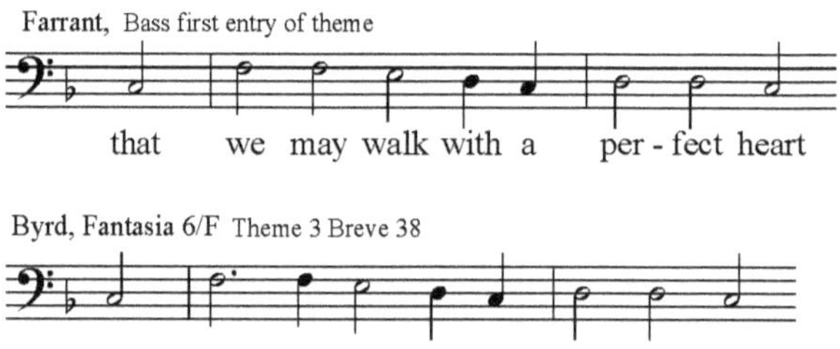

Example 6.3b Quotation from Farrant found in part one (treble) of Fantasia 6/F

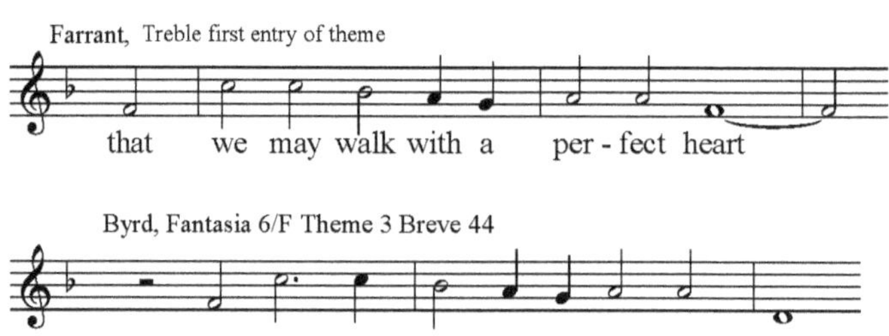

Although it is possible that Farrant was quoting from Byrd, what we know about the relationship between the two composers makes it more likely that the borrowing was the other way round.[6] The third theme of Fantasia 6/F is taken from the phrase 'That we may walk with a perfect heart' in Farrant's anthem. There is sufficient similarity between Farrant's and Byrd's melodic material for it not to be considered just a coincidence in a common musical language. Byrd is thought to have been in direct contact with Baldwin, Farrant's scribe at Windsor, supplying him with music to copy.[7] The possibility that Byrd was a chorister at St George's Windsor also gives a link with Windsor. John Baldwin's initials are stamped on the late sixteenth century leather covers of the five surviving partbooks of GB-Och MSS 979–83. Byrd would have known Farrant from his time at the Chapel Royal before he left for Lincoln in 1563. It would seem highly likely that, in sending the piece to Baldwin, the only known scribe of the Fantasia 6/F, Byrd hoped that the fantasia might come to the attention of Farrant, who would of course recognise the flattery and hopefully help his hunt for a new position. Although this is conjectural, it provides a possible scenario considering that Byrd returned to the Chapel Royal in 1572.[8] It also helps to date the fantasia and supports the hypothesis that it was written before the motet.

Further supporting this is the fact that in the index of GB-Och MSS 983, Fantasia 6/F (no. 157), is listed in Baldwin's handwriting as 'A songe of tow basses'. It is found in the manuscript with three other six-part consort works, Parsons's *The song called trumpets* (no. 158), William Daman's *Beati omnes* (no. 159), and Taverner's *Quemadmodum* (no. 160). This all suggests a small collection of consort works. *Quemadmodum* is also found in GB-Lbl Add. MS 31390 along with a work by William Mundy, *In aeternum.* Both survive without words but can have credible texts supplied for them. It seems unlikely Baldwin would have listed Fantasia 6/F as 'A songe of tow basses', if he were aware that the motet pre-dated the fantasia, especially as a copy of the *Cantiones Sacrae* of 1575 is bound with the partbooks.[9] The fact that Fantasia 6/F is referred to as a 'songe' for two basses might be taken to imply that it was of vocal origin. However, the six-part work by Parsons in the manuscript is also called a song and it is clearly an instrumental piece. Byrd included two fantasias in his 1611 publication of *Psalmes, Songs and Sonnets,* again designed for voices or viols. It is clear that 'song' being included in a title did not necessarily imply something that was sung.

Oliver Neighbour is quite clear that the fantasia came before the motet. He suggests that in his melodic style and use of imitation in his instrumental writing in Fantasia 6F, Byrd was influenced by Robert White's *Song.*[10] John Milsom also expresses his certainty that the fantasia came first in his 2014 edition of the *Cantiones Sacrae* of 1575.[11] The two notable exceptions to those who accept the fantasia came first are Gerald Strahle in an article 'Two Byrd "Fantasias" Disproven' and David Pinto, who asks, why would Byrd write 'a dull instrumental work and then compound the error by publishing it in 1575 with added words?'[12] He believes there is no evidence that *Laudate pueri* existed previously as an instrumental piece.

Structure

Examining the structure of Fantasia 6/F supports the notion that the fantasia was written first, as does looking at the placing of the textual underlay in *Laudate Pueri* and comparing the motet to the other Latin motets in the *Cantiones Sacrae* of 1575. Fantasia 6/F lasts for 109 breves and has a signature accidental of one flat. The clefs for the surviving five parts are C1, C3, C3, F4 and F4. The two bass parts each have a wide range of 12 notes. The other three surviving parts have a narrower range of nine notes and the compass is of just 20 notes. In Fantasia 6/F, Byrd was looking for a new instrumental form that could support a work of significant length. In 1597, Thomas Morley, Byrd's pupil, wrote that the Fantasy was the most important type of music made without a 'ditty'.[13] He points out that the form is primarily used in instrumental music and rarely in vocal music. Morley goes on to say there is more art in the fantasy than in any other instrumental form because the composer is not tied to anything (e.g. a chant) so may design the music as he wishes. This was obviously still a challenge for Byrd embarking on writing one of the first English fantasias; he still needed to find a structure to support the music. His solution was to use imitative symmetry relating to groups of entries divisible by 6 and 3.

Fantasia 6/F has a clear, self-contained internal structure that is not dependent on words or a cantus firmus. At 109 breves, it is almost twice as long as any of Byrd's earlier seven In Nomines, which last from between 54 to 59 breves, although the fantasia requires significant repeats to achieve this. The music falls into four sections. The first theme appears six times and repeats with modification six times (12 entries). The remaining three sections each contain an almost exact repeat so that the second theme appears 18 times (i.e. twice nine entries), the third theme appears 30 times (twice 15 entries) and the final fourth theme appears 42 times (twice 21 entries) with an added modified version of this theme at the very end.

The first theme of Fantasia 6/F has the characteristic rhythmic shape of the opening of a canzona, a semibreve followed by two minims. Both the first two imitative themes have either a rising or falling leap of a fifth or fourth after repeated pitches, also characteristic of the canzona. The canzona had its origins in the French chanson, initially being an arrangement of a chanson for instrumental use.[14] The canzona retained the sectional form of the chanson, with clear imitative points and repeated patterns. The chanson, designed for equal voices in its original form, was also highly suited for performance by viols. Byrd and his contemporaries were familiar with the continental chanson. GB-Lbl Add. MS 31390 (2), containing the largest and one of the earliest collections of textless music, includes untexted chansons, which, in this form, were obviously intended for performance without words. Philip van Wilder contributed 18 works to GB-Lbl Add MS 31390 consisting of chansons and motets. John Harper remarks that van Wilder's influence was important in establishing an abstract polyphonic tradition.[15] Unlike their continental contemporaries, English composers did not adapt the chanson for instrumental works; instead they took particular features from it, such as combining homophonic and imitative writing in the same work.[16] This will become apparent in later fantasias by Byrd.

The first six entries of Fantasia 6/F follow the recognisable canzona pattern of a semibreve and two minims with the leap of a fifth being followed by an entry with a leap of a fourth. It would appear that Byrd looked back at an earlier composition to find his opening idea for Fantasia 6/F. The opening canzona-like theme bears a close resemblance to the opening of his In Nomine 5/1 (Example 6.4).

The second theme, entering at breve 16 (Example 6.1), is faster moving than the canzona-like opening: a rising, stepwise four-note crotchet pattern follows three repeated minims and a falling fifth or fourth. The quotation from *Lord for thy tender mercy's sake* enters as the third theme at breve 38 (Example 6.5). Finally theme 4, a sustained stepwise rising and falling motif, enters at breve 63 (Example 6.6).

Example 6.4 Openings of Fantasia 6/F and In Nomine 5/1

Example 6.5 Opening of the third section of Fantasia 6/F

Example 6.6 Fantasia 6/F, fourth theme

The third theme is the most lyrical. The first entry by one of the bass parts at breve 38 quotes the first bass entry of the musical phrase from Farrant's anthem (Example 6.5). The notation of pitch is identical; there is just one small alteration of the rhythm from two minims to a dotted minim and crotchet (the sort of discrepancy found in different sources of the same piece), but the number of notes and their placing is identical. Byrd repeats Farrant's theme, containing an opening leap of a fourth or a fifth (except for an octave leap in the first bass entry in the repeated section) in all the parts, making the total of 30 entries. Sometimes it is very closely replicated, for example as in the second entry of Byrd's part one (treble) at breve 44 (Examples 6.3b and 6.5). The polyphonic section of Farrant's anthem using this phrase lasts for just over 13 breves. The third section of Byrd's fantasia using the quotation consists of two sections, each of just under 13 breves.

In contrast to In Nomine 5/5, Byrd includes few large leaps in Fantasia 6/F except in the final, fourth section. The second and third sections contain no leaps wider than a fifth except for one octave leap in the bass. In the fourth section, between breves 64 and 85, there are nine octave leaps. All are found in the two bass parts and the two surviving tenor parts. One further octave leap occurs in a tenor part at breve 91. The parts with the octave leap accompany and contrast with the fourth smooth main theme. Byrd's placing of octaves would seem to be very deliberate.

Fantasia 6/F is based on the Ionian mode transposed, displaying the influence of Alfonso Ferrabosco (I), who became one of Elizabeth I's musicians in 1562.[17] The six-part 'fantasia' (Example 6.7), found in GB-Lbl Add. MS 31390 at ff. 15v–16 (attributed to 'Alfoncius', MB 45/192), is also in the Ionian mode. It is highly probably Byrd knew the

Example 6.7 Opening of Ferrabosco I, six-part 'Fantasia'

work and was attracted by its major tonality. Although Ferrabosco's sextet may be a textless version of a chanson, it illustrates the link between the chanson and English consort music. Byrd's fantasia has a much more cohesive structure than Ferrabosco's work of 61 breves and, with its repeats, is at 109 breves distinctly longer. Ferrabosco's 'fantasia' has a compass of 23 notes, wider than that of Fantasia 6/F with its compass of 20 notes. Similarities are found between the parts in the two works. Both have wide bass parts. Ferrabosco's single bass part has a wide range of 13 notes. Byrd's two wide bass parts in Fantasia 6/F each have a range of 12 notes. The two known tenor parts in Fantasia 6/F use the same clef, C3, as two of Ferrabosco's parts and have exactly the same pitch and range of nine notes as one of Ferrabosco's parts.[18] The clef C4 might be expected for at least one tenor part (which of course may have been the case for the missing part from Fantasia 6/F).

The influence of Tallis, Byrd's teacher, can also be detected in the Fantasia 6/F. Tallis's five-part *A solfing song* (GB-Lbl Add. MS 31390, ff. 85v–86, MB 44/36) uses the Ionian mode (Example 6.8). Tallis also makes no use of the clef C4. As found in Ferrabosco's and Byrd's works, two parts contain the clef C3 and have a similar tessitura. The influence of chanson and van Wilder can be detected on *A solfing Song.*[19] Like the Fantasia 6F, it also opens with a leap of a fifth with the second part entering with a leap of a fourth. Tallis uses a pattern of three repeated minims in exactly the same breve as Byrd.

Example 6.8 Tallis, opening of *A solfing song*

The two wide bass parts in the Fantasia 6/F, to which Baldwin refers in his title of the piece, are typical of Byrd's bass parts in his six-part consort music. All three of his six-part fantasias have at least one bass part of 12 notes as do Fantasia 5/C and the *Browning* Fantasy. They play an important structural role in supporting and reinforcing the cadences.

All the structural elements of Fantasia 6/F point to its having begun life as an instrumental consort work. However, in its technical and instrumental demands and its melodic and tonal structure, it is a simpler and less demanding work than Byrd's In Nomine 5/5, although the latter is likely to have been written a little earlier. Perhaps it was because Byrd was experimenting with a new instrumental form. Recycling the fantasia as a Latin motet later helped him collect the works he needed for *Cantiones Sacrae* of 1575, published just three years after he had returned to London.[20] Byrd needed to provide 15 works to go alongside the equivalent by the more experienced Tallis. It seems quite understandable that he recycled all or some parts of earlier compositions to help him find sufficient motets for the publication.

The Cantiones Sacrae of 1575

The first book of *Cantiones Sacrae* contains 31 Latin motets or 'sacred songs', 15 each by Tallis and Byrd, and one probably by both.[21] As well as its dedication to Elizabeth I, who had granted Tallis and Byrd the printing patent, one purpose of publication was to position Byrd as the leading composer of his generation.[22] The two composers also had their eye on selling their collection on the Continent. *Laudate pueri* is the seventeenth motet contained in the collection. It is important to recognise that Elizabethan sacred songs were closer to secular instrumental music than they were to liturgical music sung in cathedrals.[23] Latin-texted polyphony no longer had a place in church music. Six of Byrd's motets in the collection have non-liturgical texts and contain free material not found in the bible or church service books. Byrd likely began composing Latin motets in the mid-1560s.[24] The three earliest motets in the *Cantiones Sacrae* of 1575 were probably composed in Lincoln.

Nine of Byrd's motets in the *Cantiones Sacrae* of 1575 are in six parts. Some were specifically composed for the collection. *Laudate pueri* (CS 1575/17)[25] is not the only motet in the collection with instrumental origins. Three other six-part motets have been identified as having – or likely to have had – origins in earlier Byrd compositions: *Attolite portas* (CS 1575/ 11), *Memento Homo* (CS 1575/18) and *Miserere mihi Domine* (CS 1575/28).[26] Two five-part motets by Tallis in the *Cantiones Sacrae* of 1575, *Absterge Domine* (CS 1575/2) and *O sacrum convivium* (CS 1575/9), can also be linked to earlier instrumental compositions.[27] All of these motets contain instrumental characteristics.

Three motets in the *Cantiones Sacrae* of 1575 display canzona-like characteristics in their opening themes: *Laudate pueri* and the two five-part motets by Tallis. Tallis's *Absterge Domine* has the characteristic rhythmic pattern in the two opening voices, although without a leap of a fourth or fifth. Of the six motets in *Cantiones Sacrae 1575* which probably derived from consort music, *Laudate pueri* is the most distinctively instrumental. Of particular significance is the presence of two bass lines. Of the nine six-part motets by Byrd in *Cantiones Sacrae 1575*, *Laudate pueri* is the only one to contain two bass parts, typical of a six-part viol consort. The structure, the canzona-like opening and the two closely related wide bass parts found in Fantasia 6/F/*Laudate pueri* all point to the fantasia's being the original work. The existence of five other motets with instrumental antecedents reinforces the likelihood that Byrd recycled Fantasia 6/F as a motet.

Looking at the compass of each of six motets in the *Cantiones Sacrae* of 1575 with instrumental origins does not help to identify them as instrumental consort pieces. None of them have a wide compass. The widest is found in Byrd's *Attollite portas*, which has a compass of 22 notes. (The wide, significantly overlapping, part ranges found in this motet are typical of post-Reformation motets.) His *Miserere mihi Domine* has a compass of 21 notes and *Memento Homo* and *Laudate pueri*/Fantasia 6/F both have a compass of 20 notes, as do Tallis's two five-part motets. Byrd's other two six-part fantasias, Fantasia 6/g1 and Fantasia 6/ g2, have a compass of 23 and 24 notes. However, his Fantasia 4/g also has a compass of only

20 notes. A compass of 20 notes does not exclude the possibility that Fantasia 6/F started life as an instrumental work.

Some common features appear in Byrd's consort works and his Latin motets. Works built round a cantus firmus are found in both, but Byrd went on writing motets with cantus firmi long after he had ceased to use them in instrumental music.[28] In his surviving consort music, there is no work with a cantus firmus by Byrd known to date from later than the mid-1560s. From his earliest days of composing, Byrd made use of canon in both consort and vocal music, as found in the early three-part consort work *Sermone blando* (Example 5.2) and his five-part fantasia. In the one eight-part motet in the *Cantiones Sacrae* of 1575, *Diliges Dominum*, Byrd apparently applied an instrumental technique to vocal writing, as it contains an eight-part palindrome, with each of the parts paired with another making four pairs in canon. The twentieth authority on Byrd's vocal music, Joseph Kerman wrote that an 'instrumental bias' is perhaps discernible in all Byrd's vocal music', particularly in the motets published in 1575.[29]

Differences between Fantasia 6/F and *Laudate pueri*

When Byrd came to underlaying the text of *Laudate pueri* to the fantasia, he had to do so round his carefully constructed symmetry. Fantasia 6/F has a greater consistency of simpler rhythm than is found in *Laudate pueri*. Both the fantasia and motet contain repeated sections. In Fantasia 6/F, the two bass parts exchange lines on all three repeats and parts two and three (tenor) exchange lines on the first and third repeats. Part one (treble) repeats exactly on all three repeats. In all the parts in *Laudate pueri*, there are a number of minor changes on repeats to accommodate the different words. Interestingly, in *Laudate pueri* Byrd takes out a leap of a sixth that exists in part two (tenor) of Fantasia 6/F in breve 103 but he adds a minim and two octave leaps to the motet bass voices in breves 106 and 107, to accommodate the words. This creates a different melodic sound to the simple answering semibreve-minim-semibreve pattern of a falling and rising minor third following a rest in Fantasia 6/F. The pattern is found previously in the second bass at breve 104 and part two at breve 105 (Example 6.9a and b).

Example 6.9a Closing breves of Fantasia 6/F

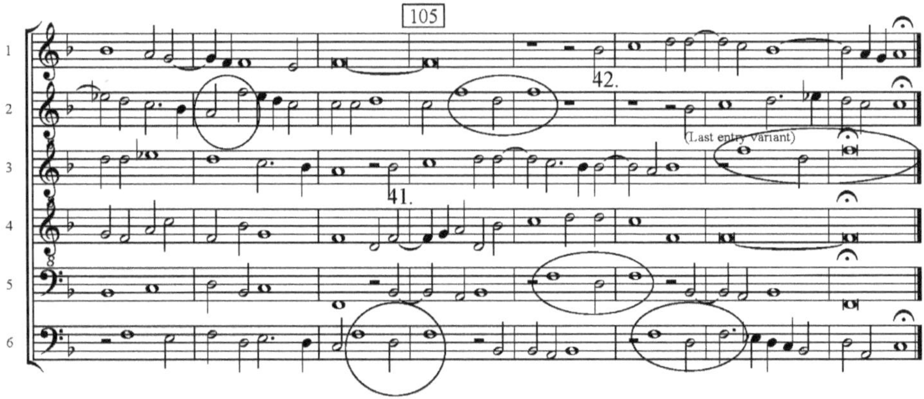

Example 6.9b Closing breves of *Laudate pueri*

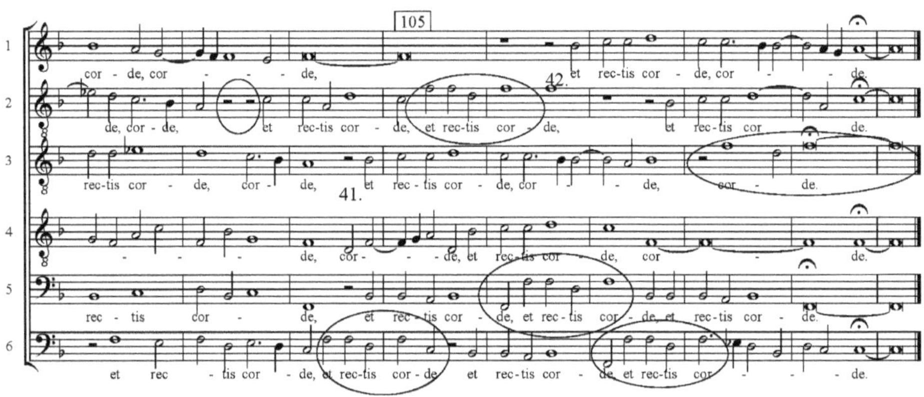

That both *Laudate pueri* and the version adapted from it with English words, *Behold now, praise the Lord*, are found copied without words suggest that they were seen as interchangeable for singing and playing.[30]

The missing part in Fantasia 6/F

It is commonly believed that the missing part from the fantasia was written for tenor viol, behaving in a similar fashion to the surviving treble, with three exact repeats. However, there is something about the relationship of all the parts to each other, which suggests that might not be the case.

The two bass parts in Fantasia 6/F are closely related; they have exactly the same range of pitch, twelve notes from F to c′, and the parts are exchanged on the repeats; two of the tenor parts (parts two and three in Example 6.1) also have exactly the same range of pitch, nine notes from f to g′, and their parts are interchanged on two of the repeats. The ranges of the treble part and part four, taken from *Laudate pueri*, are also both nine notes from c′ to d″ (octave lower in part four), suggesting a relationship between these two parts. The use of fuga in Fantasia 6/F inevitably leads to imitation between all the parts but, particularly in the arrival of the fourth theme, there is the suggestion of canon between the treble part and the missing part reconstructed from *Laudate pueri*.[31] If the reconstructed missing part is placed directly under the part one, the relationship can be seen, and indeed these two parts work as a duet if played together. (Example 6.10)

This suggests that the missing part might have originally been a second treble part part and that Byrd altered the scoring for the motet to suit singers. From a structural point of view, this would show Byrd working with three pairs of instruments and starting to explore timbre. Although raising the 'missing' part by an octave to create a second cantus part creates a momentary 6-4 chord in breve 3, and interrupts the progressive downward pattern from F to C through the first six entries, one or two other factors suggest that it is worth considering that it could be a treble part that is missing. Looking at the treble and reconstructed part, for a substantial part of the piece they are mainly in canon, particularly if some notes added to the tenor voice part to fit words are removed and also the melodic alteration made on the second repeat.[32] Byrd explored canon from his earliest compositions, as found in the second verse of his three-part *Sermone blando* and in later works such as Fantasia 5/C. The canon is echoed in the other two pairs of parts but is not as apparent as in the possible two 'treble parts'. The canonic nature of the first two entries of theme four becomes much more distinct, the initial entry of the 'second' treble being closely followed by that of the 'first'. This inevitably leads to several unison notes in these two 'upper' lines, but this is not unusual in Byrd's fantasias; ten are found in the two treble lines in Fantasia 6/g1 and eight in Fantasia 5/C. Although a reconstruction of the Fantasia 6F is inevitably conjectural, it reinforces the hypothesis that Byrd originally wrote this music as a six-part consort fantasia with a combination of two treble, two tenor and two bass viols.

Example 6.10 Fantasia 6/F, reconstruction with missing part inserted under treble part

In its only manuscript source, GB-Och MSS 979–983, Fantasia 6/F is placed with three other six-part consort works entered near the end of the manuscript. It is directly followed by Parsons's *The song called trumpets*, containing two treble parts, which in all the sources with six parts (e.g. GB-Lbl Add. MS 31390), has paired clefs (C1, C1, C4, C4, F4, F4). Daman's *Beati omnes*, which follows, is missing one part, but also has matching treble and bass clefs (C1, C1 and F4, F4) and one surviving tenor part (C4,). If the missing part is that of a tenor with the clef C4, as Doe suggests in his reconstruction of the part in *Elizabethan Consort Music II,* MB (45/191), the clef combination would be in the same pairing as found in *The song called trumpets.* Both these works therefore have two treble parts and three sets of paired parts, not common in the middle of the sixteenth century, but typical of what eventually became a common make-up of a six-part viol consort. If it is a treble part that is missing from Fantasia 6/F, it would place it as a consort for two treble, two tenor and two bass viols, collected with two similar works, grouped together for ease of access by a six-part viol consort using this combination of instruments.

Looking at the ranges of the parts in Fantasia 6/F, the interval between the highest note of the known treble part and those of two tenor parts is that of a fifth. Without the third tenor part, the interval between the highest note of two tenor parts and the bass parts would also be a fifth. Each possible pair of parts would operate in a distinct pitch range if it is a treble part that is missing,

If the missing part is a treble part, it would mean that Fantasia 6/F contains no part with the clef C4, which is unusual in English sixteenth-century consort music. The clefs would be C1, (C1?), C3, C3, F4, F4.[33] However, Byrd does not use the clef C4 in six other consort works, including the six-part Pavan and Galliard 6/C.[34] A number of consort works by other sixteenth-century composers do not contain the clef C4: Tallis's *A solfing song*, Tye's six-part In Nomine, Ferrabosco I's six-part 'fantasia' and his three five-part In Nomines, White's In Nomine III and Parsons's In Nomine a 7.[35] Tye's In Nomine contains neither C3 or C4. Tallis's *A solfing song* and Ferrabosco's 'fantasia' are of particular interest because of the influence these two works had on Fantasia 6/F.[36] Few six-part consort pieces survive from the mid-sixteenth century; ten are collected in *Elizabethan Consort Music,* MB 44 and 45. Two are of possibly of vocal origin; of the remaining eight, none contain more than two clefs of either C3 or C4.[37] In contrast, of the nine six-part motets by Byrd in the *Cantiones Sacrae* of 1575, six contain two C3 clefs and one C4 clef and two contain two each of C3 and C4. The *Browning* Fantasy is the only one of Byrd's consort pieces containing two C3 clefs and one C4. Neither of his two other six-part fantasias have more than one each of C3 or C4. Of course, what instrument a composer envisaged playing each line cannot, in many case, be identified by the clef alone. The choice of the player will relate to different viol sizes and inclination. However the use of more than two parts with either C4 or C3 clefs would seem to be uncommon. Byrd made more use of such clefs in his vocal music. The lack of a C4 clef does not exclude the possibility that the missing part in Fantasia 6/F could be that of a treble.

The contents of the partbooks of GB-Och MSS 979–983, containing five parts of Fantasia 6/F, do not all appear to be consistent in the type of part contained within them. Three of them do have a consistency of content: in MS 980, Discantus, all the parts are for tenor viol and either have the clef C4 or C3; all the parts in MS 982 have the clef C1 and are for treble viol and MS 983 contains bass parts with clef F4. The partbook MS 981, named Contra tenor, contains three bass parts (F4) and MS 979, Superius, contains two treble parts (C1) and two tenor parts (C3). So it is possible the missing partbook did contain a missing treble part for Fantasia 6/F.

Fantasia or motet

Although Fantasia 6/F never reaches the heights of Byrd's later fantasias, it has distinct elements of his instrumental style and contains characteristics that make it stand out from the other Byrd motets in the *Cantiones Sacrae* of 1575, identifying it first and foremost as an instrumental composition. The support and role of the two bass parts is of central importance as is its construction round the imitative symmetry. Byrd does not explore idiomatic rhythmic development or any dance elements, or make significant use of popular tunes as is found in the later fantasias, but contrast is found within the music. His first three themes are all related with leaps of a fourth or a fifth; his calm, walking fourth theme, lasting for over a third of the 109 breves, brings a very different feel to the music. Fantasia 6/F is undoubtedly closer to vocal music than Byrd's later six-part instrumental works. Byrd was still a relatively young man at the time of its composition; his musical expertise had been acquired in a choral tradition, within which he could develop his compositional skills, and through his experience as a viol-playing chorister. The influence of vocal music is clear, but no other work by Byrd in the *Cantiones Sacrae* of 1575 has two bass parts or displays the characteristics of the canzona. Text was clearly fitted to the music for the motet, necessitating a number of changes on repeats to accommodate different words. Byrd was, however, exploring musical structure and ideas in both his early consort music and his Latin motets written up to around 1575, and some similar characteristics can be seen in both genres.

The pairing of the bass and tenor parts suggest viol rather than vocal music and that raises the question of the missing part. Players may like to experiment with playing this part, edited from the third tenor in *Laudate pueri*, first on a tenor and then an octave higher on the treble, which brings out the relationship between this part and part one. There is no way round the problem of the 6/4 chord; players will need to make their own decisions, balancing the evidence.

It would appear that Byrd did not find his first excursion into 'free' fantasia in consort music very satisfying, and he turned to exploring the keyboard fantasia. Roughly dating his consort works suggests it was probably several years before he came back to the consort fantasia. In writing Fantasia 6/F, Byrd had found a way of supporting a much longer instrumental work, although he had to rely on repeated sections to do so. By around 1570, he had begun to explore writing longer pieces of consort music constructed on variations on a theme. The first of these, the Prelude and Ground, was probably written soon after, or around the same time he was writing Fantasia 6/F. The second, his highly successful *Browning* Fantasy using the tune *The leaves be green*, was composed after he returned to London in 1572. Both of these are examined in the next chapter.

1 McCarthy, *Byrd*, p. 118.

2 Harley, *William Byrd Gentleman of the Chapel Royal*, pp. 105–6.

3 See Richard Charteris, 'The Origin of Alfonso Ferrabosco the Elder's Six-part Fantasia C224, *Chelys*, (1987), pp. 11–14.

4 A small collection of vocal works, which contains just two textless pieces, and dates from 1610–1615.

5 EECM 56, p. 260.

6 Farrant and Byrd were possibly related through marriage. Byrd's niece, Mary, married a man named Farrant who may have been Richard Farrant's son, although this is not proven. Harley, *William Byrd Gentleman of the Chapel Royal*, p. 25.

7 As he did for the copying of *My Ladye Nevells Booke*; *ibid.*, p. 45.

8 Byrd described himself in 1577 as having being 'called' to Elizabeth's service; Harley, *William Byrd Gentleman of the Chapel Royal*, p. 42. Byrd may also have had support from influential noblemen such as Lord Paget and the Earl of Leicester; Harley, *The World of William Byrd*, pp. 109–10.

9 Baldwin apparently avoided making manuscript copies of music available in print; see Milsom (ed), *Christ Church Oxford Library Music Catalogue*, 'GB-Och Mus.979–983', http://library.chch.ox.ac.uk/music/

10 Neighbour, *The Consort and Keyboard Music of William Byrd*, p. 65

11 Milsom in EECM 56, p. 258.

12 Gerald Strahle in 'Two Byrd "Fantasias" Disproven' in *All kinds of music: in Honour of Andrew D. McCredie*, Graham Strahle and David Swale (eds) (Wilhemshaven, 1998), pp. 47–56 and David Pinto, 'Byrd and the Bees: "*In Manus Tuas*"', *The Viol* (Spring 2007/6), p. 43.

13 Thomas Morley, *A Plain & Easy Introduction to Practical Music*, ed. Alec Harman, (New York, 1963, rev. 1973), p. 296.

14 John Caldwell, 'Canzona', in *The New Grove Dictionary of Music & Musicians* online 2001, updated 2009; https://doi-org.nls.idm.oclc.org/10.1093/gmo/9781561592630.article.04804.

15 Ibid.

16 Harper, 'Ensemble and Lute Music', p. 276.

17 Harley, *The World of William Byrd*, p. 54.

18 Byrd uses the exact clef, range and pitch in two other consort works, *Christe Redemptor* and the Pavan 5/c: it is not common in other consort works, but is also found in Stonings's *Browning* Fantasy and *Mr White, his Song* (and for the cantus firmus in In Nomines by Parsley and Woodcock).

19 John Milsom. CD notes for *Thomas Tallis: The Complete Works – Volume 9, Instrumental Music and Songs*, Charivari Agréable (2004 Signum SIG42), p. 4.

20 See Milsom in EECM 56.

21 Ibid., pp. 414–16.

22 Harley, *William Byrd Gentleman of the Chapel Royal*, p. 226.

23 McCarthy, *Byrd*, p. 39

24 Harley, *William Byrd Gentleman of the Chapel Royal*, p. 205.

25 CS = *Cantiones Sacrae.*

26 Milsom in EECM 56, pp. 177, 380 and 288.

27 Ibid., pp, 17 and 128.

28 For example, in *Aspice Domine de sede*, found in the *Cantiones Sacrae* of 1589, and *Afflicte pro peccatis*, found in the *Cantiones Sacrae* published in 1591; see Kerman, *The Masses and Motets of William Byrd*, p. 341.

29 Joseph Kerman, 'Byrd's Motets: Chronology and Canon', *Journal of the American Musicological Society*, 14/3 (Autumn 1961), p. 361.

30 The manuscript containing the textless version of *Behold now, praise the Lord*, MSS 17786–91 (24), is a large collection for viol players or voices and viols, dating from the early years of the seventeenth century. It also contains parts for Byrd's five-part fantasia and Fantasia 6/g1. *Behold now, praise the Lord* is the second six-partwork entered, suggesting that this version was still understood as a fantasia to be played.

31 This inevitably leads to several unison notes in these two 'upper' lines, but this is not unusual in Byrd's fantasias; ten are found in the two treble lines in Fantasia 6/g1 and eight in Fantasia 5/C.

32 Breves 55–58 should match breves 43–45.

33 EECM 56 p. 261 contains an error: the prefatory clef should be C1 not G2.

34 Two Latin-titled works (*Sermone blando* a 3 (C1, C3, F4,), *Christe qui lux* (III) (C1, C3, C3, F4), In Nomine 5/3 (G2, C2, C2, C3, F3), In Nomine 5/4 (G2, C1, C2, C3, F3) and the Pavan and Galliard 6/C (G2, G2, C2, C3, F3, F3).'

35 Tallis's *A solfing song* (G2, C3, C3, C5, F4): Ferrabosco I's six-part 'fantasia' (G2, C2, C2, C3, C3, F4) and his three five-part In Nomines (MB 44/48–50: all G2, C1, C2, C3, F3): White's In Nomine III (MB 44/29: G2, C1, C3, F4): Tye six-part In Nomine (MB 45/195, G2, G2, C1, C2, F4, F4) and Parsons's In Nomine a 7 (GB-Lbl Add. MS 31390, ff. 25v–25r: G2, C2, C2, F4, F4, F4, F4).

36 Both *A solfing song* and Ferrabosco's six-part 'fantasia' are likely to have been written before Byrd's Fantasia 6/F, being found in GB-Lbl Add. MS 31390.

37 One each of C3 and C4, Anon. In Nomine (MB 44/72), Nicholas Strogers, In Nomine IV (MB 44/73), John Mundy, In Nomines III and IV (MB 45/193& 194); two C3s, Ferrabosco I, 'Fantasia' (MB 45/192); two of C4, Parsons *The Song called Trumpets* and probably Daman's *Beati omnes*.

Chapter 7

Variations and the first consort pavan

Byrd's earliest consort pieces have an affinity with his vocal music whereas his earliest set of variations for viol consort, the Prelude and Ground, has a strong connection with his keyboard writing. It dates from his years in Lincoln, during which time Byrd also began to write fantasias and sets of variations for keyboard. Out of this period came two linked works, based on the same ground, the Prelude and Ground and keyboard variations entitled The Second Grownde, which appears in My Ladye Nevell's Booke. The keyboard variations are the more extended work which suggests the consort variations were the earlier of the two sets.[1] Only one other consort set of variations by Byrd survives, his Browning Fantasy, probably the second consort work he wrote after returning to London in 1572.

The Pavan 5/c is thought to be the next consort work Byrd composed after the Prelude and Ground soon after his return to London. He may have been encouraged to write this by the growing interest in dance form. It also is linked to his keyboard music and appears as a keyboard piece in My Ladye Nevell's Booke. It is the only surviving five-part consort pavan by Byrd, but it seems likely that he adapted other consort pavans and galliards for keyboard. All of the sequence of pavans and galliards in My Ladye Nevell's Booke (numbered 10–25) might have originally been consort pieces.[2] What is clear is that at this stage in his career, Byrd was working at developing an instrumental style for both viols and keyboard, using similar forms. He wrote fourteen sets of keyboard variations up to c.1590 and presumably found the form particularly well suited to the keyboard, whereas only two variation sets for consort have survived. The second consort work in variation form, the Browning Fantasy, appears to have been written shortly after the Pavan 5/c and was in circulation by 1578. It is written for highly competent players, probably for those associated with the Chapel Royal. Both the Prelude and Ground and the Browning Fantasy demand advanced technical skills from viol players and Byrd must have seen the potential in variation form to develop the virtuosic style he first used in his In Nomines and learnt from Ferrabosco I.

Sources: Variations

The Prelude and Ground is found in only two manuscripts, which also contain Byrd's Browning Fantasy. The earliest is a single treble partbook, GB-Lbl MS Add. 32377 (8), dating from 1585 to 1590. It contains 80 works, of which 29 are likely to have been instrumentally conceived, four of which are by Byrd.[3] The Prelude and Ground is the second work entered after the Browning Fantasy. All five parts are found in GB-Lbl Add MSS 17792–96 (32), a much later large manuscript completed in the 1620s and 30s by John Merro, probably for the use of viol-playing choristers in Gloucester. There is little Elizabethan consort music in Merro's manuscript collections, but it is interesting that he evidently thought that the Prelude and Ground was significant enough a piece to include with Byrd's Browning Fantasy among the four Elizabethan consort pieces found among the 156 consort works in GB-Lbl Add MSS 17792–96.[4] Sadly there are significant errors in the Ground in Merro's manuscript and variations nine and ten are incomplete.[5] Thus, no known complete version of the Prelude and Ground is known to survive; Byrd's keyboard piece, The Second Grownde, based on the same ground, survives complete in My Ladye Nevell's Booke (10), which dates from 1591.

Byrd's Browning Fantasy is found in eight sources, making it his most popular consort work after In Nomine 5/5. Although undoubtedly composed later, it appears in three manuscripts that pre-date the earliest source of the Prelude and Ground. It is found in one of the very earliest and significant, GB Lbl Add MS 31390 (2). This was corrected in 1578, by which time it is likely the Browning Fantasy was added, meaning Byrd must have composed it by the late 1570s. Only music without text is found in GB Lbl Add MS 31390.

Three manuscripts identified as being completed in the 1580s contain Byrd's Browning Fantasy. In GB-Och MSS 984–8 (5) it is the first entered in a group of 19 textless works, 14 of which are consort works. Woodcock's Browning Fantasy follows Byrd's Browning variations. In Nomine 5/5 is found later in the manuscript.[6] GB-Ob MS Mus. Sch.e. 423 (6) contains four consort works by Byrd among 11 consort works, these being the Browning Fantasy, In Nomine 5/5 and the first known copies of Fantasias 6/g1 and 6/g2. The Browning Fantasy is the second consort work entered after Parsons's De la court, placing two of the most popular Elizabethan instrumental pieces together. This manuscript is of course of particular interest because it was owned by Byrd's patron John, first Lord Petre. It is likely that the four consort pieces by Byrd were played in the Petre household. The Browning Fantasy and the Prelude and Ground are both found in GB-Lbl MS Add. 32377

(8), which also dates from the 1580s.

The Browning Fantasy is the first and only consort work by Byrd found in a collection of 27 textless works US-Ws MS V.a. 408 (9) from c.1590.[7] Sixteen works are identified as consort works, mainly In Nomines and Latin-titled compositions. It is also found among 21 consort works with In Nomines 5/2 and 5/5 in GB-Ob MS Tenbury 389 (11), which contains 127 works collected over a period of time from c.1595 and completed c.1613.

The latest manuscripts to contain Byrd's Browning Fantasy were all completed in the seventeenth century. As well as being found with the Prelude and Ground in the partbooks GB-Lbl Add MSS 17792–96 (32), it was added to the keyboard manuscript GB-Lbl MS 29996 (35) in open score among madrigals. It was copied by Thomas Tomkins around 1621, who of course admired it as 'A most Excellent peice'.[8]

Sources: The Pavan 5/c

One surviving manuscript, D-Kl MS mus. 125 (22), contains all five parts of the consort Pavan 5/c. Dating from c.1600, it shows that Byrd's music had reached Germany by the end of the sixteenth century, taken there by English actor musicians. It belonged to Landgrave Moritz of Hesse-Kassel. A keyboard version of the Pavan 5/c is found in My Ladye Nevell's Booke, GB-Lbl MS Mus 1591 (10), collected in 1591. Four parts of the consort version are found in a large collection for viol players, dating from after 1606, GB-Lbl Add. MS 37402–6 (21) along with the Fantasia 6/g2 and Parsons's *De la court* and music written by the generation after Byrd; only nine pieces were originally consort music. The pavan is the only dance in the collection. Finally the keyboard version is found in a collection of dance music for keyboard, NYp MS Drexel 5612 (38) with two paired pavans and galliards by Byrd.

Prelude and Ground: Structure

John Harley identifies the ground used by Byrd in the five-part Prelude and Ground as that known as the Good night, which may have originated as a song tune.[9] The original form of the ground lasted for eight dotted semibreves, to which Byrd added two dotted semibreves in the middle and two at the end, resulting in a theme of 12 dotted semibreves (Example 7.1a and b).

Example 7.1

a) The Good Night ground

b) Byrd's version in his Prelude and Ground

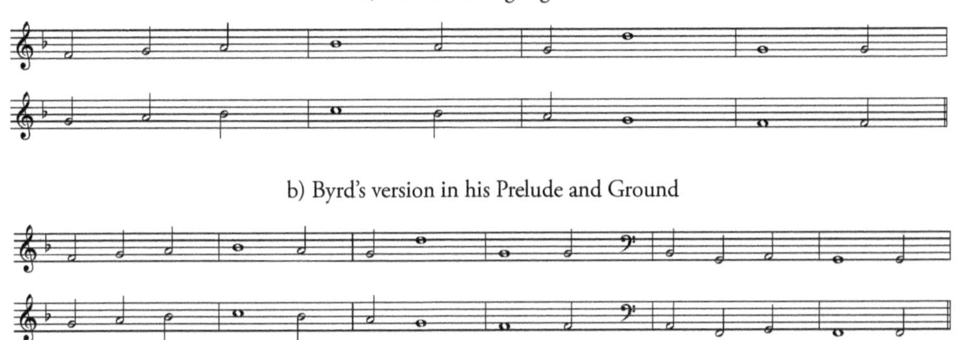

It is impossible to say whether Byrd's consort Prelude and Ground and his keyboard The Second Grownde were written simultaneously. The keyboard is the longer work, with 17 repetitions of the ground compared with eleven in the consort piece, which Harley suggests could point to The Second Grownde being the later work. Both works use Byrd's extended ground, which gave him the potential for greater harmonic variety (Example 7.1). The inclusion of a prelude suggests both the consort and keyboard works may be contemporary with Byrd's keyboard Fantasia in a, as it also has a Prelude.[10] The Prelude and Ground were also likely written around the same time as Fantasia 6/F, with which similarities can be found.[11]

In the Prelude and Ground, Byrd returned to writing for five parts, in contrast to the six found in Fantasia 6/F, but the entries of the Prelude theme occur six times at a breve's distance, as happens in the opening of the fantasia (Examples 7.2 and 6.1). The first entries in both works begin with a semibreve and two minims and move from F to C, Fantasia 6/F by a leap and the Prelude stepwise over two breves. The Prelude theme also has similarities with the last, calm stepwise theme of the fantasia. As with In Nomine 5/5 and Fantasia 6/F, the Prelude and Ground has a signature accidental of one flat. It contains the clefs G2, C1, C3, C4 and F4, the same arrangement used by Byrd in his In Nomine 5/5. It has a wide compass of 24 notes, with part one (treble) reaching a″, clearly suggesting it was instrumentally conceived. One inner part (third line, tenor) has a range of 13 notes; the fourth part and the bass have a range of 11 notes. Parts one and two each have a range of ten notes. The parts all have a different range of pitch, rather than the pairing found in Fantasia 6/F. This results in a combined range of 14 notes for the two upper parts and 15 notes for parts three and four. The lowest note of the bass sounds a fifth below the fourth part. This gives Byrd a wide compass of pitch and timbre to explore.

Example 7.2 Prelude

Byrd explores two new ideas in the Prelude and Ground: the placing of two contrasting movements together in a consort work and the use of triple metre (dotted semibreve) throughout the Ground, following the duple metre of two semibreves found in the Prelude. This implies the influence of dance music, i.e. like a galliard following a pavan. The Prelude lasts for 14 breves and opens with a sustained, stepwise rising theme found in all five parts. The rising theme is picked up by part one and the supporting fourth part in the opening of the Ground, resulting in the two movements being related. The Prelude opens with the notes f′ (repeated) g′ and a′ played by the fourth part; these three notes are found in the first dotted semibreve of the Ground in the same (fourth) part (Example 7.2 and 7.3).

Example 7.3 Opening of the Ground

The first two sections of the eleven Ground variations are calm and sustained and mainly based on movement in minims. More crotchet movement begins to occur at the end of the second repeat of the ground and intensifies in the third variation; the music feels faster through the introduction of dotted crotchet and quaver triplets and running quaver passages. The fourth variation gradually loses the quaver movement and distinctive crotchet patterns appear in the fifth repetition, reminiscent of the fourth section of Byrd's In Nomine 5/5 and the influence of Parsons (Examples 7.4, 5.15 and 5.16). The music increases in virtuosity at the end of this variation into the sixth as semiquavers are added in the last two breves. The seventh and eighth variations are much more sustained. Virtuosity then takes over in the ninth variation. It probably played an important role in the tenth variation and does so in the final, eleventh repetition of the ground. Demanding, fast-moving quaver passages require technical skill from the viol players reflecting the exploitation of technical brilliance Byrd learnt from Ferrabosco. Sadly, we cannot judge how the work finally looked due to the substantial amount of material missing from the ninth and tenth variations.

Example 7.4 Opening of Ground variation 5

The brilliance of the Ground illustrates how far Byrd had come in his writing of idiomatic instrumental music in his consort works. Unlike Fantasia 6/F, this is not a work that could be transformed into a vocal piece, but although Byrd exploits fully the capabilities of his treble and tenor viol players, the bass part is relatively simple for the greater part of the music. In the first four variations the original ground is played by part four (tenor).[12] In every four dotted semibreves out of six it acts as the bass line. The bass only enters for the last two dotted semibreves out of each group of six, playing Byrd's two patterns extending the original ground, thus making the music alternately in four and five parts. The added notes give Byrd the capacity for greater harmonic variety. The listener is drawn to the change the bass makes every time it enters. But did Byrd do this just for impact and to alter the direction of the ground? After the fourth version of the ground, the theme is passed between the parts, sometimes ornamented. The bass continues to play its two simple patterns until the sixth repetition of the ground, where it is slightly more active. Through variations seven and eight, it returns to its previous role, sometimes with slight ornamentation or variant of the original patterns. There is no accurate copy of the bass part surviving for variations 9 and 10. Seven breves survive of variation 9; it is silent in the first four and then plays the extra ground notes again.[13] It is possible that the bass played a more demanding role in variation 10 but, although the bass has significantly more notes to play in variation 11, it still is not required to play with the virtuosity demanded of the other parts. This suggests that the bass part in variation 10 was not virtuosic.[14]

The Prelude and Ground appear to have been one of the least disseminated of Byrd's consort works. Could the simple bass part be a reason for this? All the other parts require highly skilled players. There are a number of possible explanations for the simple bass part, apart from its role in guiding the tonal structure of the music and giving it freedom from the ground. Was Byrd using it to keep the music and players together? Did he play the part himself, directing the music? Or did he write it for a beginner bass viol player, perhaps one of his patrons? We can never know, but this work is unique in the way Byrd uses the bass line.

As he did in Fantasia 6/F and In Nomines 5/2 and 5/3, Byrd makes careful and strategic use of leaps of an octave or more in the Prelude and Ground. Four octave leaps are found in the Prelude. The first, found in breve 5, intimates the move from chords based on F to chords based on C. In breve nine, the return to chords centred on F is reinforced with octave leaps downwards by parts one and two from f″ and c″, and by an octave leap down by part three from f, found in breves eleven to twelve. Finally, the bass part follows in breve twelve with a leap down from a to F of an octave and a third, preparing us for the final cadence to F (Example 7.2). In the Ground variations, Byrd makes little use of octave leaps but there are two in the dotted semibreve before the fifth ground version, perhaps intended to deliberately draw attention to this variation, which is reminiscent of both Parsons's five-part In Nomine and Byrd's own In Nomine 5/5 (Example 7.4).

The use of contrasting rhythm patterns by Byrd to enhance music unencumbered by words is very apparent in the Prelude and Ground and it includes his first significant use of triplet patterns. The result is an exciting and unique composition linked to Byrd's keyboard music through its fast running scale passages as well as the common Ground melody.

Pavan 5/c

Still apparently exploring similar forms in his consort and keyboard music, Byrd probably was composing a significant number of pavans and galliards after his return to London in 1572. The consort Pavan 5/c is a stately dance eminently suitable for dance (Example 7.5). It is very different to Byrd's later six-part pavan.

Example 7.5 Opening Pavan 5/c

Source Rastall from Kassel manuscript D-Kl MS mus. 125

The Pavan 5/c consists of three repeated sections each of eight breves. The parts move mainly in minims and semibreves, as is appropriate for a slow moving dance, until the third section. In the first breve of this final section, the parts move emphatically together. Following this, it is possible to see hints of the interplay and use of small motifs that Byrd was beginning to develop in his music. The short theme that appears from breve 18 (first intimated in the fourth part in breve 17) contains a pattern of three crotchets very similar to patterns he later used in the Fantasia 4/g and Fantasia 5/C (Example 7.6).

Example 7.6 Opening of third section of Pavan 5/c

Browning Fantasy Structure

Byrd's five-part Browning Fantasy uses a popular sixteenth-century tune (Example 7.7). Other settings of the same tune are entitled 'The leaves be green' or 'the nuts be brown'.[15] One source of Byrd's Browning, in GB-Lbl Add. MSS 17792–6, has written beside it, 'The leaves be green, the nuts be brown, They hang so high they will not come down'. Tomkins titled his copy of Byrd's Browning 'The leaves be greene. A ground'.[16] There are similarities between the Browning theme and Byrd's ground in the Prelude and Ground (Examples 7.7 and 7.1b).

Example 7.7 Browning tune

As well as Byrd's version, four other consort Browning variations are known.[17] Two are in five parts, composed by Henry Stonings and Clement Woodcock; both are titled Browninge my dere and found in GB-Lbl 31390, as is Byrd's Browning Fantasy. The entry of Stonings's variations at folio 59v would suggest that his set is the earliest. Woodcock's variations appear at 101v. Byrd's Browning Fantasy was the very last work to be added to the manuscript (folio 129v), suggesting it was the last composed. The remaining two surviving consort sets of Browning variations are in three parts, written by John Baldwin and Elway Bevin (c.1554–1638). Both are found in Baldwin's Commonplace Book, GB-Lbl MS RM 24 d.2, copied between c.1580 and 1606.[18] Other compositions based on the Browning tune include two lute pieces, a set of keyboard variations and two versions for voices.[19]

Unlike the Browning Fantasies by Stonings and Woodcock, Byrd's fantasy opens with the theme in the bass (Example 7.8). His version contains 20 variations and is significantly longer than Stonings's Browning of five variations and Woodcock's version with ten variations. Byrd also decorates the theme throughout by the addition of crotchets in the third and seventh dotted semibreves.

Example 7.8 Opening of Byrd's Browning Fantasy

It is hard to ascertain what Byrd's overall plan was for the Browning Fantasy. In some place it seems as though it grew organically. It is probable that he planned 20 variations so that within a group of five variations, each instrument in turn played the theme. He then apparently changed his mind as to how the work should open, deciding to choose the bass viol to first articulate the theme affecting the order in which the theme passes between instruments. If the second variation is taken as the first, then the order in which the theme is played, corresponds exactly with the opening of Stonings's and Woodcock's fantasies (Example 7.9 a, b and c). It is likely that Byrd knew these two Browning Fantasies.

Example 7.9 Comparison of openings of

a) Henry Stonings, Browning Fantasy

b) Clement Woodcock, Browning Fantasy

c) Byrd, Browning variation 2 and beginning of 3

From variation 2 in Byrd's Browning, each viol part plays the theme in turn, through variations 2–6, and 7–11. The next four variations are missing a bass rendition of the theme, as a result of Byrd moving it to variation one. Each viol part then plays the theme in turn again in variations 16–20. This left his third set of five variations without the bass playing the theme, the result of it occurring twice in the bass line in the first set of variations.

Each of Byrd's 20 Browning variations last for eight dotted semibreves and contains the clefs C_1, C_3, C_3, C_4 and F_4. There is a signature accidental of one flat. An f# appears in all three five-part fantasies, but Byrd's fantasy is immediately distinctive through his introduction of an e♭ from the second dotted semibreve, a pitch which does not occur in the other versions. Byrd's Browning has a compass of 22 notes, narrower than that of the Prelude and Ground. However, with one exception, the individual viol parts have wider ranges than those found in the Prelude and Ground. Three parts have a range of 12 notes; the remaining two parts (tenor) have a range of 13 notes, identical pitch and the same clef (C_3). The treble part ascends only up to f″, compared with a″ in the Prelude and Ground; the bass part goes down to F, thus giving a narrower compass. The combined range of parts three and four is 15 notes, the same as found in the Prelude and Ground, but it is pitched a note lower, unusually taking one inner part down to B♭. It is impossible to know whether Byrd had access to a tenor player (and instrument) who could reliably produce a good sound on this note, or whether the bridge on the viol was moved to accommodate it (especially since the part only needs to reach up to f′).[20] There is greater overlap between Byrd's parts than is found in Stonings's Browning Fantasy, which has a compass of 23 notes. Woodcock's Browning Fantasy has a compass of 20 notes. His two upper parts only reach d″. Due to the narrower ranges in individual parts (part two has a range of 12 notes, part three a range of 11 and all other parts a range of nine notes), the overlap is also less than that found in Byrd's work. In spite of the narrower compass in Woodcock's Browning Fantasy, the content of the music makes it quite clear that all three fantasies are instrumental music. It is possible that Woodcock's work was intended for wind players, like Hackney, hence the narrower compass. Stonings's fantasy has a wide compass, typical of instrumental music, and the wide ranges of Byrd's parts indicate that it is instrumental music.

Byrd does not match his tonal development to groups of variations. It is shaped by the Browning theme and its transposition. The theme is found in its original pitch in the first four variations, with the music moving from its opening (downbeat) falling on a major chord on B♭ to closing on a major chord on F. The first transposition of the theme appears in variation 5 in the second viol part (Example 7.10). With the higher pitch and an increase of moving crotchets, the music increases in intensity through this and the following two variations. It moves between opening on a major chord on F and closing on a major chord on C. This continues in variations 6 and 7.

Example 7.10 Browning Fantasy variation 5

Real change comes in variation 8 with the second transposition of the theme, found in the treble line (Example 7.11). The theme is heard above moving crotchets in all the other

Example 7.11 Browning Fantasy variations 8 and 9

parts. Tonalities change quickly and are more ambiguous than in previous variations. The second transposition is heard again in variation 9, which ends very firmly on a cadence on to a G major chord, sustained on a semibreve by all five parts, thus bringing the music briefly to a halt. In variation 10, the music returns immediately to a major chord on F and the first transposition of the tune, which is also heard in the calmer and more sustained variation 11. The music moves through major chords on C and B♭, reaching a major chord on C at the end of variation 11.

In variations 12 to 14, the theme returns to its original pitch, but with more adventurous harmonies. The music moves through minor chords on G and major chords on F and B♭ finishing on a major chord on F in both variations 13 and 14. As it returns to a major chord on B♭ at the beginning of variation 14, the music's intensity builds up with increased use of crotchets and quavers (Example 7.12). The first and final transposition occurs once more in variation 15, which begins once again on a major chord on B♭ and finishes on a major chord on F, the intensity of the music being urged forward by different short rhythmic patterns.

Example 7.12 Browning Fantasy variations 14 and 15

The Browning theme returns to its original pitch in variations 16–20. Each variation finishes on a major chord on F. Byrd maintains the excitement and intensity of the music through his use of rhythm. In variations 16 and 17, the music fragments except for the theme until at the end of variation 17, where it launches into exuberant triplets, which continue until the end of variation 19 (Example 7.13). The last, calmer variation opens with minor chord on G, but moves through major and minor chords on C to its conclusion on a major chord on F.

Looking at the relationship between the variations, variations 2 – 3 continue the calm opening found in variation 1 (Examples 7.8 and 7.9c). As in the opening of Woodcock's Browning, Byrd's fantasy begins in three parts, which is continued in the second variation (which of course corresponds to Woodcock's first variation). This gives Byrd the opportunity to contrast the first variation, using parts two and four and the bass line (five), with the second that uses the treble (part one) and parts three and four. All five instruments play from the entry of variation 3 (Example 7.9c). From the beginning, Byrd exploits instrumental colour and varies the musical texture. In variation 4, running crotchet passages become more frequent, picking up a pattern found first in the fifth and sixth dotted semibreves. These patterns continue in variations 5–8. In variation 4, the crotchets are falling; in variation 5 they rise (Example 7.14). The crotchets behave the same way in variations 6 and 7.

In variation 8 the theme is found in the treble and the rising crotchet pattern continues from the previous variation, passing through the lower parts. In variation 9 a new pattern emerges based round a minim, four crotchets and a further minim (Example 7.11). This pattern continues in a different form in variation 10. Variation 11 returns to the more sustained movement of the opening. In variation 12, the Browning theme returns at the original pitch, maintaining the sustained movement of the previous variation. This continues until the end of variation 13. At the beginning of variation 14, the music starts to gather momentum which is carried through variation 15 to the start of variation 16 (Example 7.12). Fast, dotted crotchet/quaver patterns appear. In variation 16 short patterns reminiscent of In Nomine 5/5 proliferate (Example 7.15); this leads into variation 17, which contains reminders of the previous two variations, but in the last two bars[21] (Example 7.13) Byrd introduces his first really exuberant, extensive use of triplets in consort music, developing his use of triplets in the Prelude and Ground. Through falling and rising crotchet triplet patterns, the music moves with speed through variations 18 and 19 to the final, more sombre variation 20, in which the listener is reminded of the calm opening.

Example 7.13 Browning Fantasy from the end of variation 17

Example 7.14 Browning Fantasy end of variation 4 and beginning of variation 5

Example 7.15 Browning Fantasy variation 16

The variations appear to relate to each other as follows:

Variation1–3	Calm, opening section
Variations 4–8	Falling and rising crotchet patterns
Variations 9–10	A new short theme based on a symmetrical rhythm
Variations 11–13	Calmer sections reminiscent of the opening variations
Variations 14–16	Variations exploiting rhythmic patterns
Variations 17–19	Extensive use of triplets begins at the end of variation 17
Variation 20	Return to the calm of the opening section

Although there is a calmer section formed in the middle by variations 11–13, Byrd gradually builds up the excitement and tension in the Browning fantasy through his increased use of smaller note values and dotted rhythms. The music reaches its most exciting point with the arrival of the fast triplet patterns in variation 17.

The Browning theme behaves like a ground in five variations. In the first, the bass plays the Browning tune supporting just two other lines, parts two and four, and the first statement is heard clearly (Example 7.8). The fourth part then takes over the theme, acting as a bass for two higher parts, these being part one (treble) and part three in variation 2. The bass takes the theme back again to support all the other parts in variation 3. In the first four bars of variation 7, the Browning tune returns to the bass again in its first transposition (starting on C, a fourth up from its original pitch), supporting three voices. This means that that theme can be clearly heard at its new pitch. The music reduces to four parts for the final part of the variation leading to a chord on C. In variation 19 the bass takes over the theme again at its original pitch (Example 7.13). It provides stability for the lively, running triplet patterns in the other four parts.

In variations 13 and 20 (Examples 7.13 and 7.16), the Browning theme is found in the fourth part. In these two variations, the bass line works with part four; together they provide support for the freely moving three parts above.

Example 7.16 Browning Fantasy variation 13

Byrd carefully planned which part is playing the Browning theme at particular points in the variations. In variation 7, the bass plays the Browning theme in its first transposition beginning on C; the theme then passes in variation 8 to the treble viol playing the second transposition starting on g′, where it is heard above the other parts (Example 7.11). In variation 13, the combination of parts four and five supporting the upper parts emphasises the progression the music makes from a minor chord on D at the end of variation 12, a minor third below F, to its furthest point in G, then back through a chord on C to close on a chord on F.

In variation 20, the music operates in a similar way, moving from an F chord to G chords before the fantasy is finally brought to a close onto a chord on F. At variation 18, the treble viol takes over the theme, so it that it stands out above the triplets in the parts underneath. In variation 19, the theme passes back to the bass, with the triplets tumbling above (Example 7.13).

Byrd uses the upper ranges of his treble and bass parts very sparingly. The treble line only once reaches its highest note, f″, in variation 5 (Example 7.10). It is found at the top of an upward crotchet running passage in bar 39 just before a variation finishes for the first time on a cadence on C. Otherwise the treble part rarely goes higher than d″.

An e♭″ is found only in four places, each time occurring just before a cadence at the end of a variation as the music moves to a chord on F. Byrd uses the highest bass note, c′, only once, immediately after the first cadence onto C between variations 5 and 6, following his only use of the highest treble note two dotted semibreves earlier (Example 7.10). Frequent use is made of the lowest bass note, F, which is, of course, the first note of the Browning theme. Although Byrd allowed himself a compass of 22 notes, the music remains mainly within a compass of 20 notes, resulting in a dense texture.

As in earlier works, Byrd has planned his use of octave leaps. The Browning Fantasy contains 17 octave leaps plus one of an octave and a third. Eight octave leaps are placed to prepare for – or bring attention to – a cadence at the end of a variation. For example, in variation 2, (originally the first variation) an upward octave leap from g (bar 14, part 3) comes before downward crotchet movement that emphasises the return to a cadence onto an F chord (Example 7.8); near the end of variation 5 (bar 39, Example 7.10), a downward octave leap from c″ anticipates the first cadence onto a C chord, with part four taking over the role of bass; for four minims there is a quartet. In variation 7, a downward octave leap from f′ (bar 55, part 2) again anticipates another cadence onto a C chord. In variation 9, a downward octave leap from a dotted semibreve g (bar 72, part 5) before the final note of the variation prepares the listener for the conclusion on a major chord on G.

In some places Byrd had no choice other than to write an octave leap as parts reached their extremities, but this he puts to good use, for example in variation 10, where a bass leap brings the four lower parts, playing for five minims as a quartet without the treble, into close 'harmony' within a small compass of notes (Example 7.17). In variation 15 an octave upward leap in the treble line (bar 116) gives clarity to the line and brings the music into four parts without the bass viol for almost four breves. Variation 14 contains two wide virtuosic bass leaps, as the music becomes more demanding (Example 7.12). Finally in variation 20, two octave leaps up in the bass line from G are clearly heard in the sustained closing section, helping to return the music to a final cadence onto a chord on F (Example 7.13).

Example 7.17 Browning Fantasy variation 10

Byrd's use of pitch and range of his instruments in the Browning Fantasy is closely linked to his development of texture, contrast, transposition and modulation. In the first four variations he varies the number of instruments playing, altering the tessitura and texture. He delays using all five parts until the beginning of variation 3, the first two variations being in three parts (Example 7.8). In variation 4, the music begins in the three upper parts; Byrd then adds part four followed by the bass, returning the music to five parts (Example 7.18). No furtherthree-part writing occurs in the fantasy, but significant use of four-part writing changes texture and pitch. For example, at the end of variation 5, a downward octave leap in part four leads to this part briefly becoming the bass line, and the music moves in four parts to the conclusion on C (Example 7.10); in variation 7 an inner part is lost for just over four dotted semibreves, lightening the texture. In variations 8 and 16, more rests are found in the parts, giving the music a sparser texture (Examples 7.11 and 7.15). In variation 11 (Example 7.19), Byrd alternates the treble and bass lines as they answer each other with short phrases. In variation 14 the music becomes denser as it increases in virtuosity into the beginning of variation 15 (Example 7.12) In the middle of variation 17, the treble is silent for two semibreves and then returns to introduce the triplets that dominate variations 18 and 19 (Example 7.13). In variation 20, all the parts join together on a cadence on a G chord (bar 157) as the sense of forward momentum dissipates with the reduction of crotchet movement and the increase of semibreves and minims. Part three, briefly joined by the bass in bar 158, brings back the stepwise crotchet movement for two dotted semibreves. In the last dotted semibreve (bar 161), part three finally brings the music to rest on the third minim.

Example 7.18 Browning Fantasy variation 4

Example 7.19 Browning Fantasy variation 11

It is clear that Byrd planned providing contrast in the Browning Fantasy through his uses of individual viols and their tessitura. As mentioned before, the highest notes in both the treble and bass parts occur just once. Although each has a range of 12 notes, the treble viol mainly falls in the range of d′ and d″ and the bass in a range between F and a; the latter is required to play up to b♭ on four occasions. In parts two and three, each with a range of 13 notes, the highest note, b♭′ is carefully placed; in part two, this occurs three dotted semibreves before the final note and sounds above the treble line (Example 7.13); in part three, the b♭′ occurs at the end of variation 13 just before the cadence onto F, returning from D (Example 7.16). Again, this sounds above the treble line. Byrd mainly uses the upper register in these two parts, so that most notes lie between f and a′. In part four, with a range of 12 notes, the low b♭ is used only once, in thirds with the bass (Example 7.10), but this viol part plays the most extensively across the range from c to f′.

In the Browning Fantasy, Byrd makes extensive use of running crotchet patterns and of short melodic patterns derived from the theme. Sometimes they imitate the overall rise and fall of the melody. For example, in the opening, the second part (tenor) anticipates the first two notes of the theme with a leap of a fourth. In variations 2 and 3, Byrd makes extensive use of an upward or falling leap of a minor third, both found in the theme. In variation 11, the bass and treble viols answer each other with short phrases echoing the theme. From variation 14 the parts, excluding the theme, seem to take on a life of their own but the section is also full of minor thirds. In variation 16, the parts fragment; the short crotchet patterns still frequently incorporate a leap of a minor third. This section is reminiscent of both In Nomine 5/5 and variation 5 from the Ground.

Byrd also changes the texture of the Browning Fantasy through his pairing of instruments in thirds and sixths. Up to the end of variation 5, the moving crotchet patterns mainly follow each other with the occasional overlap of parts and incidence of parallel parts in thirds and sixths. From variation 6, parts are paired in sixths and thirds, starting with the treble and bass viols, which are paired over an octave and a third. They are followed by a pairing of parts two and four. The pairing of parts continues through variations 7, 8 and 9. Parts are paired again at end of variation 17 as the triplets move the music into variation 18. There is extensive use of paired running triplets in thirds and sixths until the end of variation 19 (Example 7.13). It adds to the complexity, texture and delight of the music and is in sharp contrast to the continuous slower-moving theme.

The Browning Fantasy requires technical skill from all the players, including the bass viol, the latter in contrast to the bass part in the Prelude and Ground. The fantasy requires highly skilled consort playing and absolute accuracy for a successful performance. It is a truly complex instrumental piece requiring exuberant viol playing, a long way from Byrd's Fantasia 6/F but following on from the idiomatic instrumental style that he developed in his In Nomines and the Prelude and Ground. The latter demands virtuosic skill in the treble and tenor viol parts, something Byrd gained greater understanding of through his acquaintance with the music of Ferrabosco. In the writing of his two consort works in variation form, Byrd produced truly instrumental music in terms of exploiting viol technique, variation in tessitura and texture, instrumental colour and contrast. What he still needed to find was a less limiting musical structure to support his developing idiomatic instrumental style.

So far as is known, Byrd did not write another set of instrumental consort variations. Presumably he felt he had explored all possibilities in the Prelude and Ground and the Browning Fantasy. Instead, he was attracted back to the fantasia, using the skills he had developed to compose in a more freely constructed form with variety and depth.

1 See Harley, *William Byrd Gentleman of the Chapel Royal*, p. 194.

2 See Richard Rastall in William Byrd, *Pavans and Galliards in Five Parts*, Richard Rastall (ed. and reconstructed) (Leeds, four-fifteen press, 1998), p. iv. Rastall believes that all up to the ninth pair in *My Ladye Nevell's Booke* were probably originally consort works.

3 The other two being In Nomines 5/2 and 5/5.

4 The other two works are by Holborne, a pavan *The Funeralls*, and Mundy, *Sermone blando*.

5 See BE 17.

6 GB-Och MSS 984–8 contains 56 works by Byrd.

7 To which eight anthems were added.

8 http://www.diamm.ac.uk/sources/4129/#/; the manuscript also contains In Nomine 5/5, part of Fantasia 5/C and Fantasias 6/g1 and 6/g2, all in keyboard score: see previous chapters.

9 Harley, *William Byrd Gentleman of the Chapel Royal*, p. 193, n.22. Harley notes that John Ward writing in *The Dublin Virginal Book* (London, 1983), pp. 44–5, identifies the ground in eleven other pieces.

10 Identified in the Fitzwilliam Virginal Book as 'Praeludium to ye Fancie'.

11 Harley, *William Byrd Gentleman of the Chapel Royal*, pp. 157 and 201.

12 It is ornamented slightly the fourth time.

13 See BE 17/10.

14 Elliott reconstructs variations 9 and 10 in BE17/10.

15 See '*Browning*' in Stanley Sadie (ed.), *The New Grove Dictionary of Music and Musicians* (1995), 3, p. 348.

16 In in GB-Lbl MS 29996, http://www.diamm.ac.uk/sources/4129/#/.

17 Not including modern versions.

18 Bevin's at ff. 120v–121r and Baldwin's at ff. 121v–122r.

19 David and Jennifer Baker, 'The Browning (1)', *Chelys*, 10 (1981), pp. 7–10.

20 The only other place Byrd uses a low B♭ is in a tenor viol part in Fantasia 4/g; a consideration is whether a small bass viol was used.

21 For ease of reference, the term 'bar' is used for each dotted semibreve. Thomas Tomkins added bar lines from variation 6 in GB-Lbl MS 29996.

Chapter 8

Fantasia 6/g1

As far as we know, after completing his first fantasia, the six-part Fantasia 6/F, around 1568, Byrd did not return to writing consort fantasias until the 1580s. Fantasia 6/g1 is among the earliest, if not the first, of his later group of fantasias. In it, the distance Byrd had travelled as a composer since writing Fantasia 6/F can clearly be seen in the overall structure, melodic development and instrumental style. He emerges as a gifted, mature composer producing an instrumental work of extraordinary variety and depth, reflecting his individual, idiomatic instrumental style. Both Oliver Neighbour and John Harley see similarities between Fantasia 6/g1 and Byrd's keyboard fantasies due to the wide range of character found in both including dance elements.[1]

It is interesting to consider why Byrd chose to publish his second six-part fantasia in g rather than the first, which is, in many ways, a more striking work. Writers such as Richard Rastall suggest that Fantasia 6/g2 has mainly been considered the better work because Byrd chose to publish it in the *Psalmes, Songs and Sonnets* of 1611 and therefore he, himself, saw it as the more successful of the two fantasias.[2] Early musicologists, such as Edmund Fellowes, barely mention Fantasia 6/g1. Neighbour, in his extensive analysis of the two works, suggests Byrd did not feel satisfied with it and wanted to improve it.[3] John Harper describes Fantasia 6g/2 as 'an altogether more accomplished work.'[4] Rastall states that it is not absolutely clear that Fantasia 6/g1 was written first and wonders why Fantasia 6/g1 is 'so satisfying to perform'. He finds it disturbing that academics have avoided what is obvious; 'Fantasia 6/g1 is a very fine piece that stands on its own merits as the first – or perhaps the second – truly great example of the English consort repertory'.[5]

It is impossible to know why Byrd chose to publish Fantasia 6/g2. It could just be that being shorter than Fantasia 6/g1, it fitted better into *Psalmes, Songs and Sonnets* or perhaps Fantasia 6/g1 was popular and already in circulation, whereas the second fantasia was not as well-known and Byrd wanted to promote it through publication. We cannot assume he preferred one to the other. It is significant that he published a six-part work as the six-part viol consort became more common at the beginning of the seventeenth century.

Sources

Fantasia 6/g1 is found in five surviving manuscripts. Chronologically it is the first of Byrd's consort fantasias to appear in a manuscript after Fantasia 6/F. It is first found in a single partbook, GB-Ob MS Mus. Sch. e. 423 (6), copied by John Bentley for Byrd's patron, John, first Lord Petre sometime between 1577 and 1589, when it was bound. Eleven consort works are found among the 48 five-part Latin sacred vocal works; they include Parsons's *De la court,* his five-part In Nomine and Byrd's *Browning* Fantasy, In Nomine 5/5 and the two six-part Fantasias 6/g1 and 6/g2. Fantasia 6/g1 is found in the third six-part section, added before 1586. If David Mateer is right about Bentley receiving works from Byrd as soon as they were complete, this would date Fantasia 6/g1 to *c.*1585–6. Fantasia 6/g2 was added at the end probably in 1589, just before binding, which suggests that Fantasia 6/g2 is the later work.

Two manuscripts owned by the Catholic aristocrat Edward Paston contain Fantasia 6/g1. Paston was part of the recusant circle within which Byrd moved and a serious collector of Byrd's music. He was related by marriage to the Petre family and lived a quiet country life.[6] Byrd and Paston may have known each other from the 1570s.[7] Fantasia 6/g1 is the only consort work included in a collection of 43 motets found in GB-Ob MSS Tenbury 379–84 (12), compiled from 1590. Of Paston's eight manuscripts containing consort works by Byrd, this is the only one devoted to six-part music, which may be why Fantasia 6/g1 was included. The manuscript contains the first 89 breves of Fantasia 6/g1; the galliard section and the coda are missing. This raises interesting questions. Did the scribe simply omit the last two sections or did the fantasia originally last for only 89 breves? Found close to the end of the manuscript, it is thought that it was entered after 1600. A complete version exists in another Paston manuscript, GB-Ob MSS Tenbury 341–4 (13) dating from the early years of the seventeenth century. Again, it is the only consort piece in a collection of 100 Latin vocal works.

Fantasia 6/g1 is found in two further manuscripts dating from the seventeenth century. In GB-Lbl Add. MSS 17786–91 (24) the fantasia is the third work copied into the manuscript, entered among five-part works following Parsons's *De la court* and Byrd's Fantasia 5/C. All the music in this manuscript is for viols or viols and voices. The first 40 works were probably collected by 1610. Fantasia 6/g1 was initially entered with the first part of 89 breves and the galliard, but no coda. This was added at a later date by a different hand. It entailed the pasting of additional slips of paper into the partbooks.[8] The appearance of the fantasia in three different guises – a fantasia of 89 breves, this plus the galliard and finally a work containing both parts and a coda – has led to the hypothesis that Byrd constructed the work in three stages, adding the galliard and then the coda at later dates.

Finally, Fantasia 6/g1 is found with Fantasia 6/g2 in a large keyboard manuscript, GB-Lbl Add. MS 29996 (35), collected over a period of around 100 years and completed around 1650, by which time it was owned by Thomas Tomkins, in whose hand the title of Fantasia 6/g1 is written. The two six-part fantasias are found with Byrd's five-part Fantasia in keyboard score, close to the end of the manuscript; his In Nomine 5/5 and his *Browning* Fantasy, the latter in open score, are found earlier in the manuscript.

Structure

Popular songs play an important role in Fantasia 6/g1. A variation of the *Greensleeves* melody is found at breve 82 (Example 8.1) and Byrd appears to make reference to two other popular tunes, *Walsingham* and *Packington's Pound* (Example 8.2a, b and c), particularly in the

Example 8.1 *Greensleeves* tune found in Fantasia 6/g1

Example 8.2 Other popular tunes referred to by Byrd in Fantasia 6/g1

a) *Walsingham*

b) *Packington's Pound*

c) Opening of third section of galliard section in Fantasia 6/g1

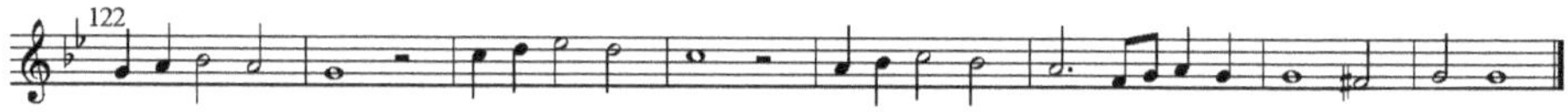

galliard.[9] In the second dotted semibreve of the galliard there is also a further reminder of the *Greensleeves* section in a short melodic phrase found in the second viol part. Richard Rastall points out that Byrd's use of popular tunes helps unite the fantasia.

Fantasia 6/g1 has a signature accidental of two flats (Example 8.3). Byrd had used a two flat signature twice before in consort works, these being his first five-part In Nomine and the Pavan5/c. Four of the fifteen motets by Byrd in the *Cantiones Sacrae* of 1575 contain a signature accidental of two flats.[10] In comparison, the *Cantiones Sacrae* of 1591, seven motets out of 21 contain a signature accidental of two flats, suggesting Byrd's increased interest in using two flats.[11]

With the clef combination C1, C1, C2, C3, C4 and F4, Fantasia 6/g1 is the only one of Byrd's three six-part fantasias that does not contain two F clefs. Part five, with the clef C4, reaches high d′. The single bass part in In Nomine 5/4 has exactly the same range, of 12 notes, but the clef F3. In Fantasia 6/g1, Byrd makes use of the whole range of the fifth part with the exception of low G, which only occurs on the last note. The use of different clefs for the two lowest parts would indicate that Byrd was writing for bass instruments with different strengths in upper and lower registers, unlike the matching paired identical ranges found in Fantasia 6/F. Part five operates up to a fifth above the low, sixth (bass) part. It rarely falls below d and only falls below c in the coda. The sixth part, with the range of g down to D, operates to a fourth below part five and the lower register is used significantly throughout. It only goes above part five on three occasions.

Like the Prelude and Ground, Fantasia 6/g1 has a wide compass of 24 notes but only the fifth part has a range of more than 11 notes. Three parts, one, four and six (treble, tenor and bass) have ranges of 11 notes; parts two and three, (treble and tenor) have a range of ten notes. Parts one and two are closest in pitch, with one part going just a note higher than the other, part one ranging from c′ to f″ and the second from c′ to e♭″. As in part five and six, an overlap is found in parts three and four. Part three ranges from b♭′ down to g and part four from g′ to d. Looking at the range of combined pairs of instruments, the two upper parts (treble) have a joint range of just 11 notes but parts three and four (tenor) have a combined range of 13 notes and the lowest two parts, a combined range of 15 notes. The lowest bass note is an octave below the lowest tenor note in part four, giving Byrd the scope to use a wide range of pitch and timbre. It illustrates how he was now able to explore the full compass of the six-part viol consort in a way he could not in earlier works.

Example 8.3 Opening of Fantasia 6/g1

As noted in Chapter three, it would seem clear that by the time Byrd wrote this fantasia, or possibly revised it, he had access to bass viols and players who could play low D with a reliable tone. All of the low Ds could be transposed up an octave without going above any upper lines except five breves before the end; here, raising a pedal D up an octave would result in part five falling below the bass line for a minim. This does not sound strange, and Byrd may have accepted this in the event of this part being played by a bass unable to reach low D. It does however suggest that basses able to play D were around before 1600 but not common. Although Byrd is believed to have composed Fantasia 6/g1 by 1586, no bass part survives before 1600. The first bass parts are found in GB-Ob MS Tenbury 384, begun in the 1590s, but the fantasia appears to have been added after 1600.

Fantasia 6/g1 consists of two main sections, these being the first section of 89 breves, and the second, a galliard of six phrases, each of which lasts for eight dotted semibreves, making a total of 48 dotted semibreves, plus a short coda of nine breves. The six galliard phrases fall into three pairs. In the first two pairs, the two treble viols take it in turn to play resulting in four phrases in five parts. The fifth set of eight dotted semibreves is also in five parts, but in the final, sixth phrase, both treble parts play, returning to a six-part texture. Finally, the coda, in six parts, returns to the more sombre mood and character of the opening.

Seven melodic ideas or short melodies that grow out of each other can be identified in the first 89 breves. The interval of a minor third, moving up from a semibreve g′ to a dotted minim b♭′, opens the first sustained theme. A rising or falling minor third can be found in all seven themes. The first theme enters seven times; six of these entries, beginning on G or D, open with the minor third (Example 8.3). One, the fourth, entering in breve five, is modified to a minor second. Byrd also adds two false entries, each beginning with a minor third, at breves seven and nine. The second theme appears in breve 12, as the music reaches a cadence on G following a major chord on D (Example 8.3). It interrupts the initial serene mood of the music. A minim is followed by a dotted crochet pattern, which is mainly stepwise in movement except for an upward minor third. At this point the parts begin to echo each other; this happens particularly between the upper voices but is also reflected in the lower parts. The second theme is quickly modified. The fourth entry is extended at the beginning by the addition of three minims (breve 14). Entries from the sixth entry have an upward leap added, mainly that of a fourth. In the final, sixteenth entry at breve 28, the theme is extended and the dotted crotchet and quaver of the previous entries are lengthened to a minim and a crotchet, bringing this second theme to a close on to a cadence finishing on a major chord on G in breve 31 (Example 8.4).

Example 8.4 Fantasia 6/g1, final entry of second theme and entry of third theme

At the entry of the third motif in breve 32 (Example 8.4), the texture is thinner as a result of the reduction to four parts from the six and five parts found at the final entry of the second theme; the part omitted continually changes. At breve 41, the treble viols pick up the syncopated rhythm from the opening statement of the third theme, a falling minor third replacing a downward step of a tone (Example 8.5). All the parts repeat variants of this theme and the music returns to six-part writing before the cadence onto a major chord on C. This is immediately followed by a minor chord beginning the fourth sustained section (Example 8.6).

Example 8.5 Fantasia 6/g1, third theme from breve 39

Example 8.6 Fantasia 6/g1, fourth theme

For ten breves the music is in three parts. In the first five, played by parts one, three and four (treble and tenor), the music moves homophonically, starting with a semibreve and minims, then moving into rising crotchets and returning to the syncopation of the previous theme before a cadence onto a major chord on G. This is answered at almost exactly an octave lower (from breve 54), played by the lower three parts. A falling minor third occurs both times in the upper line between the fourth and fifth notes (breve 50 and breve 55). From breve 61, the momentum increases with patterns based on previous ideas, reaching a cadence onto a major chord on G.

At breve 64, there is the intimation that a dance might follow. A short pattern, initially lasting for five minims, played by parts two, three and four (one treble and two tenors,) is answered by the same pattern plus an extra note played by the other treble and parts five and six. It sounds exactly like the music for partners to honour each other at the beginning of a dance (Example 8.7).[12] It is followed by the entry of the fifth theme (breve 66); this is a simple downward moving phrase that includes two pairs of falling and rising minor thirds. The second pair falls from b♭′ to g′ and back, reminding the listener of the opening theme. This melodic pattern, with slight alterations, appears nine times through the parts, giving an echo effect, particularly between the two treble parts. The sixth theme enters at breve 73; its opening takes the rising minor third of a′ to c″ from the fifth theme, with the third filled in with a crotchet b♭′ (Example 8.8). As the music changes direction, it increases in urgency. The two upper parts echo each other. Short crotchet patterns are extended from breve 75. At breve 79 the music becomes sparser and more homophonic until all six parts enter together for the entry of *Greensleeves*, the seventh theme, at breve 82 (Example 8.9). Suddenly the music becomes an exuberant dance, with a regular metre of four beats and supported by the ground-like bass line.

Example 8.7 Fantasia 6/g1, fifth theme

Example 8.8 Fantasia 6/g1, sixth theme

Throughout the first 89 breves, Byrd juxtaposes minor and major. Sometimes this is very sudden, as for example in breve 49, when a major chord on C is followed immediately by a minor chord on C (Example 8.6). In the breves before the entry of *Greensleeves* (breve 82), the music centres on G and the minor; suddenly all six parts enter together with the melody on a major chord on B♭ (Example 8.9). Following the major chords on B♭ and F in breve 82, the music continues to oscillate between major and minor. The bass line of four breves supports a repeated pattern of major tonalities on B♭ and F, a minor chord on G and a major chord on D, with the final conclusion of the first 89 breves being on a major chord on G (Example 8.10).

Example 8.9 Fantasia 6/g1, seventh theme (*Greensleeves*)

It seems perfectly logical that the *Greensleeves* dance should be followed by a galliard. Whether Byrd wrote the galliard at the same time as the first 89 breves or added it later, it is clear he composed it to go with the first part. After the major chord on G at the end of the previous section, the opening chord reverts to a minor chord on G, continuing Byrd's use of minor/major contrast. In the second and fourth dotted semibreves of the galliard is the downward four-note pattern containing two quavers found in the treble parts in breves 87–89 at the end of the first section (Example 8.10). The second appearance of this pattern in bar 88 contains the only treble high f″ found in the fantasia. This could suggest that Byrd was drawing attention to this small pattern as well as the approaching cadence.

Example 8.10 Fantasia 6/g1, end of the first 89 breves and opening of the galliard

There are other links between the galliard and the first 89 breves. The change in the galliard from 3/2 to 6/4 (in modern terminology) in bars 107 and 109 (and the repeat) is reminiscent of theme four (Examples 8.11 and 8.6). Bars 111 and 112 (plus repeat) of the galliard include two simple patterns found in the accompaniment to the *Greensleeves* theme in breve 82 (Examples 8.11 and 8.9). In alternating the treble parts in the first two pairs of phrases of the galliard Byrd continues the echo theme found in the first 89 breves. In the final sixth phrase of the galliard, the two treble parts vie with each other as they did earlier. The use of sudden juxtapositions of major and minor chords, as found in the first 89 breves, continues in the galliard, for example bars 121–122, where the major chord on B♭ at the end of the second pair of phrases is followed immediately by a minor chord on C (Example 8.12).

Example 8.11 Fantasia 6/g1, alternating 3/2 and 6/4 patterns in the galliard

Example 8.12 Fantasia 6/g1, juxtaposition of major and minor in the galliard

Byrd's use of chordal progressions helps to unify the first part of the fantasia and the galliard. Until breve 36, the music is predominantly in the minor, centring round G, From the middle of breve 36, soon after the arrival of the third theme, the music moves into the major, centred on B♭ and ending on a major chord on C before the change back to minor in the fourth theme (Examples 8.13 and 8.6). The chords develop organically from here, passing through a minor chord on C, alternating with chords on G, F, B♭ and D. In the last eight breves of the first part, a clear progression of chords is established by the bass line, these being on B♭, F, G (minor chord), D, B♭, F, G (minor chord), D, G (major chord) repeated once (Example 8.10, showing the repeat). The galliard has a clear overall chordal shape;

Example 8.13 Fantasia 6/g1, changes of tonality in the third theme

chords are based on the following notes, G, D, G, D; F, B♭, F, B♭; C (minor),G, C (minor), G. In the first section of two sets of eight dotted semibreves, the music is not sure whether it is major or minor (Example 8.10). The b♭′ in the opening chord is replaced by a b♮′ two minims later (bar 90). The second pair of phrases (from bar 106) are based firmly on major chords. This section of the galliard includes a rhythmic pattern (in bars 107 and 109, Example 8.11) that is a reminder of a similar pattern found from breves 41 to 47 (example 8.5).

The coda does not just reflect the mood of the first 89 breves; the chordal progressions relate closely to the rest of the fantasia. The major chord on G at the end of the galliard is followed immediately by a minor chord on C, opening the coda. The music moves through major chords on E♭ and F to minor chords on G and C to reach a minor chord on D. Four breves before the end, it passes quickly over a minor chord on G and a minor chord on C, to reach the final two breves centred on a major chord on G (Example 8.14). There are also reminders of the echo responses found elsewhere

Byrd makes extensive use of intervals of a minor third in six of the themes found in the first 89 breves of Fantasia 6/g1. The music opens with a rising minor third from g′ to b♭′; the same interval is found in the second theme and in the first two entries it is the only non-stepwise movement (breves 12–13, Example 8.3). Byrd then extends this theme, still maintaining a minor third in sixteen entries, thirteen of which are from g to b♭ at different pitches. Falling minor thirds are prevalent in the third theme (Example 8.5) and in the fourth, where Byrd incorporates a b♭ falling to g in the fourth and fifth notes of the theme

Example 8.14 Fantasia 6/g1, end of galliard and coda

(breve 50, Example 8.6). Theme five is full of falling minor thirds, particularly from c″ to a′(Example 8.7). The sixth starts with short three-note pattern rising from a′ to c″ and also includes the falling c″ to a′ minor third (example 8.8). In contrast, the *Greensleeves* tune opens the final section of the first 89 breves with falling and rising major thirds but upwards minor thirds reappear prominently for the last five breves ((Example 8.9).

Byrd's use of a minor third forms a link through all three sections of Fantasia 6/g1. Minor thirds are not significant in the first 32 dotted semibreves of the galliard, but the third section opens with an ornamented minor third, from g′ to b♭′, of two crotchets and a minim (bars 122 and 130), i.e. with an a′ added between them. Minor thirds starting on a′ and c″ follow, filled in the same way. The opening two phrases in the coda (breves 138 and 139) also contain a rising quaver and crotchet pattern, also creating an ornamented minor third (Example 8.15).

As he did in the *Browning* Fantasy, Byrd carefully builds a structure of contrast and variety in Fantasia 6/g1, particularly in the first 89 breves. It opens with a calm, sustained theme. The tranquillity of the music is carried through until the entry of the second theme (breve 12, Example 8.3), when the introduction of a dotted crotchet and a quaver interrupts the mood. The theme is short, initially only lasting two breves, but it is immediately changed and extended by the addition of four notes at the beginning. Varying versions of this theme emerge, continuing the feeling of change. The introduction of echo effects at this point make the music feel as if the parts are chasing each other. In contrast to the contrapuntal first theme and the use of echo effects in the second section, the third starts with syncopated homophonic part-writing (breve 32, Example 8.4) based on short phrases. The syncopated motif is then contrasted with a short sustained homophonic theme of four or five notes at breve 39 (Example 8.5). Gradually the homophony disintegrates as the patterns mix together. In contrast, the fourth section opens with sustained three-part homophonic writing lasting for almost ten breves before the music returns to six parts. Following a short linking section, hinting at the approaching dance (breve 64), with the arrival of the fifth theme (breve 66) the music begins to gather momentum (Example 8.7). From this theme with its falling and rising minor thirds and mainly descending patterns, Byrd develops his sixth theme. It begins with a simple repeating pattern of a′ b♭′ c″ causing the music to rise rather than fall. Byrd then extends this and transposes it up a tone. The music moves swiftly through this section and a short link, oscillating between minor and major, to the full impact of the *Greensleeves* tune and dance beginning in breve 82 (Example 8.9). The dance theme continues with the galliard; it carries forward the exuberant mood of the previous section. The two treble parts vie with each other for supremacy, taking it in turns to play and finally joining back together for the last six-part eight dotted semibreves of the dance. The coda brings the music back to the opening calm mood of the fantasia.

Example 8.15 Fantasia 6/g1, Byrd's use of a rising minor third

As in his previous consort works, Byrd is very selective in his use of octave or large leaps. There is only one leap greater than a fifth in the opening 89 breves of Fantasia 6/g1, that of a sixth, found in part four at breve 44 (Example 8.5). Two downward leaps of an octave are found in the bass part in the galliard at bars 107 (Example 8.11) and 115, emphasising the syncopation begun in the treble parts. A further downward leap from f in bar 135 prepares the music for the final cadence of the galliard. In contrast, six octave leaps are found in the nine breves of the coda (Example 8.14), perhaps one possible argument for the coda being added later. Byrd uses these leaps to move the music and the chords forward, for example in breve 139, as the music moves into the major, and in preparing the final cadence.

Fantasia 6/g1 contains far fewer passages involving parts moving in parallel thirds than are found in the *Browning* Fantasy, and no use of paired sixths. Byrd appears to have used parallel thirds very selectively; for example parts three and four are paired in crotchets for just over a breve in the opening theme from the middle of the third breve, accentuating the stepwise pattern rising to meet the falling treble part (Example 8.3). Part two is paired with part six at an octave and a third in similar fashion at breve nine. In the galliard, rising pairings of an octave and a third are found very briefly at the beginning of the first part of the third section (bars 122 and 123, Example 8.12). The coda opens with a descending pattern of paired thirds played by parts three and four (breve 138, Example 8.14). Byrd makes significant use of homophonic writing in Fantasia 6/g1, which may be why he uses few parallel thirds and no parallel sixths.

As he did in his *Browning* Fantasy, Byrd makes full use of the bass viol in Fantasia 6/g1 in both its overall range, technical possibilities and in support of the chordal progressions, aided by the ability he now had to use low E♭ and D. With the exception of three notes part six remains the lower, supporting line throughout. It participates fully in playing the different themes, but provides the foundation for the progression of chords and the direction in which the music moves. In places, it seems to display some of the characteristics found in Baroque bass lines, particularly where there are sustained leaps from D to G and cadences from a major chord on D to G. As Jessie Ann Owens wrote (see Chapter Two), 'English music *sounds* tonal and English music theory uses concepts associated with tonality well before either happens on the continent'.[13] This is very apparent in Fantasia 6/g1.

Byrd's themes and motifs are carefully constructed; they grow out of each other through the first 89 breves and there is a clear relationship between the galliard and coda and the first part of the fantasia. His characteristic use of a minor third unifies the music, as does his careful use of chords and their relationship to each other and of course his use of popular tunes and dance music. Byrd's juxtaposition of major and minor gives extraordinary colour and excitement to Fantasia 6/g1 as well as linking the three separate sections.

Fantasia 6/g1 is clearly instrumental and not dependent in any way on a structure related to vocal music. Byrd explores significant instrumental techniques with which he first experimented in earlier consort works. Polyphonic sections are contrasted with homophonic writing. Instrumental colour and constantly varied tessitura are used throughout the fantasia, particularly where Byrd uses smaller groups of instruments, as in the fourth section of the first 89 breves (from breve 49, Example 8.6), where a treble and two tenor parts are answered by the three lower parts. This alters the texture and dynamics of the music. In the sixth section, the music becomes sparser, with very short motifs and rests. This is followed by the entry of the *Greensleeves* tune and all six parts playing homophonically together.

The contrast between the first 89 breves, the galliard and the coda give life and colour to the music. Following Byrd's use of minims in sustained sections, as the music progresses, it becomes more exciting through increasing use of crotchets and dotted rhythms. The change of metre and tempo in the galliard plus the use of quavers at the end of the first 89 breves again increases the excitement in the music, while in the coda, it returns to the mood and tempo of the opening.

The influence of two works by Parsons, *The Song called Trumpets* and *De la court*, can be seen in Fantasia 6/g1. *The Song called Trumpets* is also in six parts, but has paired clefs, C1, C1, C4, C4, F4 and F4.The second section is a tripla section, following a definitive end to the first section, as found with the galliard in Fantasia 6/g1. The tripla theme is derived from the first theme (Example 8.16a and b). Echo effects and a suggestion of canon are found in the treble parts (Example 8.17) and Parsons builds up the music with short melodic patterns. *The Song called Trumpets* is distinctly shorter than Fantasia 6/g1, the first section lasting for just 35 breves and the tripla section for 30 dotted semibreves.

Example 8.16 Parsons, *The Song called trumpets*

a) Opening

b) Opening of tripla section

Example 8.17 Echo effects in the *The Song called trumpets*

The five-part *De la court*, containing the clefs C1, C1, C3, C4, F4, is of a significant length and, as one of the most popular pieces of sixteenth-century consort music, must have been known to Byrd. The first part, of just over 63 breves, begins with smooth imitative writing for 41 breves followed by a dance-like section. In the first 47 breves of the second section the music returns to calmer imitative writing that gradually becomes livelier with the parts echoing each other, particularly in the two treble parts (Example 8.18), leading into a tripla section of 34 dotted semibreves. *De la court* is based around G and D but Parsons uses a signature accidental of just one flat. Both *The Song called Trumpets* and *De la court* have two clearly defined sections as found in Fantasia 6/g1.

Example 8.18 Echo effects in Parsons, *De la court*

Byrd was attracted to Parsons's use of contrast and his combination of polyphonic writing and homophonic dance-like music in the same work. Both of Parsons's two works demonstrate his ability to vary his thematic ideas to build a viable, substantial piece of textless music. His approach provided Byrd with a starting point for his Fantasia 6/g1, but Byrd was able to develop Parsons's compositional techniques tonally, structurally and instrumentally. *De la court* is a well-written and polished consort work, but it does not contain the same variety of chordal progressions as Fantasia 6/g1 or exploitation of instrumental colour.

In both *The Song called Trumpets* and *De la court*, the music concludes with the tripla section. The idea of a coda section following a galliard may also reflect the influence of Ferrabosco I. A four-part *Fancy* by Ferrabosco contains a middle section of a short galliard of 14 breves which is followed by just over 17 breves in the original metre. It survives in GB-Lbl Add. MS 32377 (8), a single partbook dating from 1585–90, plus a later keyboard manuscript GB-Lbl Add. MS 30485. It is clear when looking at Byrd's Fantasia 4/g, explored in the following chapter, that Byrd knew this work. Ferrabosco I left England in 1578 and his fantasia was probably in circulation before he left. As in Byrd's Fantasia 6/g2, in his *Fancy* Ferrabosco carries the music into the galliard without the cadences found in Fantasia 6/g1. Byrd develops his galliard sections much further than Ferrabosco did in his short galliard section.

By the time Byrd wrote Fantasia 6/g1, he had found his own individual and unique idiomatic instrumental voice. It is a long way from his first fantasia; Fantasia 6/g1 is the work of a mature composer (Byrd was by this time in his 40s). The music is full of invention, originality and ingenuity. Byrd utilises all possible variations of musical contrast and exploits the full potential of the instruments available to him. Unlike his first six-part Fantasia 6/F, he does not use a restricting framework. Byrd appears to have abandoned an aesthetic of symmetry for one of constant variety combined with ideas from different genres. He employs all the instrumental compositional techniques he had developed in his In Nomine 5/5, the Prelude and Ground and *Browning* Fantasy. Fantasia 6/g1 is an extraordinary work in its combination of a serious opening section, typical of a fantasia, with dance, popular tunes and variations. Both Parsons and Ferrabosco I had begun to explore including dance elements in the fantasia, but Byrd took it to a new level. He employs imitative and homophonic writing, dance, echo patterns and popular tunes. Variety in rhythm, including syncopation, tempo and contrast in texture and tessitura all play an important role. In particular, his use of echo effects colours the music, something he also exploited in his keyboard music, which reached Europe via Peter Philips and the circulation of manuscripts, and influenced Sweelinck.[14] Byrd's use and placing of chords is new and adventurous as is his juxtaposition of major and minor. Fantasia 6/g1 illustrates that Byrd was not a conformist but an experimenter and exploiter of new ideas taking the fantasia to new heights.

It is not possible to ascertain whether the three different parts of Fantasia 6/g1 were written at the same time or whether Byrd wrote the first 89 breves and added the galliard and coda later. The fantasia could have originally finished at the end of the 89 breves. It is, however, clear that all three parts are related. The fantasia breaks new ground in Byrd's exploration into constructing music without a predetermined structure. He unites the distinct three elements into a satisfying whole. Fantasia 6/g1 is truly abstract and instrumental in its conception. It is the first of Byrd's freely constructed great instrumental works.

1 Neighbour, *The Consort and Keyboard Music of William Byrd*, p. 79; Harley, *William Byrd Gentleman of the Chapel Royal*, p. 271.

2 Richard Rastall, 'William Byrd's String Fantasia 6/g1', in Warren Drake (ed.) *Liber Amicorum John Steele*, (New York, 1997), p. 140.

3 Neighbour, *The Consort and Keyboard Music of William Byrd*, p. 84.

4 Harper, 'Ensemble and Lute Music', p. 294.

5 Rastall, 'William Byrd's String Fantasia 6/g1', p. 144–145.

6 McCarthy, *Byrd*, p. 156.

7 Harley, *The World of William Byrd*, pp. 182 and 118.

8 Monson, *Voices and Viols in England, 1600–1650*, p. 159.

9 *Greensleeves* appears in a version found in a song by William Cobbold, *New Fashions*; see Rastall, 'William Byrd's String Fantasia 6/g1', p. 160 and pp. 168–9 for further comment on the popular tunes.

10 Two of these motets are likely to have been written in Lincoln, including *Libera me Domine de morte aeterna*, the only cantus firmus motet Byrd wrote there, probably composed shortly after he had written his last consort *In Nomine*. Harley, *William Byrd Gentleman of the Chapel Royal*, p. 206.

11 In the *Cantiones Sacrae* of 1589 only one of 16 motets has a signature of two flats.

12 Suzanne Lord writes, 'the one 'rule' of Country dancing was that they began and ended with 'Honours': a bow for men and a courtesy (curtsey) for women'. Suzanne Lord, *Music from the Age of Shakespeare: A Cultural History* (Westport Connecticut, 2003), p. 139.

13 Owens, 'Concepts of Pitch in English Music Theory'; p. 183.

14 Pieter Dirksen, 'Byrd and Sweelinck: Some Cursory Notes', p. 13; *The Keyboard Music of Jan Pieterszoon Sweelinck*, p. 333.

Chapter 9

Byrd's mature consort works after Fantasia 6/g1

In his Fantasia 6/g1, Byrd displays his ability to write complex, inventive and mature consort music for viols. Eight more fantasias by Byrd survive. These consist of one six-part work, a five-part fantasia, three four-part and three three-part. The last surviving consort works are a six-part Pavan and Galliard. Dating these ten works and working out their chronological order is not easy, especially as Byrd may have revised some of them and adapted one for keyboard. Only Byrd's three six-part fantasias appear in partbooks dating from before 1600 and Fantasia 5/C is found in a keyboard version (*A lesson of Voluntarie*) in *My Ladye Nevell's Booke* (10), completed in 1591. Apart from Fantasia 6/F and possibly one other, Byrd probably wrote all his surviving fantasias over a ten-year period beginning at some point in the early 1580s. It is possible to find related material in several of the fantasias, which may be an indication of the order in which they were composed and suggests that they were written over a comparatively short period of time. Byrd continued to develop his ideas and experiment in these works.

Fantasia 5/C and Fantasia 6/g2, like Fantasia 6/g1, are both likely to date from the latter part of the 1580s. The dates of sources and the musical content in Fantasia 5/C and Fantasias 6/g1 and 6/g2 make them probably the easiest of the late fantasias to place chronologically. A direct quotation from Fantasia 6/g1 is found in Fantasia 5/C and Fantasia 6/g2 contains reminders of both works.

The two four-part fantasias in a and g were probably composed around 1590. Similarities can be seen between Fantasia 4/g and Byrd's Mass for four voices published in 1592/3. The third four-part fantasia, Fantasia 4/G, is placed earlier; it is difficult to date as only one part survives but, like Fantasia 6/F, it is closer to vocal music in style, appears as a motet, *In manus tuas*, and thus could pre-date Fantasia 6/g1. The three-part fantasias are also likely to date from around 1590 or may be a little earlier. John Harley suggests that they could be connected with Byrd's three-part song writing of the 1580s or his Mass for three voices, published in 1593–4.[1] Kerry McCarthy agrees, remarking on Byrd's interest in serious three-part vocal writing in the 1590s, and writes that his 'elegant and concise three-part string fantasias are projects in a similar vein' to the three-part Mass.[2] Oliver Neighbour places the three-part fantasias as being contemporary with music Byrd wrote for the

Gradualia of 1605 in the late 1580s and early 1590s.[3] Byrd's final surviving consort works, the Pavan and Galliard 6/C appear to date from considerably later and are contemporary with a group of late keyboard pieces that were composed just before their publication in *Parthenia* in 1612–13.[4]

Fantasia 5/C: Sources

Fantasia 5/C is found in only one set of partbooks, GB-Lbl Add. MSS 17786–91 (24), the first layer of which was completed by 1610. It is the second piece entered, and is followed by Fantasia 6/g1 (to which the coda was added later) and a textless version of the adaptation of Fantasia 6/F and *Laudate pueri* with English words, *Behold now praise the Lord.* It is found in two versions in five keyboard manuscripts. The earliest of these, *My Ladye Nevell's Booke*, GB-Lbl MS Mus 1591 (10), dates from 1591, and contains a version entitled, *A lesson of Voluntarie.* Links with the Fantasias 6/g1 and 6/g2 suggest that the consort Fantasia 5/C came before this keyboard version, dating it to before 1591. The other four keyboard sources were compiled after 1625.[5] One of these, D-Bds MS Lynar A2 (37), dating from around 1620 to before 1630, contains the version found in *My Ladye Nevell's Booke*, but the remaining three sources contain a transcription of the consort fantasia found in GB-Lbl Add. MSS 17786–91.

Fantasia 5/C: Structure

Fantasia 5/C lasts for just over 142 breves, making it a little longer than Fantasia 6/g1. There is no signature accidental and it centres round major chords on C and G. It has a compass of 24 notes and contains the clefs G2, C1, C3, C4 and F4. Parts three and four (tenor) have wide ranges of 13 and 12 notes but share the same pitch range except for one note. The two upper parts each have a range of 11 notes. Part one (treble) reaches up to a″ and down to e′, and the second part up to e″ and down to b. The bass has a range of 12 notes, the lowest of which is F. The compass of 24 notes is identical to that of Fantasia 6/g1 but the overall pitch is higher with the treble reaching a″ and the bass only going down to F, the more conventional lowest note for a bass.[6]

The central structural feature in Fantasia 5/C is a canon at the fourth in the two upper parts (Example 9.1). Twelve themes can be identified, some of which are closely linked. For example, Byrd develops his second theme, entering in the bass at the end of breve 17, from the bass pattern beginning at breve 11 (Example 9.1). From breve 49 and the entry of the fifth theme, the two upper parts each take the first three notes of the opening theme, but this time the pattern of semitone followed by a tone is reversed (Example 9.2). Between breves 82 and 89, three previously heard themes appear together. Theme seven re-appears in the canon in the upper two parts, followed by theme eight; meanwhile the two bass parts play a modified version of the sixth theme (Example 9.3).

Example 9.1 Opening of Fantasia 5/C

Example 9.2 Fantasia 5/C comparison of first and fifth themes

Example 9.3 Fantasia 5/C from breve 82

As he did in Fantasia 6/g1, Byrd makes use of popular tunes. Theme eight, which first enters at breve 78, is a direct quotation from part of the *Greensleeves* tune as used in Fantasia 6/g1, first transposed and then at the original pitch (Example 9.4). Byrd also uses a melody

Example 9.4 Comparison of quotation from *Greensleeves* tune in Fantasia 5/C with that in Fantasia 6/g1

known as *Sicke very sicke.* At first sight, there is no obvious link between the sustained opening theme moving in semibreves and minims and the *Sicke* tune, moving in minims and crotchets, but on closer examination, the first five notes of the opening theme are the reverse of the first five notes of the tune (Example 9.5a and b). The opening of the triplet section is also derived from the *Sicke* tune (Example 9.5c).

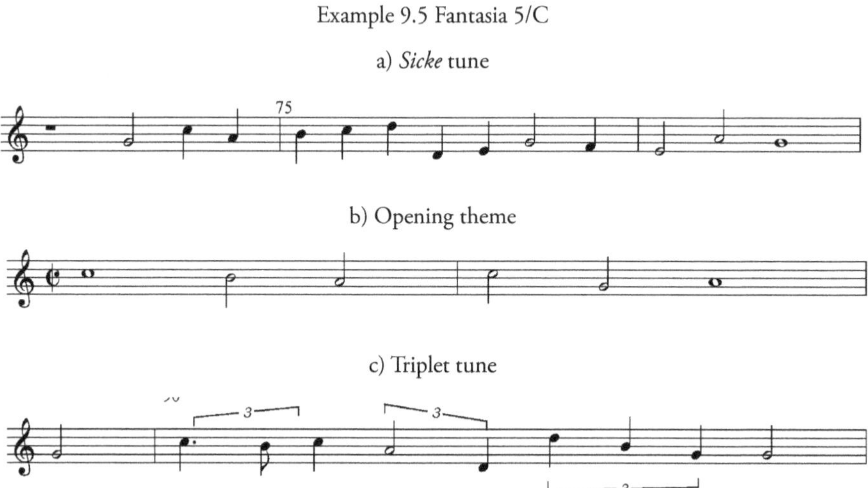

Example 9.5 Fantasia 5/C

a) *Sicke* tune

b) Opening theme

c) Triplet tune

There are distinct differences between the keyboard *A lesson of Voluntarie* and the consort Fantasia 5/C as found in GB-Lbl Add. MSS 17786–91, but they are clearly two versions of the same piece. The keyboard version could be a transcription made from an earlier consort version, no longer in existence.[7] In places the music is simplified and elsewhere Byrd occasionally adds inner parts. The consort fantasia has an extended cadence making it longer than the keyboard version by three breves. An extended cadence would have been less effective on the keyboard than it is with the more varied timbre offered by five viols. The entry of the canon is delayed by a semibreve in the consort version compared with the keyboard version (in breve eight as opposed to breve seven in the keyboard version).

Other differences between the consort and keyboard versions include dotted rhythms in the consort fantasia (breves 60 and 64), and in the part-writing in the triplet section. In the latter, there is less movement in the inner parts of *A lesson of Voluntarie,* although interestingly a sudden sustained breve (97) in the consort fantasia is omitted in the keyboard version. It is impossible to prove whether or not an earlier version of Fantasia 5/C ever existed. The two versions may just be a consort version and a keyboard adaption.

It is possible to find aspects of some of Byrd's other consort works in Fantasia 5/C, suggesting it was written after Fantasia 6/g1 and before, or at the same time as, Fantasia 6/g2. As in Fantasia 6/g1, in the five-part fantasia Byrd employs short melodies or motifs related to each other. The opening of Fantasia 5/C is slower and more sustained than that of the 6/g1, but rising stepwise crotchet patterns are introduced at breve 18 similar to those found in the six-part fantasia (Examples 9.1 and 8.3). As he does in the six-part fantasia, Byrd prepares for a change in metre, but instead of the galliard found in Fantasia 6/g1, the music launches into a triplet section without a break (Example 9.6). It is a little shorter than his triplet section in the

Example 9.6 Beginning of triplet section in Fantasia 5/C

Browning Fantasy, and dotted rhythms are introduced – something of which Byrd made significant use in Fantasia 6/g1. Unlike the section in the *Browning* Fantasy, the triplets are not paired in thirds and sixths in Fantasia 5/C, but the parts are paired in the following section, reminiscent of both the *Browning* Fantasy and 6/g1 (Example 9.7). Byrd's use of contrast in

Example 9.7 Rising paired parts in Fantasia 5/C

Fantasia 5/C is also reminiscent of the *Browning* Fantasy; the first two sections are sustained, the third and fourth themes are full of rising and falling crotchet patterns, the fifth theme recalls the calm opening, but the triplet section arrives much earlier in the fantasia. As might be expected, Fantasia 5/C opens with a single voice, this time a tenor (part three), but unlike Fantasia 6/g1 and the *Browning* Fantasy, where the music quickly falls into three parts, following the entry of part four in the second breve there is a duet for three breves. The bass is added in breve five. The low tessitura is similar to the three-part opening of the *Browning* Fantasy (Example 7.8). After this, as the other parts are added, the music alternates between four and five parts in a similar manner to the changing texture found in Fantasia 6/g1. The opening theme of the canon is initially heard in parts three and four a fifth apart before being taken up by the two upper parts in breves eight and nine (Example 9.1). At breve 125 and the entry of the twelfth theme, Byrd's use of crotchet patterns is a reminder of In Nomine 5/5 and the influence of Parsons (Examples 9.8 and 5.21 a and b).

Example 9.8 Crotchet patterns in Fantasia 5/C

Byrd had previously employed canon, unusually at the seventh, in his early *Sermone blando*. There is also a suggestion of canon at the octave in the first five breves of his In Nomine 4/1, although this develops into *fuga* (Example 9.9). If the hypothesis is correct that the missing part from Fantasia 6/F is for treble viol, then Byrd also used a canon in the upper two parts in this fantasia.

Example 9.9 Suggestion of canon in In Nomine 4/1

In places, the canon in Fantasia 5/C is also reminiscent of the echo passages in Fantasia 6/g1 (Example 9.10). Byrd's use of a major tonality in the five-part fantasia harks back to Fantasia 6/F. There is not the same significant impact of alternation between major and minor in the five-part fantasia as found in Fantasia 6/g1.

Example 9.10 Comparison of echo passages in Fantasia 5/C and Fantasia 6/g1

As he did in Fantasia 6/g1, in Fantasia 5/C Byrd makes use of invention and variation and exploits the full potential of the instruments available to him. There are a number of octave leaps in the five-part fantasia. These, as in Fantasia 6/g1, seem to have been carefully placed. For example, the first appears in part three at the first entry of the canon in breve 8 (Example 9.1). In breve 74, octave leaps are found in both part four and the bass part immediately before the entry of *Sicke very sicke* in the two upper parts, which also contain an octave leap (Example 9.11). Octave leaps are also employed in the three upper parts in the triplet section for technical brilliance. Byrd also only uses the two highest notes in each of the two upper parts twice. They are found in the last entries of *Sicke very sicke* and the theme derived from *Greensleeves* before the triplet section (Example 9.12).

Example 9.11 Octave leaps in the *Sicke* tune in Fantasia 5/C

Example 9.12 High notes in Fantasia 5/C

Although Fantasia 5/C is distinctly different from Fantasia 6/g1 in being centred on C and having no significant use of a minor third or any low Ds, it does contain many elements of Byrd's distinct idiomatic style. The conventional range bass part in Fantasia 5/C ranging from F to c′ could suggest it was written before Fantasia 6/g1, but other features suggest it came after; the lack of any low Ds could relate to the fact it is a five-part work or Byrd was writing it to be played where he knew there was no suitable bass available. The most obvious difference between the two fantasias is that Fantasia 5/C is through-composed rather than in three distinct sections, which suggests that Byrd was exploring the idea of removing clearly delineated sections, after completing the three-sectioned Fantasia 6/g1. This would place Fantasy 5/C chronologically after Fantasia 6/g1 as would the inclusion of the quotation from *Greensleeves,* as found in the six-part fantasia. As in Fantasia 6/g1, the themes of Fantasia 5/C are carefully constructed and related to one another, and popular tunes play an important role.

Fantasia 6/g2: Sources

Fantasia 6/g2 is found in five sources, one of which, GB-Ob MS Mus. Sch. e. 423 (6), dates from before 1600 (although only the second viol part survives). The fantasia is one of just 11 consort pieces in this collection of 132 pieces, which are mainly English anthems and Latin motets. It was added at the very end of the manuscript just before binding, which probably took place in 1589, thus giving us the earliest known date for this fantasia. This manuscript is significant because of its connections with Byrd's patron, Lord Petre. Three sets of partbooks containing Fantasia 6/g2 survive from the seventeenth century; these include Byrd's definitive version of the fantasia published in 1611 in *Psalmes, Songs and Sonnets* (26). The fantasia is found with the Pavan 5/c in GB-Lbl Add. MSS 37402–6 (21), an important collection for early seventeenth-century viol players, and in one of John Merro's sets of partbooks, NYp MSS Drexel 4180–5 (30), which was compiled for recreational use. The latter includes In Nomine 5/5 and Fantasia 4/g. Fantasia 6/g2 is also found with Fantasia 6/g1 in the keyboard manuscript GB-Lbl MS 29996 (35), which was eventually owned by Thomas Tomkins and completed before his death in 1656.

Fantasia 6/g2: Structure

Like Fantasia 5/C, the second six-part fantasia based on g is through-composed. It has similarities to Fantasia 6/g1, but is treated in a different way.[8] Fantasia 6/g2 is shorter than Fantasia 6/g1; the first section lasts for 79 breves (6/g1 lasts for 89 breves), the galliard for 41 dotted semibreves (6/g1, 48) and the coda for four breves (6/g1, nine breves). It shares a signature accidental of two flats with the Fantasia 6/g1 and has a compass of 23 notes, one note fewer than Fantasia 6/g1, the highest note in the treble being e♭″. Parts one and two (treble) in both fantasias have either a range of 11 or 10 notes, one part in Fantasia 6/g2 being pitched a note lower than the other three (Example 9.13a and b). Parts three and four (tenor) in Fantasia 6/g2 have a wider range, each of 12 notes, but they have the same combined range of 13 notes as parts three and four in Fantasia 6/g1. One of the bass parts (six) has a range of 13 notes and spans from D to b♭, the other a range of 12 notes, but the combined range is 14 notes, less than that of the two lower parts in Fantasia 6/g1. Byrd does not use the high d′ found in part five of Fantasia 6/g1. This is reflected in the clefs: C1, C1, C3, C4, F4 and F4. The wider ranges result in greater overlap between the parts, though not as great as is found in some of Byrd's Latin motets.

Example 9.13 Openings of

a) Fantasia 6/g1

b) Fantasia 6/g2

In the first 79 breves of Fantasia 6/g2 there are constant reminders of Fantasia 6/g1, but the themes develop and grow in a similar way to those of Fantasia 5/C. Byrd appears to quote a rising phrase (transposed) found in the five-part fantasia (from breve 111, Example 9.7) in breves 48–52 in Fantasia 6/g2 (Example 9.14). As he does in Fantasia 6/g1, Byrd includes a minor third in the first three notes of the opening theme of Fantasia 6/g2. Both fantasias begin with a single voice, though the opening part is played by the tenor in the second fantasia in contrast to the treble in Fantasia 6/g1 (Example 9.13a and b). The third theme in Fantasia 6/g2 is a direct quotation of the first theme from Fantasia 6/g1 (Example 9.15a and b). The following fourth theme is an adapted version of the second theme from Fantasia 6/g1 (Example 9.16a and b). Byrd makes some use of echo technique, for example in his fourth theme, adapted from the second of the 6/g1 (Example 9.16a), but is not as prominent.

Example 9.14 Fantasia 6/g2, quotation from Fantasia 5/C

Example 9.15

a) Third theme, Fantasia 6/g2

b) Opening theme, Fantasias 6/g1

Example 9.16

a) Fourth them, Fantasia 6/g2

b) Second theme, Fantasias 6/g1

Comparing the galliard sections of the two fantasias, in Fantasia 6/g2 parts one and two do not take turns to play as they do in Fantasia 6/g1 (resulting in 36 breves in five-parts), but the texture does alternate between five and six parts with different parts resting. The galliard in Fantasia 6/g2 is closer to that of a conventional galliard than that of the Fantasia 6/g1. It does not contain the cross rhythms introduced by Byrd at breve 107 in the 6/g1 (Example 8.11). The short coda following the galliard in the 6/g2 is also substantially different from the contrapuntal coda of the 6/g1; it moves homophonically and, almost abruptly, brings the music swiftly to a conclusion in just four breves (Example 9.17). Fantasia 6/g2 differs from Fantasia 6/g1 in Byrd's greater use of major tonalities and less contrast between minor and major than is found in Fantasia 6/g1.

Example 9.17 Conclusion to Fantasia 6/g1

In Fantasia 6/g2, the transition into a triplet section is similar to that in Fantasia 5/C, and occurs approximately four breves after the close quotation from the five-part fantasia found in breves 48–52. It then moves into a galliard section without a break, unlike Fantasia 6/g1. Both Parsons and Ferrabosco I move into dance-like sections in three in two consort pieces, *De la court* and a four-part Fancy respectively, without a break, which may have influenced Byrd (Example 9.18a, b and c).

Example 9.18 Comparison of transition to

a) Tripla section in Parsons, *De la court*

*Editorial; see Elizabethan Consort Muisc I; MB 44.

b) Galliard section in Ferrabosco I, *Fancy*

c) Transition to galliard section in Byrd, Fantasia 6/g2

The actual content of the triplet section in Fantasia 6/g2 is closer to that of the *Browning* Fantasy than the section in Fantasia 5/C. (Example 9.19a and b). There are parallel thirds between parts, particularly in breves 67–72; there are no dotted rhythms in the triplets as found in Fantasia 5/C. Six breves after the start of the triplet section, Byrd introduces a new theme that only enters four times. This has not been identified as a popular tune, but it sounds like a popular melody; Byrd could have written it or could be a sixteenth-century popular tune unknown today (Example 9.19a, from breve 62).

Example 9.19

a) Triplet section, Fantasia 6/g2

b) Triplet section *Browning* Fantasy

Like Fantasia 5/C, Fantasia 6/g2 exhibits many aspects of Byrd's distinctive idiomatic style. Its content suggests that Byrd experimented further with ideas he had for Fantasia 6/g1 and some that he explored in Fantasia 5/C. Fantasia 6/g2 could be described as more polished than Fantasia 6/g1 but it is not as exciting or colourful. In Fantasia 6/g2, the music moves seamlessly from section to section. It does not contain the contrasting homophonic sections of Fantasia 6/g1, the unexpected sudden joyful dance or the feeling of competition between the two treble parts found in the galliard section. On stylistic grounds, Fantasia 6/g2 was probably composed after Fantasias 6/g1 and 5/C; this appears to be confirmed by its entry and position in GB-Ob MS Mus. Sch. e. 423.

By the time Byrd published Fantasia 6/g2 in 1611, there had obviously been advances in both viol construction and in the capabilities of players. He was aware of the market for suitable viol music and the demand for music in six parts. Manuscripts containing music for viols compiled in the first part of the seventeenth century show a significant increase from previous collections in the number of six-part works found in them, for example as in GB-Lbl Add. MSS 17786–91 (24), which, by 1610, included such consort music, and GB-Lbl Add. MSS 17792–6 (33), begun in the 1630s.[9] By the 1670s, the six-part chest of viols was considered by some, such as Thomas Mace (1612/13–1706?), to be the 'most Compleat'. It should contain two basses, two tenors and two trebles, all 'Truly [and] Proportionally Suited'.[10] Byrd was certainly perceptive about which music to make available and there were clearly significant numbers of skilled players and good bass instruments that could cope with low Ds. Seven are found in Fantasia 6/g2, including at the start of a lively triplet passage, demanding real skill from a bass player (Example 9.18c).

Four-part Fantasias: Sources

Fantasia 4/a is found with Fantasia 4/g in a lute manuscript from the Paston collection, GB-Lbl Add. MS 29246 (14), dating from the early seventeenth century, along with the three three-part fantasias, seven of Byrd's Latin-titled consort works and his *Miserere*. (The top line is missing.) One part of Fantasia 4/a, along with one part of Fantasia 4/G, survives in a single partbook, GB-Lbl Add. MS29247 (27), dating from *c.*1612–17. The motet *In manus tuas*, found in the *Gradualia* of 1605, appears to be an adaption of Fantasia 4/G. A fragment from Fantasia 4/a is also found in a keyboard manuscript, GB-Lcm MS 2093 (41), dating from the latter half of the seventeenth century, entered before a keyboard fantasia by Byrd.

Fantasia 4/g is found in six sources. It was the second fantasia Byrd chose to publish in the *Psalmes, Songs and Sonnets* (26) of 1611. It is found in two sets of partbooks collected from the second decade of the seventeenth century. The earliest of these, NYp MSS Drexel 4180–5 (30), completed by 1625, also contains Fantasia 6/g2 and the In Nomine 5/5. The second, GB-Ob MSS Mus. Sch. D. 245–7 (31), contains 450 pieces, mostly written for viols; Fantasia 4/g is the only consort work by Byrd in the manuscript; just three parts are entered after three-part fantasias by Gibbons. As well as appearing in a Paston lute manuscript, GB-Lbl Add. MS 29246, the fantasia is found in a second lute collection, GB-Lbl MS Hirsch M.1353 (36), where it is the only intabulation of a consort work by Byrd. Finally, it is found with Fantasia 5/C in a keyboard collection dating from after 1650, F-Pc Rés. 1122 (39).

Only one of Byrd's three four-part fantasias, Fantasia 4/g, survives complete. Byrd left a definitive version when he chose to publish it. John Harley links together Fantasia 4/a, Fantasia 4/g and *A Fancie*, found at the end of *My Ladye Nevell's Booke* (number 41), as they have a similar structure in which an imitative opening section is followed by minim and crotchet syncopations.[11] This would suggest that Fantasia 4/g was composed in the late 1580s or 1590 as the keyboard *Fancie* was added to *My Ladye Nevell's Booke* shortly before its completion in 1591 (Example 9.20). It contains other features suggesting a date of *c.*1590.

Example 9.20 Comparison between melodic material found in Fantasia 4/g and in *A Fancie* in *My Ladye Nevell's Booke*

Fantasia 4/G

With only a single surviving treble part of Fantasia 4/G, it is difficult to make a true assessment of this work. There are distinct differences between this part, found in GB-Lbl Add. MS29247, and the treble voices in *In manus tuas* published in *Gradualia* in 1605. In the motet, the second treble voice contains most of the opening 17 breves of the surviving treble viol part; from breve 20, the viol part is transferred to the upper voice part through to the end of the piece, with a few minor changes. Most commentators believe that *In manus tuas* was adapted from the four-part fantasia that dated from the 1580s.[12] However, David Pinto argues that this four-part work began life as *In manus tuas.*[13] His assertion regarding this motet is more credible than his belief that Fantasia 6/F did not exist before *Laudate pueri*. *In manus tuas* is very different from the two other Byrd four-part fantasias. From breve 35 it sounds more like an English anthem than an instrumental fantasia, although there is a suggestion of a canon between the upper two parts, a device Byrd used in Fantasia 5/C and earlier consort works (Example 9.21).

Example 9.21 Suggestion of canon in *In manus tuas*/Fantasia 4/G

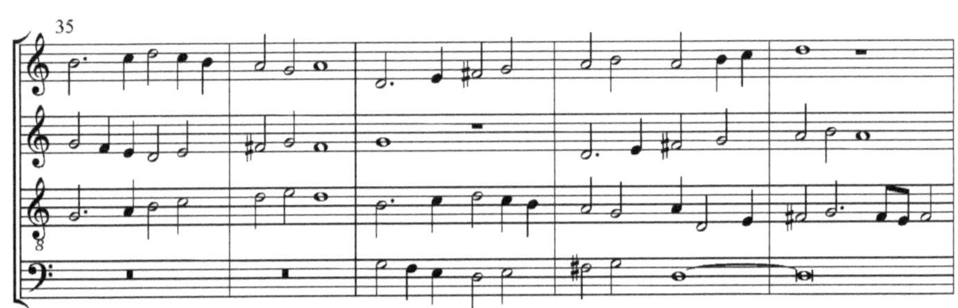

Two factors point to Byrd's having adapted the motet from a fantasia. The opening of Fantasia 4/G is strikingly similar to the opening of Byrd's Fantasia 6/g1 but has an interval of a major rather than minor third (Example 9.22a and b). Secondly there is the evidence of the single partbook, Gbl-Add. MS 29247 (27). Pinto dismisses this, saying that, as it was copied after the publication of the 1605 *Gradualia*, the copyist or his source 'simply adapted a texted piece for playing fodder'.[14] The partbook initially consisted of 30 pieces of three- and four-part consort music, including Byrd's Fantasia 4/a. Copied by Thomas Myriell, an assiduous collector of viol music, the two Byrd fantasias are found alongside identifiable instrumental fantasias by Wilbye, Lupo and Alfonso Ferrabosco II. If Pinto's view is correct, then Fantasia 4/G would likely be the only item in the collection that is not an original consort work.

The length of Fantasia 4/G is almost identical to that of Fantasia 4/g. The range of the surviving treble part is nine notes, identical to the treble part of Fantasia 4/g, although the pitch is one tone lower. It is difficult to say definitively that Fantasia 4/G was originally a consort work; perhaps *In manus tuas* was substantially recycled from an early work, written when Byrd first experimented with writing consort fantasias shortly before leaving Lincoln.

Example 9.22 Openings of

a) *In manus tuas*/Fantasia 4/G

b) Fantasia 6/g1

Fantasia 4/a

Only 13 breves of the treble part of Fantasia 4/a survive. Part two (tenor) survives complete in the single partbook GB-Lbl Add MS 29427 (27) and the two lower parts can be reconstructed from the Paston lute manuscript, GB-Lbl Add. MS 29246 (14), from which of course the top line is missing. It is therefore impossible to know the complete compass of the fantasia, as only two clefs are known. Part two has a known range of 12 notes but the exact range of the other three parts can only be conjectural (Example 9.23). Fantasia 4/a lasts for 48 breves and has no signature accidental.

Example 9.23 Opening of Fantasia 4/a

As in Fantasia 6/g1, the music opens with a solo treble, which is joined after a breve and half by part two; the two instruments pursue a duet for just over two breves until the entry of part three at the end of the fourth breve. The bass enters at the end of breve seven as the treble is silent for just under two breves. Four-part writing does not appear until the tenth breve, when the treble re-enters with the opening theme. Thus, the music gradually builds up, increasing in texture and dynamic sound. The first theme is unusual as it opens with a leap of a fourth. Except for the lower parts in two of his Consort Hymns, the only other work by Byrd which opens with a rising fourth is his *Browning* Fantasy. It is tantalising that we do not have the whole of this fantasia. What survives displays all the hallmarks of a well-constructed four-part consort piece.

Fantasia 4/g

Although Fantasia 4/g has been dated to *c.*1590, there are several features that are not typical of Byrd's later five and six-part consort works. It lasts for 59 breves and contains the clef combination of C1, C3, C4 and F4. Like Fantasias 6/g1 and 6/g2, it has a signature accidental of two flats. It has a narrow compass of 20 notes, the same as Fantasia 6/F. Part one has a range of just nine notes. Excluding Byrd's early Consort Hymns and In Nomine parts, such a narrow treble viol part is only found in Fantasia 6/F, the Pavan 5/c and in one of the two treble parts in the Pavan and Galliard 6/C. The bass has a range of just ten notes; excluding the Consort Hymns, only Fantasia 3/C1, the Pavan 5/c and the Pavan and Galliard 6/C have a bass part with as narrow or a narrower range.[15] Parts two and three (tenor) have ranges of 11 and 12 notes and a combined range of 15 notes. Part two extends up to b♭′ and part three down to B♭, as in the *Browning* Fantasy. There is a significant overlap between the parts in Fantasia 4/g, the lowest bass note being only a minor third below the lowest note in part three (Example 9.24).

Example 9.24 Opening of Fantasia 4/g

Not many four-part fantasias by English composers are known. Robert White's six four-part fantasias survive only in the Paston lute manuscript, GB-Lbl Add. MS 29246 (14), without the top line. The reconstruction of White's fantasias by Paul Doe suggest a compass of 20 to 22 notes for five fantasias and one with a compass of 23 notes.[16] One four-part fantasia or '*Fancy*' by Ferrabosco I survives.[17] Like Byrd's Fantasia 4/g, Ferrabosco's fantasia has a compass of 20 notes. At first glance, Fantasia 4/g is very different to Ferrabosco's *Fancy*. Despite having the same compass, Ferrabosco's part ranges are wider than those of Byrd's. His fantasia is longer, lasting for 65 breves plus a section of 14 dotted semibreves. From the start it is faster-moving with quavers introduced in the fifth breve, while Byrd's Fantasia 4/g feels more like a motet at the beginning. On closer examination it is, however, clear that Byrd knew Ferrabosco's fantasia and elements of it appear in Fantasia 4/g.

Fantasia 4/g: Structure

Fantasia 4/g is different from Fantasia 5/C and Fantasias 6/g1 and 6/g2. It is a more reflective work, reminiscent of vocal music, suggesting Byrd was seeking to write a more serious fantasia yet incorporate the techniques he had developed in the five- and six-part works thought to precede it. It has five themes. It opens with a calm, upward rising crotchet pattern from a dotted minim in part two (Example 9.24) that has the same feeling as Byrd's Sanctus from his Mass for four voices, published 1592/3, and also contains a signature accidental of two flats (Example 9.25a). The part ranges are similar in the two works except for the cantus part in the Sanctus, which is wider than the treble viol part, having a range of 11 notes compared with a range of nine notes in the viol part. However, the compass of the Sanctus is only 18 notes compared with 20 in the fantasia; the lowest note of the fantasia bass part is a fourth lower than that of the Sanctus bass, which is pitched high and only goes down to c, pointing to the fantasia being an instrumental work. (The mass was quite likely sung at a slightly lower pitch). The vocal-like opening of the Fantasia 4/g has a feeling of looking back, which is not surprising with its links to the four-part mass and the fact Byrd used the Sanctus from Taverner's five-part *Mean Mass* as the model for his Sanctus (Example 9.25b).

Example 9.25

a) Opening of Byrd, Sanctus from Mass for four voices

b) Opening of Taverner, Sanctus from *Mean Mass*

The first rising theme in Fantasia 4/g is answered, in breve 16, by a similar second theme with a falling crotchet pattern (Example 9.24). The music opens with a duet between the two parts; the treble plays four sustained long notes, reminiscent of a cantus firmus, over the opening theme in part two. This paired opening is unique among Byrd's fantasias. However, he did employ a paired opening at the beginning of In Nomine 5/5 (Example 5.17a), in which the first four notes of two opening parts are identical to the end of Taverner's opening Sanctus phrase (breve 3) except for the swapping of the two parts and an f natural instead of sharp. The connection is surely not coincidence; it would suggest Byrd was looking back at his In Nomine 5/5.

The four sustained notes played by the treble are at the same pitch and intervals as the opening of Fantasia 6/g1. The third part plays the same pattern from breve 3. This idea re-appears in breves 22–24 played by the treble (Example 9.26). The music reaches a cadence

Example 9.26 Sustained semibreves in Fantasia 4/g

onto a major chord on G in breve 27 before the entry of the third theme, when the music moves upwards, begins to fragment rhythmically and becomes syncopated (Example 9.27). The

Example 9.27 Entry of themes three and four in Fantasia 4/g

fourth theme follows after a cadence on to a major chord on D in breve 33 and falls in contrast to the rising third theme. It is in the fourth theme, that the influence of Ferrabosco becomes apparent. It is quite clear Byrd is quoting from him. In breve 38 Byrd quotes a short melodic pattern found in breve 30 of Ferrabosco's *Fancy*. The pitch is identical; there is a slight rhythmic alteration from Ferrabosco's original melodic pattern (the fourth note is shortened; Examples 9.28 a and b). The pattern first appears in Fantasia 4/g transposed down a fourth in breve 33. Byrd follows this with Ferrabosco's melodic pattern appearing an octave lower before it appears at the original pitch. In the last section of his *Fancy*, Ferrabosco develops the first three notes of his pattern at the initial pitch used by Byrd (Example 9.28c).

Example 9.28 Comparison of material in Ferrabosco I's *A Fancy* and Byrd Fantasia 4/g

a) Ferrabosco I, *A Fancy* from breve 30

b) Byrd, Fantasia 4/g, fourth theme

c) Ferrabosco I , *A Fancy* from breve 70

A short, initially homophonic, passage following a cadence onto a major chord on B♭ leads to the fifth and final theme (Example 9.29).[18] The first three notes of theme five are reminiscent of a three-note motif found shortly before the second theme (Example 9.30a), the opening interval of a major second being replaced with a minor second in the fifth theme.[19] The pattern is found seven times between breves 11 and 16, with a falling major third, which becomes a minor third in the fifth theme. The mood of the fantasia as it nears its conclusion is completely different from the opening, but is linked to the beginning through the incorporation of this small motif into the fifth theme. The second occurrence of the three-note motif, in breve 12 of Fantasia 4/g, contains identical notes (two octaves higher) to the opening of the second theme in Fantasia 5/C (Example 30b). This could be one indication that Fantasia 4/g was written

Example 9.29 Fantasia 4/g, end of fourth theme

Example 9.30

a) Fifth theme Fantasia 4/g, compared with three-note motif found just before the second theme

b) Second theme Fantasia 5/C

after the five-part fantasia. The fifth theme in Fantasia 4/g moves upwards in a similar to the theme in the five-part fantasia.

In the last twelve breves, Fantasia 4/g concludes in a brilliant fashion that is a complete contrast to the opening, and reflects Byrd's skill in writing for viols (Example 9.31). The parts enter headlong after each other, sometimes only a crotchet apart, threatening to disrupt the direction of the music. The first nine notes of the fifth theme fall into three groups of three crotchets, altering the flow of the music. The bass part's initial entry in breve 48 follows this pattern but then as the other three parts continue in the same way, from breve 54, the bass line takes the first four crotchet notes of the theme, to which a minim is added. The bass part becomes even and regular, playing in minims and crotchets against the groupings of three crotchets in the other parts. The extraordinary tension in the music is created by the rhythmic tussle between the bass and the other three parts, which is not resolved until the very end.

Example 9.31 Fantasia 4/g, last 12 breves

As in previous works, any leaps of an octave or a sixth have been carefully considered by Byrd. They are employed mainly in changing tessitura – for example the bass line in breve four (Example 9.24), where the treble is silent, or at breve 33 (Example 9.28b), where part three leaps up a sixth to become a high bass line as the music moves higher into three parts. (In breve 14 Byrd has to take the bass up an octave to move down to a cadence on to D as he chose to restrict the lowest bass note in this fantasia to a G, Example 9.24.)

In Fantasia 4/g Byrd continues to explore texture and tessitura through different combinations of viols and their ranges. The music alternates between four and three parts. The final section opens with a duet between parts three and four followed by a repeat of the same notes an octave higher played by parts one and two (Example 9.31). Instrumental colour and the upper and lower ranges of the notes available are exploited within the 20-note limit. The texture is varied from the start by the sustained semibreves played over and below the opening polyphonic phrases with their moving crotchets. This is found both at the opening and near the conclusion of the first theme (breves 1–4 and 22–24, Examples 9.24 and 9.26). At breve 33, the fourth theme is stated by the upper three instruments followed, with a syncopation, by the lower three (Example 9.28b).

The highest note played by the treble (e♭″) is carefully placed whenever it is used. It first appears in part one in breve 26 in the approach to a cadence in the last statement of the second theme (Example 9.27). After this, with arrival of the third theme, the music changes in mood as the texture becomes busier with the introduction of smaller note values, leaps and syncopation. Before the final fifth section, the music moves suddenly and briefly into close, homophonic part-writing (breve 45, Example 9.29) following a sudden rest in all four parts. The short three-note motif becomes syncopated and extended and is emphasised by an octave upward leap by part two. This is followed by the same motif starting on the highest treble note (e♭″) in breve 47 leading to a cadence on to a major chord on D and the entry of the final theme. The urgency of the final section is increased in the last eight breves by Byrd's use of the highest notes in parts one and two, while underneath the insistent bass line continues to fall a fifth from d to G pulling the music to its final statement on a major chord on G (Example 9.31).

What is particularly noticeable in Fantasia 4/g is the way Byrd exploits and plays with different rhythms. Sometimes he just shifts a phrase by a crotchet, as happens in the final section. The pace of the music changes through his use of different note values. It seems faster after the first two sections as the number of crotchets, dotted rhythms, leaps and syncopation increase through the third and fourth sections. The introduction of homophonic writing using minims and crotchets briefly halts the momentum of the music before the impact of the fast-moving final section with its crotchets and quavers.

In spite of having a range of just ten notes, the bass has a demanding and important role in Fantasia 4/g. The part includes fast-moving quaver passages. Even in its opening polyphonic entry (the second statement of the first theme), the bass directs the chordal progressions and tonal effect of the music. From the conclusion of this first bass entry, throughout the music the bass part repeatedly has a falling fifth from d to G, pulling the music back to G. This becomes increasingly insistent in the last ten breves.

Although not as prominent as in Fantasia 6/g1, the music moves continuously between minor and major. The interval of a rising minor third is present in the sustained semibreves accompanying the opening theme, reminding the listener of the six-part fantasia. A falling minor third is the second interval in the final fifth theme, appearing at repeated close intervals in the last ten bars (Example 9.31).

Fantasia 4/g is in many ways an enigma. It is different from Byrd's five-part fantasia and six-part fantasias in g. It has all the trademarks of a late consort work, typical of his idiomatic instrumental style. The fantasia contains reminders of Fantasias 5/C and 6/g1 and his In Nomines. The final section displays the brilliance he was achieving in viol compositions by the late 1580s.The structure is simple and effective, linked through the development of the five themes. Within this structure Byrd develops an incredible variety of related melodic and rhythmic patterns and ideas. In particular, he explores shifting rhythmic patterns in a way he had not done previously. Fantasia 4/g is similar to parts of his masses written around 1590 in the way he uses sustained, rising dotted minim and crotchet patterns. In some ways it looks back to the 1570s, with its more vocal style, reminders of the In Nomine and the influence of Ferrabosco I. Although the opening characters of Byrd and Ferrabosco's four-part fantasias are different, both open with a duet between treble and tenor viols; in each case, the upper part enters after a semibreve. In his Fancy, Ferrabosco delays longer than Byrd in bringing in a fourth part (in breve 6) and adds the fourth part in breve 8. In Fantasia 4/g, the music drops back from four to three parts in breves 7–9, lasting for two-and-a-half breves, matching Ferrabosco's three-part writing in breves 6–8. Both composers explore texture and tessitura (Examples 9.24 and 9.32). They each play with rhythm in these two fantasias and make use of parts paired in thirds. Fast moving quaver passages are found in the last section of both fantasias.

Example 9.32 Opening of Ferrabosco I, *A Fancy*

Fantasia 4/g has an unusually narrow bass line compared with most of Byrd's later consort works and a restricted compass of 20 notes, but of course it is in four rather than five or six parts. It contains no popular tunes or dance-like or triplet sections. It does not, however, appear in any source before the early 1600s. Did Byrd perhaps re-work some ideas from an earlier four-part composition, developing it into the extraordinary piece that he chose as the only four-part textless viol work in the *Psalmes, Songs and Sonnets* of 1611? Or maybe he chose the challenge of writing within a restricted compass of 20 notes. So much variety is packed into 59 breves, displaying the work of a skilled and mature composer.

Fantasias 3/C1, 3/C2 and 3/C3: Sources

Only one of Byrd's three-part fantasias is found in a source not owned by Edward Paston. All surviving sources date from after 1600. Paston's manuscript, for lute, GB-Lbl Add MS 29246 (14), is the only collection that contains all three fantasias among 29 consort works, 13 of which are by Byrd. Fantasia 3/C2 and Fantasia 3/C3, appear in GB-Lbl Add 41156–8 (17), in which, with *Ut re mi fa sol la* by Ferrabosco I, they are the only consort works. Fantasia 3/C1 and Fantasia 3/C3 are found (transposed up a fourth) in GB-Lcm MS 2036 (19) with two other consort works, one of which is Ferrabosco's *Ut re mi fa sol la.* The only manuscript not owned by Paston containing a three-part fantasia by Byrd, GB-Lbl Add MSS 34800A–C (23), is a set of anonymous partbooks containing Fantasia 3/C1 among a mixture of untexted music that includes four three-part motets from Byrd's *Gradualia* of 1605.

The limited sources for Byrd's three-part fantasias give us very little indication of when they were written. The fact that Fantasia 3/C1 is found in a manuscript containing music from the *Gradualia* of 1605 could suggest they are contemporary; aspects of the three fantasias would suggest they were written after Fantasia 5/C and Fantasia 4/g.

Three-part fantasias: Structure

The three fantasias have a compass of 17 to 19 notes and can all be played by differing combinations of viols. For example, the first could be played by treble, tenor and bass or tenor and two basses. The ranges of each part vary between the three works. The upper part has a range of 10, 12 and 11 notes respectively in each fantasia; the second line, a range of 11, 12 and 10 notes and the bass line, 9, 11 and 10. A range of nine or ten notes is narrow for Byrd's bass viol parts. The overlap between parts is similar to that in earlier fantasias. Fantasias 3/C1 and Fantasia 3/C2 have the clef combination C1, C4 and F4, and Fantasia 3/C3 has that of C1, C3 and C4. In Fantasia 3/C1 and Fantasia 3/C2, the upper part reaches no higher than d′ or c″, but in Fantasia 3/C2 it goes down to g, making this the lowest register for any upper viol part in a consort work by Byrd. None of the three fantasias has a signature accidental.

The three fantasias are very short and, as John Harley suggests, Byrd may have used them as a way of preparing to write three-part vocal music, possibly in the 1580s or the early 1590s.[20] Fantasia 3/C3 lasts for only 18 breves and displays influence of Italian style especially that of Adrian Willaert's (*c.*1490–1562) three-part ricercares published in the 1540s and 1550s. Oliver Neighbour suggests Byrd turned to the Italian ricercare, when exploring three-part writing, because there was no English consort tradition of three-part writing except as a vehicle for technical exercises.[21] Making a comparison between the opening breves of Fantasia 3/C3 and those of Willaert's three-part *Ricercare Primo*, a clear similarity can be seen (Example 9.33a and b). The opening four notes are identical in pitch. Both contain a dotted rhythm.

Example 9.33 Openings of

a) Byrd, Fantasia 3/C3

b) Adrian Willaert, *Ricercare Primo*[22]

However, the length of the two works is very different; Willaert's ricercare lasts for 142 breves whereas Fantasia 3/C3 lasts for only 18 breves, into which Byrd manages to include four melodic motifs. The fourth theme contains the three-note crotchet pattern found in Fantasias 5/C and 4/g, supporting the theory it was written after at least one of these two works. The first seven notes of the theme follow the same melodic line as entries two and four of the fifth theme in Fantasia 4/g (Examples 9.30a and 9.34).

Example 9.34 Fourth theme, Fantasia 3/C3

Fantasia 3/C1 lasts for 45 breves, making it the longest of the three fantasias. Its gentle mood is reminiscent of Fantasia 4/g. It has three melodic ideas. Byrd immediately augments the opening theme on its second entry in the bass; the resulting sustained four-note pattern is reminiscent of Fantasia 4/g and the four-note, sustained breve and semibreve pattern found in the opening of the four-part fantasia (Examples 9.35 and 9.23). Part one

Example 9.35 Opening of Fantasia 3/C1

in Fantasia 3/C1 follows with a four semibreve pattern in breve 5, rising from under part two. In the third theme, Byrd includes rising paired thirds as he did in Fantasia 5/C. Out of the 45 breves, 22 are devoted to the third theme and are full of moving crotchets. Clear similarities can be seen between the conclusion of Fantasia 3/C1 and the end of the Gloria from Byrd's Mass for three voices, written 1593–4 (Example 9.36a and b), illustrating the link between the three- part fantasias and Byrd's three-part vocal writing. Like the three-part fantasias and the four-part fantasias, the Mass for three voices is short compared with Byrd's four-part mass.

Example 9.36 Conclusions of

a) Fantasia 3/C1

b) Gloria from Mass for three voices

Fantasia 3/C2 lasts for 32 breves and contains significant movement in crotchets and quavers. It has three melodic ideas, dividing the music into three, almost equal, sections. The texture becomes denser in the second section with fast running dotted crotchet and quaver passages. Byrd provides contrast to this with his third theme, which initially consists of short, crotchet motifs (Example 9.37), similar to those found in Fantasia 5/C (Example 9.8). The fantasia concludes with a contrasting, smooth rising bass part, moving in minims supporting rhythmic patterns in shorter note values in the two upper parts. There is greater contrast in Fantasia 3/C2 than is found in the other two three-part fantasias. Byrd plays with syncopated rhythms from the fifth breve and introduces quavers in the second section.

Example 9.37 Crotchet patterns in Fantasia 3/C2

The first two three-part fantasias are more similar in character than the third and were probably written as a pair. Both reflect ideas from Fantasia 4/g and Fantasia 5/C and they have a link with Byrd's three-part vocal music of the 1590s, particularly Fantasia 3/ C1, suggesting they were composed after 1590. Fantasia 3/C2 is full of character and ideas and reflects Byrd's mature idiomatic instrumental style more than the other two fantasias. It illustrates how many ideas he could include in a short piece. Fantasia 3/C3, in the Italian style, is less interesting and has the narrowest range; it could be the first of the three, in which Byrd deliberately explored the Italian style as a way of embarking on three-part writing, may be in the 1580s, when he was writing three-part songs.[23]

Pavan and Galliard 6/C: Source

Byrd's final known consort works, the six-part Pavan and Galliard 6/C, are found in only one manuscript, a set of partbooks dating from *c.* 1635–1641, GB-Ob MSS Mus Sch. C 64–9 (34), meaning that the only surviving source dates from at least twelve years after Byrd's death in 1623. The two dances are likely to date from after 1600. The contents of the partbooks reflect the growth of viol playing in the seventeenth century and the increasing number of viol pieces in three, four and six parts. It consists almost entirely of fantasias by composers working after 1600. Byrd is the only composer of his generation with any pieces in the collection. Although five-part pieces form the biggest group in GB-Ob MSS Mus Sch. C 64–9, there are significant numbers of three-part (40), four-part (32) and six-part (33) pieces. The Pavan and Galliard 6/C may be contemporary with Byrd's keyboard *Echo* Pavan and Galliard, published in *Parthenia* in 1612–13.[24]

Pavan and Galliard 6/C: Structure

Like other pavans and galliards, Byrd's Pavan and Galliard 6/C has a narrow compass: 21 notes for the pavan and 19 for the galliard. One treble part in each dance has a range of either 11 or 12 notes. All the other parts have ranges of 10 notes or less. Both dances contain a set of high clefs, these being G2, G2, C2, C3, F3 and F3. It is possible that the music should be played a fourth or fifth lower, particularly as the bass goes down only to B♭ and up to d′.[25] Moving the music down in pitch brings it closer to a conventional arrangement of two treble, two tenor and two bass viols. The pitch would then correspond to that of Fantasia 6/g1 and Fantasia 6/g2 (Example 9.38a and b). Richard Dering (*c.*1580–1630) quotes the opening of the Pavan 6/C at the lower pitch in his first, five-part pavan supporting the theory that this is the correct pitch (Example 9.38c).

Example 9.38

a) Opening of Pavan 6/C at original pitch

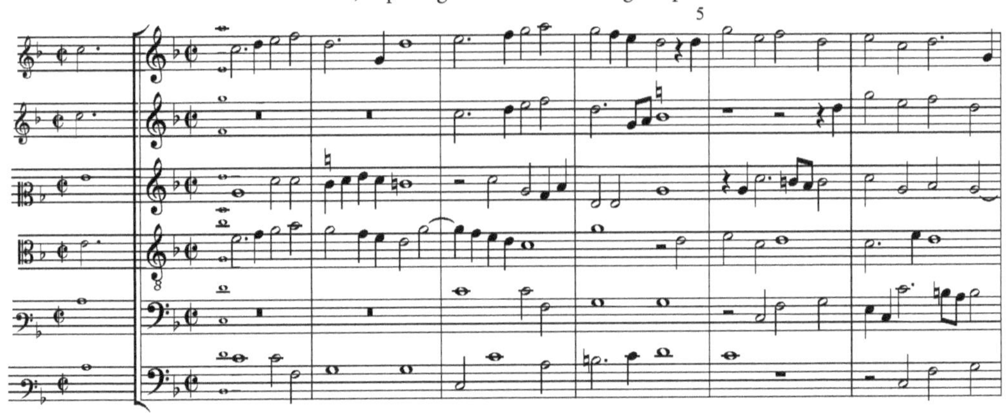

b) Opening of Pavan 6/C transposed down a fourth

c) Opening of Richard Dering, Pavan No 1[26]

Dering's quotation also supports the date of after 1600 for the composition of the Pavan 6/C. Dering was born in 1580 so it is unlikely he quoted from the Byrd pavan before 1600.

The pavan consists of three repeated sections, each of eight breves, and the galliard has three repeated sections, each of eight dotted semibreves. At the original pitch, both have a signature accidental of one flat but are centred round C and end on a major chord on C. In the first section of the Pavan, all the b♭s are raised to b♮ s; the second section has mainly b♭s. There are b♭s at the start of the third section but the last four breves contain only b♮ s. The tonal structure is quite clear; the first and last sections centre round major chords on C and the relationship with chords a fifth above or below is important. The middle section is mainly minor, but finishes on a major chord. The importance of these features in Byrd's instrumental writing support the notion that he was moving away from the modal system towards the harmonic structure of the Baroque.

The Pavan and Galliard 6/C both display the characteristic idiomatic instrumental style Byrd developed in the fantasias. In terms of melodic development, the second and third themes of the pavan grow out of the first, developed out of the second to fourth notes (Example 9.39).

Example 9.39 Themes from Pavan 6/C

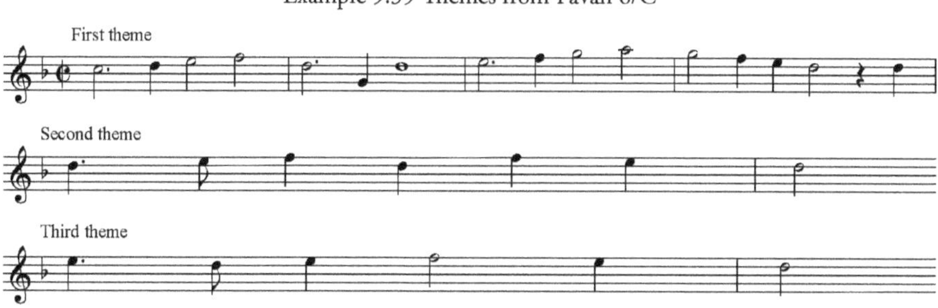

In the opening of the pavan, there is the effect of canon between the two treble parts reminiscent of Fantasia 5/C (Example 9.38a).The two dances are thematically linked; the first five notes of the pavan appear in a different rhythm at the beginning of the galliard (Example 9.40).

Example 9.40 Openings of Pavan 6/C and Galliard 6/C

In the second and third measures, Byrd makes extensive use of echo effects in the treble parts, reminiscent of Fantasia 6/g1 (Example 9.41). The use of echo technique is extended (slightly modified in places) to the bass parts in the galliard (Example 9.42). As in previous consort works, the two lowest lines (five and six) play a supporting role. In the pavan, they work as a pair, supporting the four upper parts). In the galliard, parts five and six are slightly more integrated with the other four parts, but they still support the upper lines as they interact with each other.

Example 9.41 Echo effects in treble viol parts in Pavan 6/C

Example 9.42 Echo effects in bass viol parts in Galliard 6/C

Throughout the pavan, Byrd varies the density of the music. It opens in four parts; all six parts enter in the third breve. At the start of the third section of the galliard, the tessitura is briefly varied with the upper three parts being answered by the lower three parts. He obviously enjoys playing with rhythm in both dances. Rhythmic patterns consistently change, with the introduction of quavers in the pavan and dotted rhythms in both dances. He makes use of cross rhythms, particularly in the pavan where three parts move steadily in semibreves and minims against dotted crotchet patterns grouped in threes (Example 9.43).

Example 9.43 Cross rhythms in Pavan 6/C

As he did in Fantasia 4/g, Byrd manages to pack an extraordinary amount of variety into the 24 breves of the pavan and 24 dotted semibreves in the galliard (each with a repeat, making 48 breves, plus a breve cadence in the pavan), producing a pair of highly sophisticated consort works. Pavan 6/C is very different from Byrd's Pavan 5/c, written at least 30 years earlier. The five-part pavan is much simpler and closer to dance music (Examples 7.5 and 7.6). It moves in a stately fashion, sometimes homophonically. Only in the third section of Pavan 5/c is it possible to see hints of the interplay of parts and motifs that Byrd was beginning to develop in his music. Comparing the Pavan 6/C with the Pavan 5/C shows how far Byrd had come in his development of an idiomatic instrumental style. It would be quite straightforward to dance to Byrd's Pavan 5/c, where the beat is clear but the third section of the Pavan 6/C and second section of the Galliard 6/C, with their cross rhythms, would be difficult for dancers. It is not music for dancing.

Byrd must have been approaching seventy when he wrote the Pavan and Galliard 6/C and it is interesting to ponder what inspired him to return to writing consort music. Perhaps it was to show that he could produce a work for six-part viol consorts that rivalled that of the younger, Jacobean composers. The two dances would seem to be contemporary with the *Psalmes, Songs and Sonnets* of 1611, in which Byrd chose, for the first time, to include two of his consort pieces in a published collection of music. It was his last publication. Harley points out the great care Byrd took over the 1611 *Psalmes, Songs and Sonnets* and the importance this collection had in his 'old yeares', which, as he wrote, 'are desirous of rest'.[27]

In his consort music written after the Fantasia 6/g1 it can be seen that Byrd continued to explore and combine different ideas, refining his instrumental writing and producing contrasting compositions. His final two surviving consort works, the Pavan and Galliard 6/C, may be short works, but they are full of variety and contrast displaying Byrd's continued mastery and skill.

1 Harley, *William Byrd Gentleman of the Chapel Royal*, p. 273.

2 McCarthy, *Byrd*, pp. 136–7.

3 Neighbour, *The Consort and Keyboard Music of William Byrd*, p. 95.

4 Ibid., p. 87.

5 GB-Lbl MS Mus 1591, *My Ladye Nevell's Booke* (10); GB-Lbl MS 29996 (35); D-Bds MS Lynar A2 (37) and GB-Lbl MS 29996 (35).

6 Unlike the low D in the six-part fantasias.

7 Oliver Neighbour believes Byrd ended up improving the original five-part fantasia in producing a second version. He argues that Byrd would not have taken out the delay of the canon entry to breve eight found in the consort version. See Neighbour, *The Consort and Keyboard Music of William Byrd*, p. 74 and Harley, *William Byrd Gentleman of the Chapel Royal*, p. 270 n.65.

8 See Lionel Pike, 'Byrd's 'Echo' Fantasias', *Annual Byrd Newsletter*, 10 (2004), p.7.

9 The number of available works in three and four-parts also increased; see, for example, GB-Lbl Add MS 29427 (27) completed c.1612–17.

10 Thomas Mace in Bryan, '"Choice Consorts….(Rare Chests of Viols)": The Evidence of the Repertory', p.39.

11 Harley, *William Byrd Gentleman of the Chapel Royal*, p. 272.

12 Neighbour, *The Consort and Keyboard Music of William Byrd* p. 92; John Milsom, Review, 'A Century of English Song', in *Early Music*, 33/4 (Nov. 2005), p. 722; Philip Brett, ed. Joseph Kerman and Davitt Moroney, *William Byrd and His Contemporaries, Essays and Monograph*, (Oakland, 2007), p. 163; Richard Rastall, 'Tunes, Textures and Tonalities: Some Thoughts on Structure in English Consort Music', *The Viol*, 5 (2006–7), pp. 8–15; William Byrd, *Fantasia 4/G & Dances Reconstructed for Viol Consort a 4*, ed. Richard Rastall, VdGS 218 (Viola da Gamba Society of Great Britain, 2007).

13 David Pinto, 'Byrd and the Bees: "*In Manus Tuas*"' in *The Viol*, 6 (Spring 2007), pp. 41–3.

14 Ibid., p. 41.

15 If the bass part in the motet *In manus tuas* is correct, then the bass in Fantasia 4/G had a narrow range of 10 notes; if the bass part of Fantasia 4/a is correctly reconstructed from the lute manuscript, it has a range of 11 notes.

16 MB 44, numbers 6–11.

17 Found in GB-Lbl Add. MS 32377 (8), f. 4r and GB-Lbl Add. MS 30485, f. 43v; MB 45/127.

18 Richard Turbet points out the similarity between this short homophonic section, found at breve 45, and a similar phrase found in an anonymous consort song, *Come tread the paths*. He suggests that one possible composer is Richard Farrant and, if he is right, then this would be the second occasion on which Byrd quotes from Farrant in a consort work. See Richard Turbet, 'Notes of Dule: Byrd and *Guichardo*', *The Viol*, 42 (Spring 2016), pp. 14–19.

19 This three-note pattern is also found in Tallis's *A solfing song* and could be a deliberate reference by Byrd.

20 Harley, *William Byrd Gentleman of the Chapel Royal*, p. 273; McCarthy, *Byrd*, p. 137.

21 Neighbour, *The Consort and Keyboard Music of William Byrd*, p. 95.

22 Found in Robert Judd (ed.), *Fantasie recercari contrapunti a tre voci, Venice 1551*: *Italian Music of the Sixteenth and Early Seventeenth Centuries* (New York, Garland, 1994), p. 14.

23 Harley, *William Byrd Gentleman of the Chapel Royal*, p. 273.

24 See Neighbour, *The Consort and Keyboard Music of William Byrd*, p. 87.

25 This would follow the practice of chiavette relating to a set of high clefs. Adriano Banchieri and others advocate transposing down a fourth if there is a signature accidental of a flat.

26 MB 101/22.

27 Harley, *William Byrd Gentleman of the Chapel Royal*, p. 341.

Chapter 10

Byrd's achievements in his consort music

Although Byrd only wrote a small number of consort works compared with his output of vocal and keyboard music, they were obviously important to him. His 33 surviving consort compositions are a significant output compared with other sixteenth-century English composers with the exception of Tye, the greater part of whose consort compositions consists of In Nomines. Byrd's consort works are unique among sixteenth-century compositions in the variety found within them, the exploration of different forms (Latin-titled works containing a cantus firmus, In Nomines, variations, dances and fantasias) and his exploitation of instrumental technical skill. In publishing two of his fantasias in *Psalmes, Songs and Sonnets* of 1611, he showed that he believed that their value was equal to that of the vocal music in the collection. It was also of course astute of him to publish these two works with the growth of demand for such music in the early years of the seventeenth century. The placing by scribes of his two six-part Fantasias 6/g1 and 6/g2 next to Latin motets in a number of sources may have been for convenience next to other six-part works, but it similarly suggests they were understood to be of equal worth.

Byrd's consort fantasias are of particular significance in the history and development of abstract instrumental music. They are self-contained and not dependent on external constraints such as the presence of words, a cantus firmus or a theme and subsequent variations. Byrd experiments in his fantasias, combining elements of different genres. Morley defines a Fantasy as relating to 'serious' vocal forms; [1] Byrd combines *fuga* with dance elements and variations of popular tunes to create his own unique brand of fantasia. His fantasias exist as autonomous, abstract music.

By placing Byrd's consort music in approximate chronological order, it is possible to trace the development of his compositional skills and the emergence of a particular idiomatic instrumental style that culminated in the fantasias of the 1580s and early 1590s. From his earliest In Nomines, particularly In Nomine 5/2, it is possible to see Byrd searching for a way of developing a style unique to instrumental music, and using the technical possibilities offered by a skilled consort of viol players. His consort music illustrates the divergence of instrumental consort music from vocal music. His earliest textless Latin-titled consort pieces could just as easily have been sung to solmization syllables and his first fantasia was easily adapted for voices; by the time he composed his last In Nomine 5/5, the music is clearly instrumental and could not be performed vocally. This reflects the progression from music that could be played on viols to music that was written specifically for viols. In Byrd's earlier consort compositions, there are common traits shared with his vocal music, seen especially when comparing his Latin motets and Fantasia 6/F, in which he first explored writing in an instrumental form not reliant on a cantus firmus. As the diverse instrumental elements found in his consort music increased and developed, these similarities decrease. Byrd's later fantasias are undoubtedly pieces written for viols.

Byrd learnt from his predecessors and contemporaries, particularly Tallis, Parsons and Ferrabosco I. Tye influenced his In Nomines. Byrd took ideas that appealed to him and in which he saw potential for further development. This can be traced through his seven In Nomines and on through to his last fantasias, where he developed these ideas to a new level of instrumental writing. Byrd's music was influenced by his knowledge of the chanson and canzona and his choral background. It is the combination of these influences with his use of popular tunes, dance rhythms, canon, contrast of major and minor and his careful development of harmonic progression relating to his use of melodic themes, combined with his understanding of the possibilities achievable by a skilled consort of viol players that resulted in his idiomatic instrumental style. He became skilled at exploiting the ranges playable by viols by the late sixteenth century and the virtuosity of players. By the time he was writing his fantasias in the late 1580s, the quality of the instruments and the greater security with which a wide range of notes could be played allowed him to do this.

His development of melody, melodic and rhythmic patterns all contributed to this unique idiomatic style. Byrd found a way of constructing music based on an abstract form in which the parts are imaginatively related and the music is full of variety. How he developed his use of bass lines also contributed to his development of an individual musical style. From the *Browning* Fantasy onwards, Byrd's bass parts became more demanding as he took advantage of the technical advances in bass instruments and the developing skill of players. The role the bass plays in creating and moving on chordal progression in his fantasias is very significant.

It seems that Byrd was consistent in how he notated his consort music, if we can assume that scribes were accurate; certainly, a small number of them, such as Baldwin, appear to have received the music directly from him. There are also two published consort works that support the notion Byrd was consistent in his use of notation, in particular his use of clefs. The consistency with which he used clefs and his choice of signature accidentals indicates that he had a clear understanding of what viols could play reliably and how he wanted his music notated.

Where Byrd uses a cantus firmus or incorporates popular tunes into his music, mode influences the sound but, as John Harley notes, it is impossible to separate this from Byrd's notion of key and his use of major and minor.[2] Byrd is writing in a new tonal language within which the bass plays an important role. As well as directing the chordal progressions in his music, particularly in his fantasias, the bass line supports the upper lines. Byrd's use of chords a fifth apart from each other and contrast between major and minor support this new language. His fantasias can be seen as a bridge between sixteenth-century English music and the music of composers such as Orlando Gibbons, writing at the beginning of the seventeenth century. From the tonal language of English composers like Gibbons, as Candace Bailey suggests, comes the style known as 'Baroque'.[3] Walter Kreyszig describes the transition from Renaissance to Baroque music as being from the *stile antico* to the *stile moderno*. Kreyszig defines the *stile moderno* as denoting 'a relaxation of the strictness of compositional practices'.[4] He sees the *Cantiones Sacrae* of 1575 as a 'testimony to the upholding of traditional practices infused with new ideas'.[5] Kreyszig believes this combination of old and new techniques can be seen particularly in Byrd's keyboard music, for example in *Fantasia super Ut re mi fa sol la* from *My Ladye Nevell's Booke* and Praeludia in C and G found in the Fitzwilliam Virginal Book, where Byrd can be seen 'delicately' and 'elegantly' negotiating between the *stile antico* and the *stile moderno*.[6] The combination of the tradition of sixteenth-century English consort music and new ideas can also be seen in his consort music. Byrd's music is on the cusp of the Renaissance and Baroque.

The technical improvements in the making of viols and the emergence of highly skilled viol players provided Byrd with the opportunity to write challenging and highly sophisticated music. Exploiting technical skill, something Byrd learnt from Ferrabosco I, is an essential element of his consort music. It is first seen in In Nomine 5/4, and particularly apparent in Byrd's two variation works, the Prelude and Ground and the *Browning* Fantasy. Fast-moving crotchet and quaver patterns are common in Byrd's consort music. He makes complex use of triplet figures in his Fantasias 5/C and 6/g2, which he first explored in the *Browning* Fantasy. Using the upper and lower ranges of viols gave Byrd the means to utilise contrast of tessitura and to vary instrumental colour in his music as he does, for example, in the Fantasia 6/g1.

Starting with his earliest consort compositions, Byrd was exploring how to find a successful means of structuring music that was not reliant on words. His fantasias contain a sophisticated level of *fuga* that includes canon, echo technique and the development of themes and short motifs that relate to each other. He makes use of long melodic phrases, which can be found in his Latin motets, but also extensive use of short snatches of melodic pattern, something not commonly found in his vocal music. The exception to this are his consort songs, composed for voice and four viols. Such an example, *In fields abroad*, can be found in *The Psalmes, Sonets and Songs* of 1588, which Byrd published as a collection of five-part music for voices, but all of the pieces were adaptions of consort songs, and thus originally four of the five parts were written for viols.[7]

It is impossible to know definitively for whom Byrd wrote his consort music. It seems highly likely that most of it was written for viol players associated with the Chapel Royal, though perhaps some of his music was not composed with anyone in mind but simply to explore ideas. This would seem to be true of the three-part fantasias and their link to Byrd's three-part vocal music. His Latin-titled works were undoubtedly student works written before he left London for Lincoln, as were his early In Nomines. The latter may have been written partly for teaching purposes. The circumstantial evidence relating the composition of the Fantasia 6/F to Byrd's wish to leave Lincoln and return to London points to the reason for its composition. The Prelude and Ground and the *Browning* Fantasy must have been composed with professional viol players in mind and the later fantasias require skilled viol players.

Of all his patrons, Byrd was closest to John, first Lord Petre. GB-Ob MS Mus. Sch. e.423 (6) was copied by John Bentley for John Petre between 1577 and 1589. It contains two five-part pieces by Byrd, In Nomine 5/5 and the *Browning* Fantasy, and two six-part, Fantasias 6/g1 and 6/g2. Byrd stayed with and played for the Petres; it is recorded that after one such visit at Christmas 1589, Byrd received payment for five musicians from London.[8] It is possible that Byrd wrote some of his consort music for John Petre to be performed for him by Byrd and his fellow professional viol players, but there is no way of knowing for certain. It is thought John Bentley was a skilled musician, so he could have made a sixth player for performing six-part music.[9]

It has been suggested that, as so many of Byrd's compositions appear in Edward

Paston's manuscripts, much of it may have been premiered and frequently performed in Paston's home.[10] The latter is probably true for a significant amount of Byrd's consort music, but it is unlikely that any of it was premiered there. With one exception, all of Paston's manuscripts date from after 1600 whereas the source situation suggests that Byrd had completed most of his consort music by 1590.

With the exception of the Pavan and Galliard 6/C, all of Byrd's consort music was written before the increase in the number of non-professional viol players at the end of the sixteenth century.[11] Only ten surviving sources of Byrd's consort music were completed before 1600. Only three of these sources survive from the 1590s, the decade in which he completed writing almost all his consort music. Thirty-one sources have completion dates of after 1600, reflecting the growth in amateur viol playing, the continuing interest in Byrd's music and its adaption for lute and keyboard.

Byrd obviously felt inspired to come back to writing for viol consort after a break of many years in the composition of his Pavan and Galliard 6/C. He had retired from public life by that date so presumably was attracted to writing for the increased demand for viol music and possibly to show he could rival the younger generation of composers in writing consort dances. That also must have encouraged him to publish two consort works in the *Psalmes, Songs and Sonnets* of 1611. Although in his seventies, Byrd had not lost his eye for a business opportunity. The number of later sources containing his consort music illustrate that his music was valued and admired by musicians composing in the seventeenth century, such as Thomas Tomkins. His influence continued into the seventeenth century through his pupils, Thomas Morley and Peter Philips, and through the dissemination of his keyboard music reaching Sweelinck. In particular his use of echo effects, used to great effect in his fantasias, passed into Continental keyboard music.[12] Byrd continued to write keyboard music until around 1614, utilizing features he had developed in his consort music – for example in his Fantasia d1 in which he developed further the syncopations and tonal structure found in Fantasia 4/g, reflecting his movement away from the Renaissance towards the Baroque.

John Harley aptly sums up the quality of Byrd's music as showing 'competence, invention, originality and unexpectedness'.[13] To this should be added a comprehensive understanding of the possibilities of the viol, a visionary understanding of musical structure and a love of instrumental sound.

1 Morley, *A Plain and Easy Introduction to Practical Music*, p. 296.

2 Harley, *William Byrd's Modal Practice*, p. 29.

3 Candace Bailey, 'Orlando Gibbons, Keyboard Music and the Beginnings of the Baroque: New Considerations of a Musical Style', pp.136–7.

4 Walter Kreysig, 'William Byrd's My Ladye Nevells Booke (1591): Negotiating between the *Stile Antico* and the *Stile Moderno* in the Solo Keyboard Repertory', in John Kitchen and Andrew Woolley (eds), *Interpreting Historical Keyboard Music: Sources, Contexts and Performance* (Abingdon, 2016), pp. 31–40, p. 32.

5 Ibid., p. 33.

6 Ibid., p. 39.

7 William Byrd, *Psalmes, Sonets and Songs (1588)*, BE 12, p. viii; John Bryan discusses the ranges and adding of texts to instrumental parts, with particular reference to the *Psalmes, Sonets and Songs* of 1588 in '"Choice Consorts....(Rare Chests of Viols)": The Evidence of the Repertory', pp. 17–22.
In 29 songs in *The Psalmes, Sonets and Songs*, Byrd designates which of the voices should serve as a first singing part. These parts were the original voice parts in the consort songs and are usually distinctly narrower in range than the original, untexted viol parts. They are more syllabic, have fewer text repetitions and usually enter last. Ten first singing parts have a range of eight notes and 14 a range of nine notes. This illustrates a difference between Byrd's vocal and instrumental parts in his secular music. See Bryan, p.18.

8 Mateer, 'Oxford, Christ Church Music MSS 984–8', p. 27.

9 Ibid., p. 34.

10 William Byrd, *Psalmes, Sonets and Songs (1588)*, p. xi.

11 Ian Woodfield writes that he believes that the steady influx of ex-choristers into universities, Inns of Court and private establishments contributed to the development of amateur viol playing, as did the growth of children in private households learning to play the viol in the 1590s: Woodfield, *The Early History of the Viol*, p. 227.

12 Pieter Dirksen, 'Byrd and Sweelinck: Some Cursory Notes', p. 13; Pieter Dirksen, *The Keyboard Music of Jan Pieterszoon Sweelinck*, p. 333; Taylor and Jürgensen, 'Politics, Religion, Style and the Passamezzo Galliards of Byrd and Philips', p. 72; David Smith, 'The Interconnection of Religious, Social and Musical Networks: Creating a Context for the Keyboard Music of Peter Philips and its Dissemination' in Smith and Taylor (ed.), *Networks of Music and Culture in the Late Sixteenth and Early Seventeenth Centuries*, pp. 11 and 22.

13 Harley, *William Byrd Gentleman of the Chapel Royal*, p. 369.

Bibliography

Abbreviations

BE Byrd Edition

EECM Early English Church Music

MB Musica Britannica

Andrews, H.K.. *The Technique of Byrd's Vocal Polyphony* (London and New York, 1966).

Anon. *The First and Second Prayer Books of Edward VI* (London, 1910).

Ashbee, Andrew. 'A further Look at Some of the Le Strange Manuscripts', *Chelys*, 5 (1974), pp. 24–50.

——. 'John Merro's Manuscripts Revisited', *Viola da Gamba Society Journal*, 7 (2013).

Ashbee, Andrew, Robert Thompson, and Jonathan Wainwright (eds). *Viola da Gamba Society Index of Manuscripts Containing Consort Music,* http://vdgs.org.uk/indexmss (Authored 2014).

Bailey, Candace. 'Concepts of Key in Seventeenth-Century English Keyboard Music', in Christle Collins Judd (ed.), *Tonal Structure in Early Music* (New York, 1998), pp. 247–74.

——. 'William Ellis and the Transmission of Continental Keyboard Music in Restoration England', *Journal of Musicological Research*, 20 (2001), pp. 211–42.

——. 'Orlando Gibbons, Keyboard Music and the Beginnings of the Baroque: New Considerations of a Musical Style', *International Review of the Aesthetics and Sociology of Music*, 37/2 (2006), pp. 135–56.

Baker, David. 'The Instrumental Consort Music of Robert Parsons', *Chelys*, 7 (1977), pp. 4–20.

Baker, David and Jennifer. 'The Browning', *Chelys*, 10 (1981), pp. 4–10.

Baldwin, David. *The Chapel Royal Ancient & Modern* (London, 1990).

Bassano, Augustine *Pavans* and *Galliards*, ed. Albert Folop, IMSLP Petrucci Music Library 164722, 164733, 164745 and 164765, https://imslp.org/wiki/Pavans_and_Galliards_for_5_Viols_(Bassano_Augustine) (Authored 2011).

Bent, Margaret. 'The Grammar of Early Music: Preconditions for Analysis', in Christle Collins Judd (ed.), *Tonal Structure in Early Music* (New York, 1998), pp. 15–59.

Bevin, Elway. *A Briefe and Short Instruction of the Art of Musicke*, ed. Denis Collins (Aldershot, 2007).

Bowers, Roger. 'To Chorus from Quartet', in John Morehen (ed.), *English Choral Practice 1400–1650* (Cambridge 1995), pp. 1–47.

——. 'Chains of (Rehabilitated) Gold', *Early Music Review*, 159 (April 2014), pp.10–17.

Bray, Roger. 'Music and Musicians', in Roger Bray (ed.), *The Blackwell History of Music in Britain: The Sixteenth Century* (Oxford 1995).

Breig, Werner. 'Die Lübbenauer Tablaturen Lynar A1 und A2. Eine quellenkundliche Studie', *Archiv für* Musikwissenschaft, 25/2 (1968), pp. 96–117.

Brett, Philip. 'Edward Paston (1550–1630): A Norfolk Gentleman and his Musical Collection', *Transactions of the Cambridge Bibliographical Society*, (1964), pp. 51–69.

——. Kerman, Joseph and Davitt Moroney (eds). *William Byrd and His Contemporaries: Essays and a Monograph* (Oakland, 2007).

Brookes, Virginia. 'In Nomine: An Obscure Designation', *The Viol*, 6 (Spring 2007), pp. 22–5.

Brown, Alan and Richard Turbet (eds). *Byrd Studies* (Cambridge 1992).

Bryan, John. '"Not Unlike a Confused Singing of Birds in a Grove": An Introduction to the In Nomine', *The Viol*, 6 (Spring 2007), pp. 15–29.

——. '"Full of Art and Profundity": The Five-part Consort Pavan as a Medium for Sophisticated Musical Expression and Compositional Cross-reference in Late Renaissance England', in David J. Smith and Rachelle Taylor (eds), *Networks of Music and Culture in the Late Sixteenth and Early Seventeenth Centuries* (Farnham, 2013), pp. 185–202.

——. '"Choice Consorts......(Rare Chests of Viols)": The Evidence of the Repertory', in Michael Fleming and John Bryan (eds), *Early English Viols* (Abingdon and New York, 2016), pp. 13–64.

Bull, Henry. *Christian Prayers and Holy Meditations, as Well for Private as Public Exercise*, collected 1566 (Cambridge, Parker Society, 1842).

Butler, Katherine. 'Printed Borders for Sixteenth Century Music or Music Paper and the Early Career of Music Printer Thomas East (*c.*1540–1608)', *The Library*, 19/2 (2018), pp. 174–202.

——. 'From Liturgy and the Education of Choirboys to Protestant Domestic Music-Making: The History of the 'Hamond' Partbooks (GB-Lbl Add. MSS 30480–4)', *Royal Musical Association Research Chronicle*, 50/1 (2019), pp. 29–93.

Byrd, William. *Cantiones Sacrae I (1589)*, ed. Alan Brown, BE 2 (London, Stainer and Bell, 1988).

——. *Cantiones Sacrae II (1591)*, ed. Alan Brown, BE 3 (London, Stainer and Bell, 1981).

——.*Latin Motets I*, ed. Warwick Edwards, BE 8 (London, Stainer and Bell, 1982).

——. *The English Services*, ed. Craig Monson, BE 10a (London, Stainer and Bell, 1983).

——. *The English Anthems*, ed. Craig Monson, BE 11 (London, Stainer and Bell, 1983).

——. *Psalmes, Sonets and Songs (1588)*, ed. Jeremy Smith, BE 12 (London, Stainer and Bell, 1987).

——. *Psalmes, Songs and Sonnets (1611)*, ed. John Morehen, BE 14 (London, Stainer and Bell, 1987).

——. *Consort Music*, ed. Kenneth Elliott, BE 17 (London, Stainer and Bell, 1971).

——. *My Ladye Nevells Booke* ed. Hilda Andrews and Blanche Winogron (New York, Dover, 1969).

——. *Pavans and Galliards in Five parts* ed. Richard Rastall (Leeds, four-fifteen press, 1998).

——. *Fantasia 4/g and Dances Reconstructed for Viol Consort a 4* ed. Richard Rastall, VdGS 218 (Viola da Gamba Society of Great Britain, 2007).

Caldwell, John. 'Preston, Thomas', in Deane L. Root (ed.), *The New Grove Dictionary of Music & Musicians*, online 2001, updated 2009;

https://doi-org.nls.idm.oclc.org/10.1093/gmo/9781561592630.article.40009 .

——. 'Canzona', in Deane L. Root (ed.), *The New Grove Dictionary of Music & Musicians*, online 2001, updated 2009;

https://doi-org.nls.idm.ocle.org/10.1093/gmo/9781561592630.article.04804.

Carter, Tim. *Music in Late Renaissance & Early Baroque Italy* (London, 1992).

——. 'Secular Vocal Music' in Roger Bray (ed.), *The Blackwell History of Music in Britain: The Sixteenth Century* (Oxford 1995).

Carwood, Andrew. CD notes for *William Byrd: The Great Service and Other Works*, Cardinall's Musick (2005 Hyperion CDA67533).

Charlton, David. 'A National Catalogue of Music Microfilms', *Royal Musical Association Research Chronicle*, 11/1 (1973) pp. 1–70.

Charteris, Richard. 'A Memorial for Alfonso Ferrabosco the Elder', *The Musical Times*, 129/1746 (August 1988), pp. 393–6.

——. 'New Connections Between Eastern Europe and Works by Philips, Dowland, Marais and Others', *Chelys*, 29 (2001), pp. 3–27.

Christophers, Harry. CD Notes for *Philip & Mary – A Marriage of England & Spain*. COR16037: (CORO, 2006).

Cockshoot, John V. and Field, Chistopher D.S.. 'Ferrabosco family, in Deane L. Root (ed.), *The New Grove Dictionary of Music & Musicians*, online 2001;

https://doi-org.nls.idm.oclc.org/10.1093/gmo/9781561592630.article.09507 .

Craig-McFeely, Julia. 'English Lute Manuscripts and Scribes 1530-1630' (DPhil dissertation, University of Oxford, 1992); https://www.cs.dartmouth.edu/~wbc/julia/

(Authored 2000).

D'Accone, Frank. *London British Library MS Egerton 3665, The Tregian Manuscript by Frances Tregian* (New York, Garland, 1988).

Dakers, Lionel (ed.). *The New Church Anthem Book* (Oxford, OUP 1994).

Di Grazia, Dona. 'New Perspectives on Thomas Myriell's *Trisititae Remedium* and Add MS. 2947', *Early Music*, 38/1 (2010), pp. 101–112.

Dirksen, Pieter. *The Keyboard Music of Jan Peterszoon Sweelinck* (Utrecht, 1997).

——. 'Byrd and Sweelinck: Some Cursory Notes', *Annual Byrd Newsletter*, 7 (June 2001), pp. 11–20.

——. 'New Perspectives on Lynar A1', in Christopher Hogwood (ed.), *The Keyboard in Baroque Europe* (Cambridge, 2003), pp. 36–66.

Dodds, Gordon and Andrew Ashbee (eds). *Viola da Gamba Society Thematic Index of Music for Viols,* http://vdgs.org.uk/thematic (Authored 2004).

Doe, Paul (ed.). *Elizabethan Consort Music I,* MB 44 (London, Stainer and Bell, 1979).

——. (ed.). *Elizabethan Consort Music II,* MB 45 (London, Stainer and Bell, 1988).

——. revised David Mateer. 'Tye, Christopher' in Deane L. Root (ed.), *The New Grove Dictionary of Music and Musicians* online 2001, updated 2009; https://doi-org.nls.idm.oclc.org/10.1093/gmo/9781561592630.article.28665.

Doe, Paul and Roger Bowers; revised Hugh Benham. 'John Taverner' in Deane L. Root (ed.), *The New Grove Dictionary of Music and Musicians* online 2001, updated 2009; https://doi-org.nls.idm.ocle.org/10.1093/gmo/9781561592630.article.27571.

Dreyfus, Lawrence. 'The Five and Six Part Music of William Byrd', *The Viol,* 1 (2005–2006), pp. 20–21.

Edwards, Richard ed. Hyder Edward Rollins. *The Paradise of Dainty Devices* (Cambridge Mass., 1927).

Edwards, Warwick. 'The Sources of Elizabethan Consort Music' (PhD Dissertation, University of Cambridge, 1974).

——. 'The Walsingham Consort Books', *Music & Letters,* 55/2 (April 1974), pp. 209–14.

Elcombe, Keith. 'Keyboard Music', in Roger Bray (ed.), *The Blackwell History of Music in Britain: The Sixteenth Century* (Oxford 1995).

Fenlon, Iain. 'Music and Society' in Iain Fenlon (ed.), *The Renaissance (Man & Music)* (London, 1989), pp. 1–62.

Fenlon, Iain and John Milsom. '"Ruled Paper Imprinted": Music, Paper and Patents in Sixteenth-Century England', *Journal of the American Musicological Society,* 37/1 (1980), pp 139–63.

Ferguson, Howard. 'Keyboard Music, §I, 2: 16th century', in Stanley Sadie (ed.), *The New Grove Dictionary of Music & Musicians,* 10 (London, 1995) p. 14.

Ferrabosco I, Alfonso. *Pavans & 3 In Nomines a 5,* ed. Richard Charteris, VdGS 159, (Viola da Gamba Society of Great Britain, 2004).

Fleming, Michael. 'An "Old Old Violl" and "Other Lumber": Musical Remains in

Provincial, Non-Noble England *c.*1580–1660', *The Galpin Society Journal,* 58 (May 2005), pp. 89–99.

——. '"Such As Do Lawfully Exercise Any Art, Mistery or Manual Occupation": Viol Making As a Trade or Occupation', in Michael Fleming and John Bryan (eds), *Early English Viols: Instruments, Makers and Music* (Abingdon & New York, 2016), pp. 149–83.

Flynn, Jane. 'The Education of Choristers in England during the Sixteenth Century', in John Morehen (ed.), *English Choral Practice 1400–1650* (Cambridge, 1995), pp. 180–200.

Ford, Robert. 'Clement Woodcock's Appointment at Canterbury Cathedral', *Chelys*, 16 (1987), pp. 36–43.

Fuller-Maitland, J.A. & W. Barcley Squire. (eds). *The Fitzwilliam Virginal Book Volume I*, (New York, Dover, 1963).

Gair, Reavley. *The Children of St Paul's: The Story of a Theatre Company, 1553–1608* (Cambridge, 1982).

Gervers, Hilda. 'A Manuscript of Dance Music From Seventeenth-Century England: Drexel Collection MS 5612', *Bulletin of the New York Public Library* (1977), pp. 503–52.

Greer, David, and Fiona Kisby. 'William Cornysh (ii)' in Deane L. Root (ed.) *The New Grove Dictionary of Music & Musicians*, online 2001; updated 2009; https://doi-org.nls.idm.ocle.org/10.1093/gmo/9781561592630.article.06536 .

Grimshaw, Julian. 'Sixteenth-century English *Fuga*: Sequential and Peak-note Subjects', *The Musical Times* 148/1900 (Autumn 2007), pp. 61–78

——. '"Fuga" in Early Byrd', *Early Music*, 37/2 (May 2009), pp. 251–265.

Harley, John. *William Byrd Gentleman of the Chapel Royal* (Aldershot, 1997).

——. *William Byrd's Modal Practice* (Aldershot, 2004).

——. '"My Ladye Nevell" Revealed', *Music and Letters*, 86/1 (2005), pp. 1–15.

——. *The World of William Byrd* (Farnham, 2010).

——. *Tallis* (Farnham, 2015).

Harper, John. 'Ensemble and Lute Music', in Roger Bray (ed.), *The Sixteenth Century (Music in Britain)* (Oxford, 1995), pp. 263–322.

Herrisone, Rebecca. *Music Theory in Seventeenth-Century England* (Oxford, 2000).

Holborne, Anthony. *Pavans, Galliards, Almains 1599*, ed. Bernard Thomas (London, London Pro Musica, 1980).

Holman, Peter. *Four and Twenty Fiddlers* (Oxford, 1995).

Humphreys, David. 'Wilder and Byrd: Wilder's *Aspice Domine a 6*', *Annual Byrd Newsletter*, 10 (2004), p. 26.

Irving, John. *The Instrumental Music of Thomas Tomkins 1572–1656* (London and New York, 1989).

Jeffries, Mathew. *Consort, Full, and Verse Anthems*, ed. John Cannell (Madison, A-R Editions, 1998).

Johnson, Robert and Joseph Lupo. *A Knell of Johnson* and *Pavan*, ed. Virginia Brookes, VdGS 199 (Viola da Gamba Society of Great Britain, 2005 and 2013).

Johnstone, Andrew. '"As It Was in the Beginning": Organ and Choir Pitch in Early Anglican Church Music', *Early Music*, 31/4 (2003), pp. 507–24.

Judd, Cristle Collins. 'Introduction: Analyzing Early Music', in Cristle Collins Judd (ed.), *Tonal Structures in Early Music* (New York and London, 1998).

Judd, Robert (ed.). *Fantasie recercari contrapunti a tre voci, Venice 1551*: *Italian Music of the sixteenth and early seventeenth centuries* (New York, Garland, 1994).

Kerman, Joseph. 'Byrd's Motets: Chronology and Canon', *Journal of the American Musicological Society*, 14 (1961), pp. 359–82.

——. *The Masses and Motets of William Byrd* (London, 1981).

——. revised Kerry McCarthy. 'William Byrd' in Deane L. Root (ed.) *The New Grove Dictionary of Music & Musicians*, 2001 print and online; updated 2014; https://doi-org.nls.idm.oclc.org/10.1093/gmo/9781561592630.article.04487.

Kim, Hyun-Ah. *Humanism and the Reform of Sacred Music in Early Modern England* (Aldershot, 2008).

Klotz, Martin. *Instrumentale Konzeptionen in Der Virginalmusik Von William Byrd* (Tutzing, 2005).

Kreysig, Walter. 'William Byrd's My Ladye Nevells booke (1591): Negotiating Between the *Stile Antico* and the *Stile Moderno* in the Solo Keyboard Repertory', in John Kitchen and Andrew Woolley (eds), *Interpreting Historical Keyboard Music: Sources, Contexts and Performance* (Abingdon, 2016), pp. 31–40.

Leach, Arthur Francis. *A History of Winchester College* (London, 2013).

Lord, Suzanne. *Music from the Age of Shakespeare: A Cultural History* (Westport Connecticut, 2003).

Marsh, Christopher. *Music and Society in Early Modern England* (Cambridge, 2010).

Martin, Anne. 'The Consort Music of William Byrd and Its Relationship to Preceding and Contemporary Consort Music' (M Mus Dissertation, University of Surrey, 1998).

Mateer, David. 'Oxford, Christ Church Music MSS 984–8: An Index and Commentary', *Royal Musical Research Chronicle*, 20 (1987), pp. 1–19.

——. 'The Gyffard Partbooks: Composers, Owners, Dates and Provenance', *Royal Musical Research Chronicle*, 26 (1993), pp. 19–43.

——. 'William Byrd, John Petre and Oxford Bodleian MS Mus. Sch. E. 423', *Royal Musical Research Chronicle*, 29 (1996), pp. 21–46.

McCarthy, Kerry. 'William Mundy's *Vox Patris Caelestis* and the Assumption of the Virgin Mary', *Music and Letters*, 85/3 (2004), p. 355.

——. 'Byrd, Augustine and *Tribue, Domine*', *Early Music*, 32/4 (2004), pp. 569–76.

——. 'Evidence of Things Past', *Journal of the Royal Musical Association*, 135/2 (2010), pp. 405–11.

——. *Byrd* (New York, 2013).

——. *Tallis* (New York, 2020).

McCoy, Stewart. 'Edward Paston and the Textless Lute-Song', *Early Music*, 15/2 (1987), pp. 221–27.

Milsom, John. 'Music', in Boris Ford (ed.), *16th Century Britain*, The Cambridge Cultural History of Britain, 3 (Cambridge, 1992), pp. 168–207.

——. 'Tallis, Thomas (*c.*1505–1585)', in *Oxford Dictionary of National Biography* print and online 2004, revised 2008; https://doi-org.nls.idm.oclc.org/10.1093/ref:odnb/26954.

——. CD notes for *Thomas Tallis: The Complete Works – Volume 9, Instrumental Music and Songs*, Charivari Agréable (2004 Signum SIG42).

——. 'A Century of English Song', *Early Music*, 33/4 (Nov. 2005), p. 721–3.

——. 'A Composer's-Eye View of the In Nomine', *The Viol*, 6 (2007), pp. 26–30.

—— (ed). *Christ Church Oxford Library Music Catalogue*, 'GB-Och Mus.979–983', http://library.chch.ox.ac.uk/music/ (Authored 2005/2011).

Monson, Craig. 'Byrd and the *Cantiones Sacrae-2*', *Musical Times*, 117 (1976), pp. 65–67.

——. *Voices and Viols in England, 1600–1650* (Michigan, 1982).

Morehen, John (ed.). *English Choral Practice 1400–1650* (Cambridge, 1996).

Morley, Thomas. *A Plain and Easy Introduction to Practical Music*, ed. Alec Harman (New York, 1973/2nd ed.).

Mould, Alan. *The English Chorister; A History* (London, 2007).

Neighbour, Oliver. *The Consort and Keyboard Music of William Byrd* (London, 1978).

——. '*Instrumentale Konzeptionen in der Virginalmusik von William Byrd*: By Martin Klotz', *Music and Letters*, 87 (2006), pp. 672–75.

Otterstedt, Annette. *The Viol: History of an Instrument* (Kassel, 2002).

Owen, Dorothy. *A History of Lincoln Cathedral* (Cambridge, 1994).

Owens, Jessie Ann. 'Concepts of Pitch in English Music Theory, c. 1560–1640', in Cristle Collins Judd (ed.), *Tonal Structures in Early Music* (New York and London, 1998), pp. 183–246.

—— (ed.). *Charles Butler's Principles of Musick (1636)* (Aldershot, 2009).

Parrott, Andrew. 'Performing pitch', *Early Music*, 32/2 (May, 2004), p. 349.

Parsons, Robert. *Latin Sacred Music*, ed. Paul Doe, EECM 40 (London, Stainer and Bell, 1994).

Payne, Ian. 'The Provision of Teaching on the Viols at some English Cathedral Churches, *c.*1594–*c.*1645: Archival Evidence', *Chelys*, 19 (1990), pp. 3–15.

——. 'New Light on "New Fashions" by William Cobbold (1560–1639) of Norwich', *Chelys*, 30 (2002), pp. 4–10.

Philips, Peter and Richard Dering. *Consort Music*, ed. David J. Smith, MB 101 (London, Stainer and Bell, 2016).

Pike, Lionel. 'Byrd's "Echo" Fantasias', *Annual Byrd Newsletter*, 10 (2004), pp. 7–10.

Pinto, David. 'Byrd and the Bees: "In Manus Tuas"', *The Viol*, 6 (2007), pp. 41–43.

Popović, Tihomir. *Mäzene — Manuskripte — Modi: Untersuchungen zu My Ladye Nevells Booke* (Stuttgart, 2013).

Poulton, Diana. 'Lute §7: Repertory', in Stanley Sadie (ed.), *The New Grove Dictionary of Music & Musicians*, 11 (London, 1980), p. 361.

Powers, Howard. 'From Psalmody to Tonality', in Cristle Collins Judd (ed.), *Tonal Structures in Early Music* (New York and London, 1998), pp. 275–340.

Rasch, Rudolf. 'Modality in Sweelinck's Psalm Compositions', in Pieter Dirksen (ed.), *Sweelinck Studies: Proceedings of the International Sweelinck Symposium Utrecht 1999* (Utrecht, 2002), pp. 147–70.

Rastall, Richard. 'William Byrd's String Fantasia 6/G1', in Warren Drake (ed.), *Liber Amicorum John Steele: A Musicological Tribute* (New York, 1997), pp. 139–70.

——. 'Tunes, Textures and Tonalities: Some Thoughts on Structure in English Consort Music', *The Viol*, 5 (2007), pp. 8–15.

Ravens, Simon. "A Sweet Shrill Voice': The Countertenor and Vocal Scoring in Tudor England', *Early Music*, 26/1 (February, 1998), pp. 122–134.

——. 'Countertenor counterblast', *Early Music*, 28/3 (August, 2000) pp. 507–8.

Rayment, Louise. 'A New Context for the Manuscript of *Wit and Science*', *Early Theatre*, 17/1 (2014), pp. 49–73.

Redford, John. *Wit and Science*, ed. Ben Byram-Wigfield (London 2013).

Scherb, Victor I. 'Playing at Maturity in John Redford's *Wit and Science*', *SEL Studies in English Literature 1500–1900*, 2 (2005), pp. 271–97.

Schofield, Bertram and Thurston Dart. 'Tregian's Anthology', *Music & Letters*, 32/3 (1951), pp. 209–15.

Sequera, Hector. 'House Music for Recusants in Elizabethan England: Performance Practice in the Music Collection of Edward Paston (1550–1630)' (PhD dissertation, University of Birmingham, 2010).

Sheppard, John. *Masses,* ed. Nicholas Sandon, EECM 18 (London, Stainer and Bell, 1976).

Skinner, David. 'The Works of John Merbecke', Programme Note in *Missa per arma iustitie, Domine Ihesu Christie, Ave, Dei patris filia*, The Cardinall's Music, Andrew Carwood/ David Skinner, (Recorded 1994, notes 1996, Gaudeamus 148, Released 2010).

Smith, David J. 'The Instrumental Music of Peter Philips: Its Sources, Dissemination and Style'

(DPhil dissertation, University of Oxford, 1994).

——. 'Byrd Reconstructed: in Search of Consort Models for Keyboard Dances by Byrd', *Annual Byrd Newsletter* 5 (1999), pp.6–8.

——. 'A Legend? Frances Tregian the Younger as Music Copyist', *Musical Times*, 143 (2002), pp. 7–16.

——. 'The Nature of Musical Influence: Jan Pieterszoon Sweelinck and English Composers Active in the Southern Netherlands', in Pieter Dirksen (ed.), *Sweelinck Studies* (Utrecht, 2002), pp. 65–84.

——. 'Making Connections: William Byrd, "Virtual" Networks and the English Keyboard Dance', in John Kitchen and Andrew Woolley (eds), *Interpreting Historical Keyboard Music* (Farnham, 2013), pp. 20–30.

Smith, David J. and Rachelle Taylor (eds). *Networks of Music and Culture in the Late Sixteenth and Early Seventeenth Centuries* (Farnham, 2013).

Spring, Mathew. *The Lute in Britain: A History of the Instrument and its Music* (Oxford, 2005).

Strahle, Graham. 'Two Byrd "Fantasias" Disproven', in Graham Strahle and David Swale (eds), *All Kinds of Music: In Honour of Andrew D. McCredie* (Willemshaven, 1998), pp. 47–56.

Tallis, Thomas and William Byrd. *Cantiones Sacrae 1575,* ed. John Milsom, EECM 56 (London, Stainer and Bell, 2014).

Taverner, John. *Four- and Five-Part Masses,* ed. Hugh Benham, EECM 35 (London, Stainer and Bell, 1989).

Taylor, Philip William. 'Music and Recusant Culture: The Paston Manuscript Collection and William Byrd's Songs' (PhD dissertation, University of Lancaster, 2007).

Thompson, Ruby Reid. 'The "Tregian" Manuscripts: A Study of their Compilation', *British Library Journal*, 18/2 (1992), pp. 202–204.

——. 'Francis Tregian the Younger as Music Copyist: a Legend and an Alternative View', *Music & Letters*, 82/1 (February 2001), pp.1–31.

Thorby, Philip. 'A Question of Status', *The Viol*, 54 (2019), pp. 8–11.

Tomkins, Thomas. *Keyboard Music*, ed. Stephen D. Tuttle, MB 5 (London, Stainer and Bell, 1964).

Trinity College Dublin. *Early English Church Music Primary Source Data Base*, http://eecm.tcd.ie/volumes.

Turbet, Richard. 'Wings of Faith', *Musical Times*, 138 (1975), p. 5.

——. (ed.). *A Byrd Celebration: Lectures at the William Byrd Festival Portland Oregon 1998–2008* (Richmond, 2008).

——. *William Byrd: A Research and Information Guide* (New York and London, 2012/3rd ed.).

——. 'Notes of Dule: Byrd and *Guichardo*', *The Viol*, 42 (2016), pp. 14–19.

Tye, Christopher. *English Sacred Music*, ed. John Morehen, EECM 19 (London, Stainer and Bell, 1977).

——. *Masses*, ed. Paul Doe, EECM 24 (London, Stainer and Bell, 1980).

——. *Ritual Music and Motets*, ed. Nigel Davison, EECM 33 (London, Stainer and Bell, 1987).

——. *Complete Consort Music*, ed. Bernard Thomas (Brighton, London Pro Musica, 1991).

University of Oxford. *Digital Image Archive of Medieval Music*, http://www.diamm.ac.uk (Authored 1998).

White, Robert. *Ritual Music and Lamentations*, ed. David Mateer, EECM 32 (London, Stainer and Bell, 1986).

Wiering, Frans. 'Internal and External Views of the Modes', in Cristall Collins Judd (ed.), *Tonal Structures in Early Music* (New York and London, 1998).

Willetts, Pamela J. 'Musical Connections of Thomas Myriell', *Music and Letters*, 49/1 (1968), pp. 36–42.

——. 'The Identity of Thomas Myriell', *Music and Letters*, 53/4 (1972), pp. 431–33.

——. 'Thomas Myriell' in *The New Grove Dictionary of Music & Musicians*, online 2001, updated 2009; https://doiorg.nls.idm.ocle.org/10.1093/gmo/9781561592630.article.19499 .

Williamson, Magnus and Julia Craig-McFeely (project leaders). *Tudor Partbooks,* joint project of universities of Newcastle and Oxford, http://www.tudorpartbooks.ac.uk/ (Authored 2016).

Windram, H. and Terence Charlston (eds). *English Keyboard Music c. 1650–c. 1700 Vol 1: Royal College of Music London MS 2093* (Oslo, 2015).

Woodfield, Ian. *The Early History of the Viol* (Cambridge, 1984).

Wulfstan, David. 'Byrd, Tallis and Ferrabosco', in John Morehen (ed.), *English Choral Practice 1400–1650* (Cambridge, 1996), pp. 109–142.

Appendix One

Manuscript details for each of Byrd's consort pieces listed by genre

Number in bracket as found in BE17

Other numbers = manuscript listing by Anne Martin

P = Paston manuscripts

Dances

Pavan 5/c (14)

Manuscript	Date	Folio	Instrument
10. *My Ladye Nevell's Booke* (GB-Lbl)	1591	No. 10	Keyboard
21. GB-Lbl Add. MSS 37402–6	completed after 1606	ff.98v, 89v, 91v, 86v	
22. D-Kl MS mus. 125 *c.*1600			
38. NYp MS Drexel 5612	1630s	p.132	Keyboard

Pavan & Galliard 6/C (15a & b)

Manuscript		Date / Folio
34. GB-Ob MMS Sch. C 64–9		*c.*1635–1641
	Pavan	ff.203v, 153v, 75v &140v, 212v, 4v
	Galliard	ff.203v, 153v, 75v & 140v, 212v, 4v

Fantasias

Fantasia 3/C1 (1)

Manuscript	Date	Folio	Instrument
14. GB-Lbl Add. MS 29246 (P)	early 17th century	f.22r	Lute
19. GB-Lcm MS 2036 (transp. up a 4th) (P)	early 17th century	f.4v	
23.GB-Lbl Add. MSS 34800A–C	after 1600 to *c.*1618	f.15v, 17v	

Fantasia 3/C2 (2)

Manuscript	Date	Folio	Instrument
14. GB-Lbl Add. MS 29246 (P)	early 17th century	f.22v	Lute
17. GB-Lbl Add. MSS 41156–8 (P)	early 17th century	f.11v	
19. GB-Lcm MS 2036 (transp. up a 4th) (P)	early 17th century	f.5v	

Fantasia 3/C3 (3)

14. GB-Lbl Add. MS 29246 (P)	early 17th century	27v	Lute
17. GB-Lbl Add. MSS 41156–8 (P)	early 17th century	f.9v	

Fantasia 4/a (5)

14. GB-Lbl Add. MS 29246 (P)	early 17th century	f.39r	Lute
27. GB-Lbl Add. MS 29427	*c.*1612–1618	f.45	
41. GB-Lcm MS 2093 (fragment)	1660s–1670s	f.25	Keyboard

Fantasia 4/g (4)

14. GB-Lbl Add. MS 29246 (P)	early 17th century	f.41v	Lute
26. (Print) *Psalmes, Songs and Sonnets*	(London 1611)	No. 15	
30. NYp MSS Drexel 4180–5	*c.*1615–1625	ff.180v, 184v, 166v 151v	
31. GB-Ob MSS Mus Sch D. 245–7	c.1610–after 1634	pp. 104, 105, f.23v	
36. GB-Lbl MS Hirsch M.1353	after 1620–1	f.21v	Lute
39. F-Pc MS Rés. 1122 (early version?)	1646–1654	f.16	Keyboard

Fantasia 4/G (34) (*In manus tuas* in *Gradualia* 1605)

27. GB-Lbl Add. MS 29427	*c.*1612–1618	f.45v	

Fantasia 5/C (8)

10. *My Ladye Nevell's Booke* (GB-Lbl) *A lesson of Voluntarie*	1591	No. 29	Keyboard
24. GB-Lbl Add. MSS 17786–91	before 1610–1620s (1st layer completed *c.*1610)	f.2v	
35. GB-Lbl MS 29996# opening missing	mid-16th – mid-17th	f.210–210v	Keyboard
37. D-Bds MS Lynar A2 (as in *My Ladye Nevell's Booke*	after 1620– before 1630	f.60	Keyboard
39. F-Pc MS Rés. 1122	1646–1654	f.38	Keyboard
40. GB-Och MS 1113 Fragment	after 1650	p. 161	Keyboard

Fantasia 6/F (11)

4. GB-Och MMS 979–983 *c.*1575–1581 No. 157
(*Laudate pueri* in Cantiones Sacrae 1575)
(24. GB-Lbl Add. MSS 17786–91 before 1610–1620s; 1st layer completed *c.*1610
Behold now praise the Lord; untexted f.33v)

Fantasia 6/g1 (12)

6. GB-Ob MS Mus. Sch. e. 423 after 1577–1589 No. 28 p.303a
12. GB-Ob MSS Tenbury 379–84 (P) started 1590s? f.42v
(no galliard or coda)
13. GB-Ob MSS Tenbury 341–4 (P) early 17th century ff.55v, 68, 67v, 57v, 58v
24. GB-Lbl Add. MSS 17786–91 before 1610–1620s
(1st layer completed *c.*1610)
(coda added later) f.3v
35. GB-Lbl MS 29996 mid-16th– mid-17th f.211–213v Keyboard

Fantasia 6/g2 (13)

6. GB-Ob MS Mus. Sch. e. 423 after 1577–1589 No. 30 p.307
21. GB-Lbl Add. MSS 37402–6 completed after 1606 ff.50, 49v, 53, 70, 51v
26. (Print) *Psalmes, Songs and Sonnets* (London 1611) No. 26
30. NYp MSS Drexel 4180–5 *c.*1615–1625 ff.168v, 179v, 183v, 165v, 150v, 71v
35. GB-Lbl MS 29996 mid-16th –mid-17th f. 213v–216 Keyboard

In Nomines

In Nomine 4/1 (16)

15. GB-Ob MSS Tenbury 354–8 (P) early 17th century f.17v
25. GB-Ob MSS Mus. Sch. d. 212–6 completed *c.*1610 f.14v

In Nomine 4/2 (17)

25. GB-Ob MSS Mus. Sch. d. 212–6 completed *c.*1610 f.17v

In Nomine 5/1 (18)

2. GB-Lbl Add. MS 31390 — from *c.*1568; corrected 1578 — ff. 43v–44r

In Nomine 5/2 (19)

3. GB-Ob MS Tenbury 1464 — 1570–1575 — f.8
8. GB-Lbl Add. MS 32377 — 1585–1590 — f.9v
11. GB-Ob MS Tenbury 389 — *c.*1595–1613 — f.72
25. GB-Ob MSS Mus. Sch. d. 212–6# — completed *c.*1610 — f.7 (bassus f. 33)

In Nomine 5/3 (20)

25. GB-Ob MSS Mus. Sch. d. 212–6 — completed *c.*1610 — ff.36, 10
33. GB-Lbl Add. MSS 39550–4 — 1630s–1644 — p. 56

In Nomine 5/4 (21)

2. GB-Lbl Add. MS 31390 — from *c.*1568; corrected 1578 — ff. 58v–59r
25. GB-Ob MSS Mus. Sch. d. 212–6 — completed *c.*1610 — ff.40, 14
33. GB-Lbl Add. MSS 39550–4 — 1630s–1644 — p. 60

In Nomine 5/5 (22)

2. GB-Lbl Add. MS 31390 — from c. 1568; corrected 1578 — ff. 120v–121r
5. GB-Och MMS 984–8 1581–1588 — No. 85/6
6. GB-Ob MS Mus. Sch. e. 423 — after 1577–1589 — No. 50 p.182
7. GB-Lbl Add. MS 22597 — 1580s? — f.35v
8. GB-Lbl Add. MS 32377 — 1585–1590 — f.8v
11. GB-Ob MS Tenbury 389 — *c.*1595–1613 — f.71
15. GB-Ob MSS Tenbury 354–8 (P) — early 17th century — f.43v
16. GB-Lbl Add. MSS 29401–5 (P) — *c.*1613 — f.55v
18. GB-Lbl Add. MS 34049 (P) — early 17th century — f.47v
25. GB-Ob MSS Mus. Sch. d. 212–6 — completed *c.*1610 — f.53
28. GB-Lcm MS 2049 — early 17th century — ff.15v, 12v, 13v
29. GB-Lbl Egerton 3665 — *c.*1613–19 — f.156v
30. NYp MSS Drexel 4180–5 — *c.*1615–1625 — ff.71v, 71r, 73v, 67v, 48v

35. GB-Lbl MS 29996 mid-16th –mid-17th f.68v–69 Keyboard

Latin-titled works

***Sermone blando* a 3** (23)

14. GB-Lbl Add. MS 29246 (P)	early 17th century	f.14v	Lute
20. GB-Lbl Add. MSS 18936–9 (P family)	*c.*1615	f.6v	

***Christe qui lux* (I)** (24)

14. GB-Lbl Add. MS 29246 (P)	early 17th century	f.46r	Lute
15. GB-Ob MSS Tenbury 354–8 (P)	early 17th century	f.24v	

***Christe qui lux* (II)** (25)

1. GB-Lbl Add. MSS 30480–30484	*c.*1570–1590s	f. 70, 74v, 69v, 71v	
15. GB-Ob MSS Tenbury 354–8 (P)	early 17th century	f.24	

***Christe qui lux* (III)** (26)

15. GB-Ob MSS Tenbury 354–8 (P)	early 17th century	f.23	

Christe redemptor (27)

14. GB-Lbl Add. MS 29246 (P)	early 17th century	f.48v	Lute
15. GB-Ob MSS Tenbury 354–8 (P)	early 17th century	f.22	

Miserere (28)

14. GB-Lbl Add. MS 29246 (P)	early 17th century	f.48	
Lute			
15. GB-Ob MSS Tenbury 354–8 (P)	early 17th century	f.23	
20. GB-Lbl Add. MSS 18936–9 (P family)	*c.*1615	ff.20v & 3v	

Salvator mundi (29)

14. GB-Lbl Add. MS 29246 (P)	early 17th century	f.47v	Lute

***Sermone blando* a 4 (I)** (30)

14. GB-Lbl Add. MS 29246 (P)	early 17th century	f.15v	Lute

***Sermone blando* a 4 (II)** (31)

15. GB-Ob MSS Tenbury 354–8 (P)	early 17th century	f.23r	

***Te lucis* (I)** (32)

14. GB-Lbl Add. MS 29246 (P)	early 17th century	f.44v	Lute

***Te lucis* (II)** (33)

14. GB-Lbl Add. MS 29246 (P)	early 17th century	f.41v	Lute

Variations

***Browning* Fantasy** (10)

2. GB-Lbl Add. MS 31390	from *c.*1568; corrected 1578		
		ff. 124v–125r	
5. GB-Och MMS 984–8 1581–1588		No. 73	
6. GB-Ob MS Mus. Sch. e. 423	after 1577–1589	No. 29 p.149	
8. GB-Lbl Add. MS 32377	1585–1590	f.2r	
9. US-Ws MS V.a. 408	*c.*1590	f.1	
11. GB-Ob MS Tenbury 389	*c.*1595–1613	ff.86–88	
32. GB-Lbl Add. MSS 17792–96	1620s–30s	ff. 72v, 73r, 72v, 43r, 71r	
35. GB-Lbl MS 29996	mid-16th –mid-17th	f.153v	Keyboard

Prelude & Ground (9)

8. GB-Lbl Add. MS 32377	1585–1590	f.2r	
10. *My Ladye Nevell's Booke* (GB-Lbl) *The Seconde Grownde*	1591	No. 30	Keyboard
32. GB-Lbl Add. MSS 17792–96 (Prelude only)	1620s–30s	f. 58r in all except 17795, f.28r	

Appendix Two

Further details of sources containing Byrd's consort music listed in probable chronological order.

Manuscripts from before 1580

GB-Lbl Add. MSS 30480–4 (1)

This is the only early source to contain a Latin-titled work by Byrd. Although probably begun *c.*1570, the manuscript was not completed for nearly 50 years.[1] The eight textless pieces among the eclectic collection of 87 texted and untexted vocal works are a mixture of instrumental music and vocal pieces transcribed without text for instrumental performance, including one In Nomine.[2] The partbooks belonged to Thomas Hamond (d. 1662) from near Bury St Edmunds in Suffolk, who acquired them when they were around 45 years old.[3] The paper in these partbooks have been dated from the mid-1560s.[4] In her research into printed borders in sixteenth-century music papers, Katherine Butler links these partbooks to the printer Thomas East through the use of a decorative border fleuron, and particularly to the slightly later period of 1567–1572, when East was working with Henry Middleton.[5] The manuscript is the work of several scribes, is well-used and full of corrections. [6]

Christe qui lux (II) is entered into the manuscript after Latin motets by Byrd, Tallis, Sheppard and White and is followed by a galliard and Parsley's 'Clock' (*The Song upon the dial*). An In Nomine and an untitled work are found a few folios later. Part of Parsons's *De la court* was added soon after. At a later date, Parsons's *Ut re mi* and a *Lachrimae* by Thomas Weelkes (1576–1623) were inserted in the manuscript.[7] Katherine Butler has suggested that *Christe qui lux* (II) was entered at the end of the first layer in the 1570s.

The texted music consists mainly of English services and anthems, and the untexted of Latin motets and consort songs. Composers include Tallis, William Mundy, Tye and White and a small number of continental composers. The origin of the manuscript is unknown but it may have been collected in East Anglia or London. [8]

GB-Lbl Add. MS 31390 (2)

Add. MS 31390 contains three of Byrd's five-part In Nomines and his *Browning* Fantasy. Consisting of one table book, it contains the largest collection of textless music copied in

England in the sixteenth century, written so that the performers play or sing sitting round a table. Composers of the consort works include Strogers, Ferrabosco I, Parsons, Tye, Edward Blancks (*c.*1550–1633), Robert Johnson (*c.*1500–1560) and Clement Woodcock as well as Byrd. The remaining music consists of untexted vocal works, mainly motets and secular pieces, by English composers including Byrd, and continental composers including Clemens, Nicolas Gombert (*c.*1495–*c.*1560) and Orlando de Lassus (1530/32–1594). The 66 consort pieces are carefully grouped by numbers of parts. Several genres are represented, including 42 In Nomines, as well as Latin-titled works, fantasias, *Browning* fantasies and Parsons's *De la court.* The manuscript was most likely compiled between 1568 and 1578. Its scribe is unknown, but the manuscript probably has links with the Chichester area.[9]

In Nomine 5/1 is the fourth In Nomine to be entered in the five-part section. In Nomine 5/4 was added a little later and In Nomine 5/5 at the end of the manuscript. Byrd's *Browning* Fantasy was probably the last work to be added.[10] As well as the In Nomines, the consort works include 11 Latin-titled works, *Browning* Fantasies by Woodcock and Henry Stonings, *Hackney*, also by Woodcock, Parsons's *De la court* and *The song called trumpets* and Ferrabosco I's six-part 'fantasia'. As well as almost all of Tye's consort works (28 out of 31), the manuscript contains eighteen textless vocal works by van Wilder, mainly chansons. Add. MS 31390 would appear to have been corrected in 1578; the corrections are in the same hand as the rest of the music but copying could have started a number of years earlier, possibly 1568.[11] It can only be conjecture as to whether the manuscript was used for singing, viol playing or a mixture of voices and viols or other instruments. The parts could have been copied for viol players.

GB-Ob MS Tenbury 1464_(3)

This manuscript, thought to date from before 1580, consists of a single bass part and contains 62 works. These are mainly Latin motets. Fifteen textless works are found near the beginning of the manuscript; eleven, mainly In Nomines, have been conceived without a text. Five of the consort works are by Tye. Byrd's In Nomine 5/2 is the first of a group of eight In Nomines that follows Latin motets and an extract from Taverner's *Mean Mass*. Composers of the motets include Robert Fayrfax (1464–1521), Tallis, Taverner, Johnson, White, Clemens, Lassus, van Wilder and Gombert. This collection was probably aimed at singers. Joseph Kerman dates this manuscript to *c.*1570–75.[12] It contains almost all of the known music of Osbert Parsley, who was a singing man at Norwich Cathedral and additions at the end include music by William Cobbold (1560–1639) who was organist at Norwich from 1595, which suggest a close association between the manuscript and Norwich. Edwards states that the majority of the music contained in the manuscript was probably written by the mid-1560s'.[13]

Manuscripts from the 1580s

GB-Och 979–983 (4)

Copied between *c.* 1575–81 by John Baldwin, who may have intended it to be a collector's anthology,[14] this collection is made up almost exclusively of Latin motets by English and Scottish composers. Vocal music with sacred texts dates from pre- to post-Reformation and includes motets later published by Byrd in 1591. It contains 30 Latin motets by Byrd and over 40 vocal pieces by Sheppard, as well as significant contributions by Tallis, Taverner, Mundy and White. There are just three works by continental composers. As well as four six-part consort works by Byrd (Fantasia 6/F) Parsons, Daman and Taverner, a further two consort works – three-part pieces by John Baldwin and Elway Bevin (*c.*1554–1638) – follow a little later in the manuscript, plus the copy of the 1575 *Cantiones Sacrae.*

The partbooks consist of sheets of paper presumed to have been issued by Tallis and Byrd under their 1575 patent.[15] Baldwin was astute in selecting which material he collected and he must have had access to excellent sources, probably associated with the Chapel Royal.[16] There are no In Nomines in the manuscript.

GB–Och 984–988 (5)

Known as the Dow part books, this is also probably a collector's anthology, copied mainly by Robert Dow. (Two works were added by John Baldwin.) Dow was made a Fellow of All Souls College, Oxford in 1575 and was Bursar of Law at the College from 1585 until 1587.[17] The manuscript contains paper identified by Fenlon and Milsom as having been issued by Tallis and Byrd, meaning it must date from after 1575.[18] Nineteen textless works are found in a collection of 127 works, mostly English anthems, Latin motets and consort songs of which fourteen are consort pieces. The textless works are entered as a group following consort songs, suggesting this was a collection for viol players, especially with the inclusion of Byrd's and Woodcock's *Browning* fantasies.

The music falls into three sections; the first 54 works are (numbered) Latin motets by a wide range of sixteenth-century English composers (including Byrd, White, Strogers, Ferrabosco I and Parsons) and two by Lassus. In contrast to the previous manuscript there is just one vocal Latin work each from Sheppard and Taverner. The second section contains English anthems and consort songs, mainly by Byrd, followed by the group of 19 works without text. These open with the *Browning* fantasies by Byrd and Woodcock followed by a *Miserere* by Mallorie (*fl.* *c.*1575). Tye's *Rubem quem* and Parsons's *De la court* come next, interspersed with four chansons by Maillard, Lassus, Verdelot and van Wilder. There then follows a group of nine In Nomines by Parsons, Byrd, Strogers, Bull, White, Tye and Woodcock. Byrd's In Nomine 5/5 is the second of these after Parsons's five-part In Nomine. The section concludes with a mixture of music including five consort songs by Byrd and another In Nomine by Brewster (*fl* mid-sixteenth century). The final section mainly consists of English songs.

The partbooks ended up at Windsor through a Fellow of All Souls, Giles Thomson, who became Dean of Windsor in 1603, hence the presence of two additional works copied into the manuscript by Baldwin.[19] The collection might been Dow's way of commenting on the religious persecution prevalent in 1581 and 1582.[20]

GB-Ob MS Mus. Sch. e. 423 (6)

This is a single bass partbook, containing only 11 consort pieces in a collection of 132 works, owned by Byrd's patron John, first Lord Petre. Like GB-Och 984–988, this manuscript contains mainly English anthems and Latin motets. It consists of three sections, the second being devoted to five-part works and the third to six-part. These three sections initially existed separately, each with its own numbering system. It was assembled with empty folios between the sections. The earliest manuscript paper, found in the second and third sections, has a watermark dated to 1577, indicating the earliest date for copying. These two sections were started before the first and the scribe, John Bentley, worked on them concurrently.[21]

The first section consists of 37 pieces of English vocal works beginning with anthems by Parsons, Tallis, Sheppard and Byrd, mainly in five parts. The second section contains 48 five-part sacred Latin vocal works, mainly motets by Byrd, Mundy, Ferrabosco I, Taverner, White and Parsons. Among these are nine consort works by English composers. The first group of three consist of Parsons's *De la court*, Byrd's *Browning* Fantasy and *Sermone blando* by Mundy. Tye's *Amavit* and *The point* by a little known composer, Gregorie Ballard, are entered separately and four In Nomines are entered as a group, the third and fourth of which are Byrd's In Nomine 5/5 and Parsons's five-part In Nomine. The third six-part section contains 27 six-part Latin sacred vocal pieces by most of the composers found in the first and second sections plus three works by Sheppard and William Whitbroke (*fl.* 1520–50) and initially ended with Byrd's Fantasia 6/g1 added by 1586.[22] At some time after 1586, five consort songs by Byrd were added at the very beginning of the manuscript.[23] The manuscript appears to have been bound in 1589, by which time an Italian song by Ferrabosco I had been added at the end of the third section and finally Byrd's Fantasia 6/g2.[24] No motets published in the 1575 *Cantiones Sacrae* are included in MS Mus. Sch. e. 423, supporting the dating of the 1580s.[25] Some motets not published until 1589 and 1591 are found in the manuscript.

GB-Lbl Add. MS 22597 (7)

One partbook survives of this manuscript, which originally contained 56 works, some of which are missing;[26] most of the music replicates pieces found in Add. MS 31390 (2). Fenlon and Milsom give the late 1570s as the earliest possible copying date.[27] A distinctive figure of eight pattern is found in the borders that is not found in printed English works before 1584.[28] There are, however, subtle differences in the figure-of-eight pattern found in the manuscript compared with other English papers, making its provenance hard to determine; the paper may have been imported from the Continent.[29] The layout of Add. MS 22597 is similar to that of the Dow partbooks, suggesting that it was compiled in the 1580s.[30]

The manuscript falls into two sections. The first consists of 18 texted pieces, mainly English anthems by Byrd, Tallis, Mundy, Parsons and van Wilder, plus anonymous works and two pieces by Lassus; van Wilder's *Aspice Domine* was added without text after the 18 texted works. The second section probably originally contained 34 untexted works, including three chansons by van Wilder and an Italian madrigal as well as three texted anthems. The fourteen surviving (out of 16) consort works include eight In Nomines found two groups of four. The first group consists of In Nomines by Tye, Poynt (*fl. c.*1555–84), Byrd (In Nomine 5/5) and Parsons (five-part). Tye's *Rubem Quem* is also included in this group. The second group are by Tallis and White. Part of Parsons's *De la court*, Tye's *Amavit* and Johnson's *The Bells* (or *A Knell of Johnson*) are also found in the manuscript.

GB-Lbl MS Add. 32377 (8)

This is a single partbook, mainly consisting of treble parts. The manuscript begins with 47 untexted works, 29 of which appear to be consort music. The 20 In Nomines, mainly in five parts, include works by Ferrabosco I, Byrd, Parsons, White, Tye, Brewster, Strogers and Parsley. The manuscript opens with Byrd's *Browning* Fantasy, the Prelude and Ground and Ferrabosco I's four-part *Fantasy*. The group of 20 In Nomines are found from folio 7, beginning with Ferrabosco I's In Nomines III and I, followed by Byrd's In Nomines 5/5 and 5/2. The remaining consort pieces include Parsons's *De la court* and (William?) Mundy's *O mater mundi*. Latin motets in five and six parts by Sheppard, White, Mundy, Tallis, Byrd and Parsons make up most of the rest of the music, the majority of which are texted. Daman's six-part *Beates Omnes* is found among these.

The manuscript may be associated with Exeter Cathedral. On folio 80, the county of Dorset is mentioned several times and Somerset once; the same page also contains the words 'Mr Hugh Geare His boock'.[31] Geare was a vicar general at Exeter Cathedral from 1572. Add. MS 32377 would seem to have been intended for viol players. Viols were known to have been acquired by Exeter Cathedral in 1550 and it is highly likely that the vicars choral were playing viols later in the century, performing the music found in Add. MS 32377.[32] The dates 1585 and 1588 appear on the final page of the manuscript indicating when it may have been completed.[33]

Manuscripts *c.* 1590–1600

US-Ws V.a. 408 (9)

What is likely to have been the earliest manuscript from the decade, US-Ws V.a. 408 (9), is a single surviving cantus partbook. The 35 works consist of a mixture of secular continental pieces, motets, anthems and consort music. Originally a collection of 27 textless works, eight texted English anthems were added later.[34] There are 16 consort works which include six In Nomines, and several Latin-titled works. Byrd, Ferrabosco I, Edward Blancks, (William?) Mundy, Tye and Johnson (II) are the most prominent composers of this music. Seven of the remaining textless works are madrigals by Orlando Merulo (1533–1604) and Lassus. Byrd receives prominence with the *Browning* Fantasy being the first work to be entered. The last, untitled, textless piece in the manuscript and the anthems were added by a different hand from the rest. The manuscript might have belonged to Matthew Jeffries (*c.*1558–*c.*1615), who was at Wells Cathedral from the 1580s. The seven anthems at the end of the manuscript are by Jeffries and four consort works by him, including two In Nomines, are also found in the manuscript.[35]

My Ladye Nevell's Booke (10),

This collection of Byrd's keyboard music, copied by Baldwin, consists of forty-two numbered pieces made up of grounds, paired pavans and galliards, variations, voluntaries, fantasias and a suite of descriptive pieces.[36] Placed among keyboard variations is a version of Byrd's Fantasia 5/C adapted for keyboard, entitled *A lesson of Voluntarie*, a keyboard version (*The Second Grownde*), of the ground used by Byrd in his consort Prelude and Ground, and a keyboard version of the consort Pavan 5/c. This 'First Pavan' is the first of nine pavans, seven of which have an accompanying galliard. The consort version is presumed to pre-date this keyboard version of the Pavan 5/c. Richard Rastall writes that 'stylistically the consort version must be the original', an opinion also held by Neighbour.[37]

GB-Ob MS Tenbury 389 (11)

The Tudor Partbooks Project suggests that this single cantus partbook dates from *c.*1595–1613.[38] It was certainly copied over a significant period of time. The majority of the 127 pieces consists of texted Latin motets (65), English anthems and songs.[39] Eighteen of the 21 consort pieces are In Nomines or have Latin titles. [40] A large number of composers are represented in the manuscript including Byrd, Sheppard, Tallis, van Wilder, Clemens, Parsons, John Redford (*c.*1500–1547), Lassus, Ferrabosco I and Gombert.

The manuscript falls into five distinct sections. It opens with three texted five-part motets taken from the *Cantiones Sacrae* of 1589 followed by seven five-part textless pieces, the first of which is Parsons's five-part In Nomine and the second, *De la court.* The second section consists mainly of five-part textless anthems and two textless songs by Philip van Wilder. The third and fourth sections contain motets. The first part of the fifth section consists of a group of nine textless pieces, eight of which are In Nomines. The first entered is an In Nomine by Tye followed by Byrd's In Nomine 5/5 and In Nomine 5/2. Others are by Taverner, Johnson and Tallis. Up to this point entries are mainly in the same hand, probably writing in the 1590s. After that, the manuscript was added to in a haphazard order and different hands appear.[41] The remaining works are a mixture of motets, songs and anthems and nine further consort pieces. Byrd's *Browning* Fantasy, entered in the original hand, follows shortly after between Latin motets by Redford and Parsons. After that, a number of textless works appear at random, including Taverner's *Quemadmodum*, three In Nomines and right at the end, two Misereres. The provenance of the manuscript is unknown.

Manuscripts from after 1600

The Paston manuscripts (*c.*1590 to the early 1600s)

GB-Ob MSS Tenbury_379–84 (12)

The first 89 breves of Fantasia 6/g1, distinctly shorter than the version known from other sources with its galliard and coda, are found near the end of the manuscript devoted to 43 six-part motets, the majority of which are by continental composers, including Giovanni Pierluigi da Palestrina (1535/6–1594), Thomas Crecquillon (d. 1557?), Lassus, Merulo, and Gombert; a small number are by Ferrabosco I and Byrd. The fantasia is entered after the second part of a Byrd motet, *Circumspice Jerusalem*, and it is thought it was added after 1600.[42]

GB-Ob MSS Tenbury 341–4 (13),

Most of the music in this set of partbooks consists of Latin motets plus Lamentations and excerpts from Mass settings. Almost all the music is by English composers, with 27 contributions by Byrd and significant numbers of works by Taverner, Tallis and Ferrabosco I. Fantasia 6/g1 is entered between Byrd's Latin motet, *Attollite portas*, and his anthem, *Christ is risen*. The hand in this manuscripts is that of William Corbett, who also copied Paston's lute books. He has been identified from his writing of English texts in the Tenbury manuscripts, where the writing is identical to that found in a letter which he wrote for Paston to the Earl of Rutland in 1587.[43]

GB-Lbl Add. MS 29246 (14)

A partbook for the upper voice for this manuscript collection of music for lute has never been found. William Corbett is identified as the copyist.[44] The bulk of the music is made up of Latin motets, and mass settings by English composers including Byrd, Fayrfax, Taverner, Sheppard, Tallis, White, Tye, and Mundy, with a small number of works by continental composers.[45] Byrd's three-part and first four-part *Sermone blando* are entered after 46 Latin motets (this is the only source for the first four-part *Sermone blando*). Fantasias 3/C1 and 3/C2 are added a little later following three works by Lassus. Fantasia 3/C3 appears after five of Byrd's Latin motets. A group of consort works then appears after Latin motets by continental composers. This consists of eight fantasias by White and Byrd, the latter's Fantasia 4/a being the second and Fantasia 4/g the fifth in the group, followed by eight Latin-titled works, two by White and six by Byrd. These include two further works by Byrd that appear only in this manuscript, *Te lucis* (I) and *Salvator Mundi*. Finally seven In Nomines by White, Tallis, Taverner, Parsons and Strogers are found near the end of the collection following five Latin vocal works by White.

GB-Ob MSS Tenbury 354–8 (15)

The music in these partbooks mainly comprises liturgical and non-liturgical Latin vocal music by a wide range of English composers, with significant contributions from Taverner, Fayrfax, White, Tallis and Byrd. There is just one English-texted work (by Tallis). The music is organised in two sections, the first of four-part works and the second of five-part. Very little of the first section is fully texted; there is greater accuracy and consistency in the five-part section.[46] A group of 13 consort works are found at the end of the four-part vocal works. Seven are In Nomines, of which four are by White; the third entered is Byrd's In Nomine 4/1. Taverner's original four-part In Nomine is the last entered. Six Latin-titled consort works by Byrd then follow this, including *Christe qui lux* (III) and *Sermone blando* a 4 (II), which appear only in this manuscript. Four In Nomines are found almost at the end of the second section. Byrd's In Nomine 5/5 is the last of these entered.

GB-Lbl Add. MSS 29401–5 (16)

This set of partbooks is one of two sets of Paston partbooks dedicated to Byrd's English-texted songs in which four five-part In Nomines are included at the end of a collection of 55 works. Parsons's is the first entered and Byrd's In Nomine 5/5 is the last. The other two are by Bull and White.

GB-Lbl Add. MSS 41156–8 (17)

The vast majority of music in these three partbooks comprises sections of the Mass and 40 motets for three voices or three-part sections from larger works. A significant number are anonymous; the remaining works include Tomas L. de Victoria (*c.* 1548–1611), Byrd, Parsons, Taverner and Tallis among the composers. A group of six three-part textless works, of which three are consort works, are found in the manuscript. *Ut re mi fa sol la* by Ferrabosco I is followed by Fantasia 3/C3, three Byrd songs without text and Fantasia 3/C2 which is copied before Byrd's *Ave maris stella.* An anonymous fantasia appears in the four-part music.

GB-Lbl Add. MS 34049 (18)

Only a cantus partbook survives from the original set. It contains 22 five-part works, both texted and untexted; all are Latin motets and masses, except for three In Nomines by White, Bull and Byrd (5/5), found at the end of the collection. The vocal music is by Fayrfax, Tallis, Taverner and White with one work each by Johnson (I), Mundy and Byrd. The last two works in the manuscript are Byrd's In Nomine 5/5 and his *Beata es virgo Maria.*

GB-Lcm MS 2036 (19)

This is a set of three partbooks in which four works out of 53 are consort works. Fantasias 3/C1 and 3/C2 are entered after Latin motets and mass extracts by Victoria and Lassus and before an Agnus Dei by Taverner and motets by Byrd. Ferrabosco I's *Ut re mi fa sol la* is found later as is an anonymous fantasia. The rest of the music consists of sacred and secular vocal music, mainly by Lassus (seven pieces), Victoria (five) and Byrd (eleven), a substantial part of which is untexted. All the music is transposed up a fourth.[47]

GB-Lbl Add. MSS 18936–9 (20)

Associated with the Paston household, this manuscript consists of four partbooks surviving from of a set of five, containing over 200 works including sections or parts of Masses and Magnificats, 32 motets, 49 English secular works and nine identifiable consort pieces. The latter consist of seven Latin-titled works, an In Nomine and fantasia, entered individually throughout the manuscript and not in any particular order. Byrd's three-part *Sermone blando* is the first to be entered near the beginning of the manuscript; his *Miserere* follows after Latin motets. The composers of the vocal music are mainly English with a significant contribution by Byrd. There are also 13 Latin vocal works by Victoria.

Manuscripts not in the Paston collection dating from *c.* 1600 to the 1640s

GB-Lbl Add. MS 37402–6 (21),

As well as music by English composers, this collection contains two unattributed works by Lassus, which are followed by Byrd's Fantasia 6/g2. Parsons's *De la court* is entered shortly after. The Pavan 5/c, of which one part is missing, is the last consort work found in the manuscript. The other consort pieces in the manuscript consist of an unattributed fantasia, *Laudes Deo* by Tye, a fantasia by Peerson and three 5-part fantasias by Thomas Lupo (1571–1627). The Pavan 5/c is the only dance in the collection.

Little is known about the original owners or scribes of the manuscript but the paper has been identified as having been printed between 1575 and 1600.[48] Textless madrigals were probably entered in 1596, the scribe being interested in them for instrumental performance.[49] James Pearson acquired the manuscript in 1600. He entered vocal music, almost all by English composers, that was suitable for performance by viols. This included transforming some five-part vocal music into consort songs for vocal duet and three viols. The madrigals were copied with the words contained in just the two upper parts.[50] The manuscript was completed sometime soon after 1606.[51]

Kassel MS mus. 125, (22)

A complete set of parts for Byrd's Pavan 5/c is found in the five partbooks of this German manuscript, copied around 1600 and devoted almost entirely to 53 pavans. All are apparently by English composers including John Dowland (1563–1626), Holborne, Morley, Strogers and Philips, or in an English style.[52] The paper found in the manuscript is local to Kassel. Many of the pavans, unlike Byrd's five-part pavan, appear to have been adapted from four-part works and pieces for mixed consort.

GB-Lbl Add. MSS 34800A–C (23)

Byrd's Fantasia 3/C1 is found at the beginning of a second section of a set of three partbooks containing 50 pieces. The music is a mixture of untexted vocal music and fantasias. Each partbook has four sections and the contents were probably copied in the order in which they now stand.[53] The first part is thought to have been copied before 1605; it contains untexted canzonets by Morley and six three-part fantasias by Blancks. The second section, in a different hand, begins with Fantasia 3/C1, which is followed by accurate copies of extracts from Byrd's *Gradualia* of 1605. This suggests that the manuscript is also an accurate source for the fantasia. The third section contains three-part untexted works including fantasias by Gibbons copied after 1620 from the print of that date. The final section contains a piece for three viols by Henry Losemore (1607–1670) added later, as were three-part consort pieces by Michael East (1580–1648), and some other seventeenth century pieces.

GB-Lbl Add. MSS 17786–91 (24)

Several of the composers of the music in this collection have a particular connection with New College and Magdalen, in particular Richard Nicolson (*c.*1563–1638),William Wigthorpe (*c.*1570–*c.*1610) and John Okeover (?1595–1663).[54] Forty-five of the 80 works are identifiable as consort music and the remainder are for voices and viols. It includes play songs that were suitable for use by Oxford choristers, either informally, for training or for use in dramatic performances, and music for viol consort.[55] Five books are textless; the sixth supplies a duplicate voice part for some of the consort songs in the manuscripts.

The music is divided into groups of five, six and seven parts. Six consort pieces open the manuscript; the first three consist of Parsons's *De la court* followed by Byrd's Fantasia 5/C and three parts of Fantasia 6/g1, found among the five-part works. The five-part section concludes with pavans and fantasias by Okeover, Richard Dering (*c.*1580–1630) and John Ward (1590–1638). The six-part music consists mainly of almains and fantasias by Peerson. Two seven-part works are anthems by Weelkes and Thomas Tomkins. Two bass viol duets by John Coperario (or Cooper, after 1570–1626) are also found in one partbook, MS 17790.

Composers of the vocal music in the manuscript include Parsons, Farrant, Weelkes and Nicolson and a large number of the consort songs are by Wigthorpe. MSS 17786–91 contain the largest known collection of his compositions. Craig Monson suggests that the manuscript would appear to be the work of one scribe, probably Wigthorpe himself, who matriculated in 1598, and that it was begun before 1610.[56] David Smith agrees, pointing to some music ascribed to Wigthorpe being actually arrangements of other composers including Dowland.[57]

GB-Ob MSS Mus. Sch. d. 212–6 (25)

This manuscript consists of two sets of five partbooks; it is the only known anthology devoted solely to the In Nomine. The first 64 In Nomines, consisting of 24 four-part followed by 40 five-part pieces, are clearly a collection of loose sheets that have been bound together.[58]

The composers include Tye, Taverner, Parsons, White, Byrd, Ferrabosco I, Bull, Gibbons and Stonings. These In Nomines do not include any works later than those by Gibbons. Edwards suggests they were copied by 1610 as otherwise the collection would have included In Nomines by other Jacobean composers.[59] Nine In Nomines added later include works by John Ward (1590–1638) and Simon Ives (1600–1662), dating this section to several years later. Finally, ten anthems for voices and viols, including works by Bull, Nicolson, Thomas Tomkins and Byrd, were added as an appendix, probably after 1632.[60] The 24 four-part In Nomines begin with works by Tye and Taverner. Byrd's In Nomine 4/1 is the twelfth entered after one by Henry Mudd (d. *c.*1588) and his In Nomine 4/2 appears shortly after, this being its only source. In the 40 five-part In Nomines, Byrd's In Nomine 5/2 is entered fifth after a work by John Mundy. In Nomine 5/3 is entered eighth between Ferrabosco I's In Nomines I and II and In Nomine 5/4 twelfth after Ferabosco I's In Nomine II. Parsons's five-part In Nomine is the nineteenth entered and Byrd's In Nomine 5/5 is the twenty-fifth after an In Nomine by White.

The scribe of the In Nomines is unknown. Monson believes the compiler who added the anthems was Richard Nicolson, organist at Magdalen College Oxford and the first Heather Professor of Music who worked with choristers, which would seem to support the belief that In Nomines were still being played by choirboys.[61]

***Psalmes, Songs and Sonnets* (26)**

Kerry McCarthy describes Byrd's publication of 1611 as 'retrospective'.[62] The music is suitable for performance solely by viols, or by a mixture of voices and viols. Fantasia 4/g is the last but one of the four-part pieces, found between *What is life and worldly pleasure* and *Come let us rejoice unto our Lord.* Fantasia 6/g2 is placed second in the six-part works between *Have mercy upon me O God* (voices and three treble, two tenor and one bass viols) and the motet *This day Christ was born* for six voices. McCarthy and John Morehen both remark about the accuracy of the 1611 edition.[63]

GB-Lbl Add. MS 29427 (27)

Following his graduation from Cambridge, the compiler of this manuscript, Thomas Myriell (*c.*1580–1625, was ordained and after a post in Essex, became Rector of St Stephen's Walbrook, in the City of London, in 1616. He was a friend of John Tomkins (1586–1638), who also moved from Cambridge to London in 1619 to become organist at St Paul's cathedral.[64]

Add. MS 29427 reflects Myriell's musical life moving from Cambridge to London; it appears to have grown haphazardly and is the work of several scribes.[65] It contains three kinds of music: instrumental fantasias and In Nomines, textless versions of Italian madrigals and English vocal works for voices and viols. The collection seems to have initially been made up of 30 pieces of consort music, all three- and four-part fantasias (including Byrd's four-part fantasias 4/a and 4/G), that were combined with another collection of four In Nomines and instrumental versions of 22 Italian madrigals. To this was added a large group of English vocal works. Many of these vocal works are by composers from the London circle round St Paul's, such as John Milton the elder (*c.*1563–1647), Peerson, Thomas Ravenscroft (*c.*1582–*c*1635), Giles Farnaby (c. 1563–1640) and John Tomkins.

The collection opens with ten three-part fantasias by Thomas Lupo, followed by four-part fantasias by Wilbye and Gioseffo Guami (*c.*1540–1611). Vocal pieces were then inserted into the manuscript. A group of 21 textless works follow, 19 of which are consort pieces. The first two are Byrd's Fantasias 4/G and 4/a. The following works include, thirteen four-part fantasias by Alfonso Ferrabosco II (before 1578–1628) and Ferabosco I's five-part In Nomines I and III. All that survives of the original Fantasia 4/G is the altus part found in this manuscript. Byrd recycled it as the motet *In manus tuas* in the *Gradualia* of 1605.

GB-Lcm MS 2049 (28)

Four out of six partbooks contain 36 pieces; 17 are without text, of which 12 were likely to have been instrumentally conceived. These include five-part In Nomines, pavans by Weelkes, *Sermone blando* by (William?) Mundy, a Fancy by Johnson II and part of Parsons's *De la court.* A group of four of the consort works (two of which are fragments) are found after sixteen songs; the third entered is a five-part In Nomine by Poynt (?early to mid-sixteenth century) followed by Byrd's In Nomine 5/5. Works by Lassus and Alexander Striggio (*c.*1536/7–1591) are also found without text in the partbooks. Composers of the songs include Byrd, Dering, Farnaby and Parsons. The source is unknown but the manuscript was likely copied early in the seventeenth century.[66]

MS Egerton 3665 (29)

The 1038 pieces in this manuscript in score, probably copied by Francis Tregian (1574?–1617), are ordered into eleven distinct sections. Section eight contains over a hundred consort works, mainly fantasias, by a number of composers including Thomas Lupo, East, Dering, and John Coprario (*c.*1570–1626) and In Nomines by Parsons, Byrd, Strogers and Mundy. (Byrd's In Nomine 5/5 is entered between Parsons's and Mundy's five-part In

Nomines.) Section ten is devoted to five-part fantasies and pavans by Ferrabosco II and the final, eleventh section of dances has contributions by Philips, Ferrabosco I, Joseph Lupo, Holborne and Thomas Tomkins.

NY-MSS Drexel 4180–5 (30)

This is the largest of John Merro's (d.1639) manuscripts, which he started copying around 1615 and completed by 1625.[67] Certainly it appears to be the first of the three manuscripts to be completed.[68] The last entry is an Ode composed by Gibbons for Charles I's marriage in 1625 suggesting it was bound around this time. More than 80 of the 250 pieces in three to six parts are entered without text; 33 of these are consort works, the remainder are vocal works, mainly Italian madrigals without text.

The first and oldest layer consists of sacred works by Tallis and his contemporaries. Merro appears to initially have set out to make a serious collection of vocal music.[69] As it grew, the nature of the music changed. Madrigals by English composers such as Thomas Tomkins, Weelkes and Wilbye were inserted, as were Italian madrigals, some with titles translated into English and some no titles at all. It seems that the madrigals were intended for performance by viols.[70] The continental motets entered in the manuscript also have no text except for titles. There are four groups of consort works: the first is made up of four fantasias by Thomas Lupo and Dering. The second set, sandwiched between texted English anthems and textless Italian madrigals, is a group of five works in five-parts, these being four In Nomines, the first of which is Byrd's In Nomine 5/5, followed by Parsons's In Nomine, Ferrabosco I's In Nomine I and one by Brewster, and finally Parsons's *De la court.* Three further consort works, Mundy's *Sermone blando*, Parsons's *The song called trumpets* (*Cante cantate*) and Johnson's *Johnson's Knell*, are found following a group of Latin motets. The final group of 21 consort pieces contains Byrd's Fantasia 6/g2 and Fantasia 4/g.

GB-Ob MSS Mus. Sch. D. 245–247 (31)

This is likely to have been the first set of manuscripts Merro started copying, probably around 1610; he added to it until at least 1634.[71] Andrew Ashbee describes these partbooks as the most remarkable of Merro's three manuscripts with its collection of 450 pieces. It includes three-part fantasias by Okeover, Thomas Tomkins, Jenkins, Gibbons and Ferrabosco II. Three parts of Byrd's Fantasia 4/g fall on folio 23 following nine three-part fantasias by Gibbons. Edwards suggests it was copied from Byrd's *Psalmes, Songs and Sonnets* of 1611.[72] A small number of songs are included in the collection, mainly by Morley and Thomas Ford (?–1648?), arranged for viols.

GB-Lbl, Add. MSS 17792–6 (32),

The repertoire contained in the manuscript indicates that copying could not have started before 1620–22 and that it continued into the 1630s. It was complete by Merro's death in 1639.[73] An original final flyleaf piece named 'Tennor' and with Merro's initials 'I.M.' is pasted into one of the modern bindings. The collection is planned in separate sections for each grouping of parts. Byrd's Prelude and Ground[74] (*Praeludium*) and Mundy's *Sermone blando* are entered just before the first pavans by Thomas Tomkins. This is the only source for the Prelude and Ground except for the single cantus part found in GB-Lbl Add, MS 32377. The *Browning Fantasy* is found following songs by Byrd. This version is the only one where the tune is texted each time it appears. In four of the partbooks it is found before a section of fantasias and two In Nomines. (One partbook, Add. MS 17795, contains music, mainly dances, in lute tablature that does not appear in the other partbooks.)

The 156 consort pieces consist of fantasias by composers such as Thomas Tomkins, Gibbons, Jenkins, and William Lawes (1602–1645), and pavans, almains and airs by a variety of composers plus the four five-part Elizabethan consort works including the two pieces by Byrd. The partbooks also contains 44 English anthems as well as motets and consort songs, including works by Byrd, carefully inserted round the instrumental music. Anglican service music by John Lugge (c.1587–after 1647) is a later addition, showing Merro's close connection with cathedral music.

Significantly the partbooks include consort songs for solo voice and viols, especially those by Byrd, which are copied in this form rather than in part-song versions that had become more fashionable by the 1620s. David Smith suggests that all three sets of the Merro partbooks may have deliberately contained duplicate pieces, such as Gibbons three-part fantasias, to provide sufficient material for teaching consort-playing choristers.[75]

GB-Lbl Add. MSS 39550–4 (33)

The owner of GB-Lbl Add. MSS 39550–4, was Sir Nicholas Le Strange (1603–1655), a known viol player from his days at Eton and at Trinity College Cambridge, a centre of viol playing.[76] Music from the first half of the seventeenth century makes up the bulk of the manuscript, consisting mainly of fantasias ('Fancies') in five and six parts including a large number by Coprario and Thomas Lupo. Byrd's In Nomine 5/3, followed by Ferrabsoco I's three five-part In Nomines and finally Byrd's In Nomine 5/4 are found after seven fantasias by Dering.

GB–Ob MSS Mus Sch. C 64–9 (34),

This set of six partbooks containing the Pavan and Galliard 6/C was completed after 1640 and probably compiled in Gloucestershire and Oxford. George Stratford, who matriculated in Oxford in 1625, may have been one of the scribes, as his name appears in the manuscript. Watermarks identify the paper as coming from the 1630s.[77] The 150 consort pieces include music by Gibbons, Thomas Tomkins, Ferrabosco II, Ives, Jenkins, Thomas Lupo and Ward. The bulk of the music consists of fantasias, but sixteen In Nomines are included, none of which are by the first generation of Elizabethan composers.

Keyboard and lute manuscripts completed in the seventeenth century

GB-Lbl Add. MS 29996 (35),

Owned by Thomas Tomkins, this manuscript falls into two parts.[78] It is associated with Winchester, London and Worcester, the latter being where Tomkins was organist, and completed by his death in 1656. The first part, compiled in the mid-sixteenth century, consists of liturgical organ music entered as early as the 1540s, possibly by Richard Wynslate (d.1572), organist and Master of Choristers at Winchester Cathedral.[79] It contains an antiphon for organ by Wynslate and a section devoted to the organ music of Thomas Preston (d. after 1559), organist at St George's Chapel Windsor.[80] Following this are Parsons's five-part In Nomine and Byrd's In Nomine 5/5. The scribe of the Byrd five-part In Nomine added a number of decorations to this keyboard arrangement not found in the original.

The second part of the manuscript contains music for keyboard and music in open score, including fancies (fantasias) by Ferrabosco II, nine Byrd songs, 39 English madrigals and pavans. Byrd's *Browning* Fantasy is found among madrigals after Ferrabosco II's Fancies. His Fantasia 5/C and the two six-part Fantasias 6/g1 and 6/g2 in keyboard score are found later in the manuscript following keyboard music by Nicholas Carleton II (c. 1573–1630) and *A Fancy* by Thomas Tomkins.

GB-Lbl MS Hirsch M.1353 (36);[81]

There is disagreement over the date of this manuscript containing music from the late sixteenth century. Julia Craig-McFeely describes the music as coming from the English repertory of *c.*1595.[82] She believes that the manuscript may have been a copy, or partial copy, made in the early seventeenth century from an earlier manuscript dating from 1595, with the addition of some later pieces. She points out that the folio size of the volume is similar to that of lute collections dating from the 1620s. A variety of papers are found in the manuscript including some manufactured between 1580 and 1596. Other writers have dated the manuscript to 1597.[83] Byrd's Fantasia 4/g must have been inserted in the manuscript after 1611 as it was copied from the 1611 published version. The music comprises 59 pavans, galliards, courants, In Nomines and fantasias. It is a mixture of music by lute composers such as Francis Cutting (c.1550–1595/6), Dowland and Francesco da Milano (1497–1543) and adaptations of consort music for lute. Fantasia 4/g is entered between a Fantasia by Emmanuel Adrianssen (*c.*1554–1604), a Flemish lutenist, and before Richard Allison's (before 1570–before 1610) *Sharp Pavan.*

D-Bds Lübbenau MS Lynar A2 (37)

This manuscript contains a significant number of works by Byrd and Gibbons. It opens with twelve keyboard works, comprising toccatas, canzonas, ricercari and a fugue by Christian Erbach (c.1570–1635) followed by eleven works by Giovanni Gabrieli (*c.*1553–1612) and Tarquinio Merula (1595–1665), including sonatas. The rest of the music consists of 18 works by Byrd and Gibbons and one by Bull, mainly pavans, galliards, and preludes from *Parthenia.* Fantasia 5C is found at the end of the manuscript place next to Byrd's keyboard Fantasia G2.

The manuscript is a companion to D-Bds MS Lynar A1. Opinions have differed as to the origin and dating of the two companion manuscripts. Research in the early 1960s placed them as being of Dutch origin from *c.*1615–20 or German from the 1650s.[84] Further research suggested the manuscripts were compiled *c.*1630 in southern Germany.[85] In more recent research, Pieter Dirksen puts MS Lynar A2 and its companion A1 as having been started *c.*1620 and mainly completed by 1630 in north Germany. MS Lynar A1 is a rich source of Sweelinck's keyboard music and Dirksen points to the use of Anglo-Dutch notation placing both manuscripts close to the tradition of German pupils of Sweelinck.[86]

US-NYp MS Drexel 5612 (38)

This collection of keyboard music, was probably copied in Salisbury.[87] Hilda F. Gervers identifies a watermark in the paper that corresponds to a book published in 1627.[88] This and the manuscript's contents suggest it was compiled between 1620 and 1660. Many of 191 pieces are keyboard arrangements of music for viols. The music mainly consists of pavans, galliards, allemandes, courants, sarabands and jigs, both for court and country and arrangements of well-known melodies. The manuscript is also an important source of keyboard arrangements of viol fantasias by Orlando Gibbons which were added in the 1630s and seven works from *Parthenia,* including Byrd's keyboard Pavan and Galliard, *The Earl of Salisbury.* Seven scribes can be identified; the first copied 120 pieces and planned the organisation of the manuscript.

The composers contributing to the manuscript mainly consist of those working in the latter part of the sixteenth century and first part of the seventeenth century. Byrd, Bull and Gibbons appear prominently in the collection, contributing 63 works between them. The keyboard version of Byrd's viol Pavan 5/c is placed with a galliard before two other paired keyboard pavans and galliards by Byrd.

F-PC MS Rés. 1122 (39)

This manuscript, mainly of Thomas Tomkins's own compositions, includes In Nomines, dances and keyboard versions of his viol fantasies, three pieces by Bull and six by Byrd, including keyboard arrangements of Fantasias 4/g and 5/C. The manuscript opens with two keyboard pieces entitled *Ut re mi fa* by Byrd and Bull. These are followed by the arrangements of the two Byrd consort fantasias, 4/g and 5/C, which in turn are followed by two consort fantasias by Tomkins adapted for keyboard.[89]

Both of Tomkins's keyboard arrangements of Byrd's two works are of interest. The adaptation of Fantasia 4/g, because it appears to have been copied from an early version[90] and the keyboard version of the five-part Fantasia is important because of its accuracy, in spite of added ornamentation by Tomkins.

GB-Och MS 1113 (40)

The 55 pieces in the first 130 pages of this manuscript are mainly of Italian origin, with a significant number by Girolamo Frescobaldi (1583–1643). The remainder of the manuscript is devoted almost exclusively to keyboard works by English composers, including ThomasTomkins, Bull, Gibbons and Philips. Byrd's keyboard Fantasia G2 is found towards the beginning of the collection of English music after a voluntary attributed to Benjamin Cosyn (*c.*1580–1653). A fragment of Fantasia 5/C follows a fantasia attributed to Gibbons and another voluntary contributed to Cosyn.[91] There is disagreement as to the scribe of MS 1113 but the most likely candidate is William Ellis, organist at St John's College Oxford from 1639.[92] Candace Bailey argues that the manuscript dates from sometime in the early 1650s, linking it Johann Jakob Froberger's visit to London in 1652 or 1653, when it is likely he brought Frescobaldi's music to England.[93]

GB-Lcm, MS 2093 (41)

This is a retrospective compilation collected over several decades from the 1660s containing thirteen bars of Byrd's Fantasia 4/a.[94] Twenty-one pieces are preludes or voluntaries, and the remainder are grounds, fantasias, a trumpet air, song arrangements and dances and a figured-bass exercise by a number of composers including Bull, John Blow (1649–1708), Dowland,

Gibbons, Matthew Locke (*c.*1621–1677) and Weelkes. The fragment of Fantasia 4/a is found in the middle of the collection following a voluntary and song by Blow and before Byrd's keyboard Fantasia C3 and voluntaries by Weelkes.[95] The manuscript is an important source for keyboard performance practice.[96]

1 Edwards, 'The Sources of Elizabethan Consort Music', pp. 122–5; Butler, 'From Liturgy and the Education of Choirboys to Protestant Domestic Music-Making: The History of the 'Hamond' Partbooks (GB-Lbl: Add. MSS 30480-4)', p. 29.

2 Neighbour, *The Consort and Keyboard Music of William Byrd*, p. 55n.

3 Katherine Butler, 'From Liturgy and the Education of Choirboys to Protestant Domestic Music-Making: The History of the 'Hamond' Partbooks (GB-Lbl: Add. MSS 30480-4)' *Royal Musical Association Research* Chronicle, 50/1 (2019),p. 29.

4 Fenlon and Milsom, '"Ruled Paper Imprinted": Music Paper and Patents in Sixteenth-Century England', p. 161.

5 Butler, 'Printed Borders for Sixteenth Century Music or Music Paper and the Early Career of Music Printer Thomas East (*c.* 1540–1608), p. 4; Butler, 'From Liturgy and the Education of Choirboys to Protestant Domestic Music-Making', p.31.

6 Butler, 'From Liturgy and the Education of Choirboys to Protestant Domestic Music-Making', p. 36.

7 Edwards, p. 125.

8 Butler, From Liturgy and the Education of Choirboys to Protestant Domestic Music-Making', p. 64.

9 A petition dated 1596 regarding the living of Pagham found on folio 28 on behalf of William Whalley links the manuscript with the Chichester area. Whalley was vicar of the next village, Sidlesham, from 1597 to 1625. John Harper draws attention to the fact that the copyist of this manuscript is likely to have had access to sources associated with the court.

10 Edwards, 'The Sources of Elizabethan Consort Music', p. 93; Neighbour, *The Consort and Keyboard Music of William Byrd*, pp. 20 and 70. Neighbour suggests the original compiler used a finer pen and narrower stave for the *Browning* Fantasy.

11 Ibid. Edwards, p. 94. Edwards quotes Joseph Kerman as suggesting that virtually all the music contained in the manuscript was composed by 1568.

12 Joseph Kerman, 'Byrd's Motets: Chronology and Canon', *Journal of the American Musicological Society*, 14 (1961), p. 360.

13 Edwards, 'The Sources of Elizabethan Consort Music', p. 99.

14 Harper, 'Ensemble and Lute Music', p. 273.

15 Fenlon and Milsom, '"Ruled Paper Imprinted": Music Paper and Patents in Sixteenth-Century England', p. 149.

16 Roger Bray, 'Music and Musicians', in Roger Bray (ed.), *Music in Britain The Sixteenth Century* p. 11.

17 David Mateer, 'Oxford, Christ Church Music MSS 984–8: An Index and Commentary', *Royal Musical Association Research Chronicle*, 20 (1986–7), p. 2.

18 Fenlon and Milsom, '"Ruled Paper Imprinted": Music Paper and Patents in Sixteenth-Century England', p. 149.

19 David Mateer, 'Oxford, Christ Church Music MSS 984–8: An Index and Commentary', p. 4.

20 Ibid., pp. 6–7; Mateer points out that 1581, the year Dow began copying, was a significant year in English and religious history, ending with the execution of Edmund Campion and two other priests. Many in England were shocked and this may account for some of Dow's choice of music, including White's five-part *Lamentations*.

21 David Mateer, 'William Byrd, John Petre and Oxford, Bodleian MS Mus. Sch. E. 423', *Royal Musical Association Research Chronicle*, 29 (1996), pp. 38 and 36.

22 Ibid., p. 37.

23 Ibid. p. 41 and Edwards, 'The Sources of Elizabethan Consort Music', p. 115.

24 Mateer, 'William Byrd, John Petre and Oxford', p. 40.

25 Edwards, 'The Sources of Elizabethan Consort Music', p. 114–15.

26 The missing works are listed in the index but the folios containing them have been lost; GB-Lbl Add MS 22597, Tenor Inventory, The Tudor Partbooks Project, http://www.tudorpartbooks.ac.uk/; Edwards, 'The Sources of Elizabethan Consort Music', p. 138.

27 Fenlon and Milsom, '"Ruled Paper Imprinted": Music Paper and Patents in Sixteenth-Century England', p. 161.

28 Butler, 'Printed Borders for Sixteenth Century Music or Music Paper and the Early Career of Music Printer Thomas East (*c.*1540–1608)', p. 25.

29 Ibid., p. 27.

30 Monson, *Voices and Viols in England, 1600–1650*, p. 135.

31 Edwards, 'The Sources of Elizabethan Consort Music', p. 136.

32 Ian Payne, 'New Light on "New Fashions" by William Cobbold (1560–1639) of Norwich', *Chelys*, 30, (2002), p. 31.

33 Edwards, 'The Sources of Elizabethan Consort Music', p. 135.

34 The Tudor Partbooks Project, US-Ws V.a. 408, Treble Inventory, http://www.tudorpartbooks.ac.uk/; Edwards, 'The Sources of Elizabethan Consort Music', pp. 158–9; DIAMM, www.diamm.ac.uk/sources/2677/#/.

35 Matthew Jeffries, *Consort, Full and Verse Anthems*, ed. John Cannell (Madison, A-R Editions, 1998), p.xii.

36 John Harley, '"My Ladye Nevell" Revealed', *Music and Letters*, 86/1 (2005), p. 2.

37 William Byrd, *Pavans and Galliards in Five Parts*, edited and reconstructed by Richard Rastall (Leeds, 1998), p. iv: Neighbour, *The Consort Music of William Byrd*, p. 183; David J. Smith, 'Byrd Reconstructed: in Search of Consort Models for Keyboard Dances by Byrd', *Annual Byrd Newsletter* 5 (1999), p.6.

38 The Tudor Partbooks Project, GB-Ob Tenbury 389, Discantus Inventory, http://www.tudorpartbooks.ac.uk/.

39 One piece, *Ut re fa so la*, by Parsley is missing.

40 The Tudor Partbooks Project, Gb-Ob Tenbury 389, Discantus Inventory, http://www.tudorpartbooks.ac.uk/.

41 Edwards, 'The Sources of Elizabethan Consort Music', p.131.

42 Trinity College, Dublin, 'Early English Church Music (EECM) Primary Source Data Base', http://eecm.tcd.ie/volumes/.

43 Brett, 'Edward Paston (1550–1630): A Norfolk Gentleman and his Musical Collection', p. 58.

44 Ibid., p. 57.

45 Sequera, 'House Music for Recusants in Elizabethan England: Performance Practice in the Music Collection of Edward Paston (1550– 1630)', pp.165–81; DIAMM, http://www.diamm.ac.uk.

46 Ibid., Taylor, p. 45.

47 Edwards, 'The Sources of Elizabethan Consort Music', p. 178.

48 Fenlon and Milsom, '"Ruled Paper Imprinted": Music Paper and Patents in Sixteenth-Century England', p. 153.

49 Monson, *Voices and Viols in England, 1600–1650*, p. 209.

50 Ibid., p. 221.

51 Ibid., pp. 210 and 223–224.

52 David J. Smith, 'The Instrumental Music of Peter Philips: Its Sources, Dissemination and Style' (DPhil dissertation, University of Oxford, 1994), vol. 1, p. 234.

53 Edwards, 'The Sources of Elizabethan Consort Music', p. 186.

54 Monson, *Voices and Viols in England, 1600–1650*, p. 174.

55 Ibid., p. 206.

56 Ibid., p. 172.

57 MB 101, p.185.

58 Monson, *Voices and Viols in England, 1600–1650,* p. 193.

59 Edwards, 'The Sources of Elizabethan Consort Music', p. 204

60 Monson, *Voices and Viols in England, 1600–1650*, pp. 193 and 205.

61 Ibid., p. 194.

62 McCarthy, *Byrd*, p. 194.

63 Morehen in BE 14, p. 183; McCarthy, *Byrd*, p. 205.

64 Monson, *Voices and Viols in England, 1600–1650*, p.7.

65 Ibid. Monson, p.6; Donna M. Di Grazia, 'New perspectives on Thomas Myriell's *Tristitiae remedium* and Add. Ms. 2947, *Early Music,* 38/1 (2010), p. 103.

66 Edwards, 'The Sources of Elizabethan Consort Music', p. 209.

67 Monson, *Voices and Viols in England, 1600–1650*, pp. 133 and 138.

68 Ashbee, Thompson and Wainwright (eds), http://vdgs.org.uk/indexmss/, 1/02, p. 10.

69 Monson, *Voices and Viols in England, 1600–1650*, p. 139.

70 Ibid., p. 140.

71 Ashbee, 'John Merro's Manuscripts Revisited', pp. 7 and 19.

72 Edwards, 'The Sources of Elizabethan Consort Music', p. 229.

73 Ashbee, 'John Merro's Manuscripts Revisited', p. 6.

74 Unfortunately with errors.

75 MB 101, p. 185.

76 MB 101, p. xxvi.

77 John Irving, *The Instrumental Music of Thomas Tomkins 1572–1656* (New York and London 1989), p. 146.

78 Keith Elcombe, 'Keyboard Music', in Roger Bray (ed.), *The Sixteenth Century*, pp. 216, 221 and 251.

79 Bray, 'Music and Musicians', p. 50.

80 Elcombe 'Keyboard Music', p. 221; John Caldwell, 'Preston, Thomas', in *The New Grove Dictionary of Music*, https://doi-org.nls.idm.ocle.org/10.1093/gmo/9781561592630.article.40009; (Authored 2001 and 2009).

81 The manuscript is named after the twentieth century owner, Paul Hirsch.

82 Julia Craig-McFeely, 'English Lute Manuscripts and Scribes 1530–1630' (DPhil dissertation, Oxford University 1993), https://www.cs.dartmouth.edu/~wbc/julia/; p. 201.

83 Ibid., p. 202.

84 David J. Smith, 'The Instrumental Music of Peter Philips', vol. 1, p. 133.

85 David Charlton, 'A National Catalogue of Music Microfilms', *Royal Musical Association Research Chronicle*, 11/1 (1973), p.14. See also Werner Breig, 'Die Lübbenauer Tablaturen Lynar A1 und A2. Eine quellenkundliche Studie', *Archiv für Musikwissenschaft*, 25 Jahrg. H.2 (1968), p. 98.

86 Pieter Dirksen, 'New Perspectives on Lynar A1', in (ed.) Christopher Hogwood, *The Keyboard in Baroque Europe* (Cambridge, 2003), p. 66.

87 Candace Bailey, 'Orlando Gibbons, Keyboard Music and the Beginnings of the Baroque: New Considerations of a Musical Style', *International Review of the Aesthetics and Sociology of Music* (IRASM), 37/2 (2006) p. 142.

88 Hilda F. Gervers, 'A Manuscript of Dance Music from Seventeenth-century England', *Bulletin of the New York Public Library*, (1977), p. 504.

89 Thomas Tomkins, *Keyboard Music,* ed. Stephen D. Tuttle, MB 5 (London, 1964), pp. 155–62.

90 Neighbour, *The Consort and Keyboard Music of William Byrd*, p. 93.

91 Christ Church Oxford, 'GB-Och Mus 1113', http://library.chch.ox.ac.uk/music/.

92 See Candace Bailey, 'William Ellis and the Transmission of Continental Keyboard Music in Restoration England', p. 214; Irving disagrees, giving 1620, quoting John Caldwell; *The Instrumental Music of Thomas Tomkins (1572–1656)*, p. 19; David Smith suggests that the manuscript may have been copied in Italy by an Englishman in the 1620s: David J. Smith, 'The Instrumental Music of Peter Philips', pp. 127 and 129.

93 Frescobaldi's pupil Johann Jakob Froberger (1616–1667) visited early in the 1650s and probably brought his teacher's music with him: see Candace Bailey, 'William Ellis and the Transmission of Continental Keyboard Music in Restoration England', p. 218; John Milsom suggests the copyist may have been a member of Ellis family: see Christ Church Oxford, http://library.chch.ox.ac.uk/music/.

94 Heather Windram and Terence Charlston (eds), *English Keyboard Music c.1650–c.1700*, 1; *Royal College of Music Library London, MS 2093*, (Oslo, 2015), cover.

95 London, Royal College Music Catalogue, pp. 421–2. Ashbee lists a fourth three-part Byrd fantasia in MS 2093 but this is an error based on its arrangement by Fellowes in his edition of Byrd consort music (1948): Dodds and Ashbee (eds), http://vdgs.org.uk/thematic; see Edwards, 'The Sources of Elizabethan Consort Music', p. 215; Neighbour includes Fantasia C3 in Byrd's keyboard music: see *The Consort and Keyboard Music of William Byrd*, p. 225.

96 Windram and Charlston (eds), *English Keyboard Music c.1650–c.1700*, p. 1.

Appendix Three

Biographical details of composers who influenced Byrd

Chrisopher Tye (c.1505–1573)

Tye was master of choristers and organist at Ely cathedral from the 1540s. Before that, he was a lay clerk at King's College, Cambridge, having been awarded the degree of B.Mus in 1536. Documents relating to his degree mention he had experience in composition and had taught boy choristers for ten years, which suggests Tye was working as an adult musician from around 1525. It is thought that he became acquainted with Dr Richard Cox, a Protestant reformer, during his time at King's. Cox was an undergraduate at the college and went on to become Archdeacon at Ely in 1541 and eventually Bishop of Ely. It is likely Cox influenced Tye's appointment at Ely. Dr Cox was also tutor to Prince Edward from 1544–1550 and seemingly introduced Tye at court. Tye is known to have been associated with the Chapel Royal – one confirmation of this is a record of his livery for Mary Tudor's coronation.

Tye seems to have sustained his connection at Ely through most of his career. He left in 1560, when he was ordained and appointed to livings in Ely diocese, where he served until his death in 1573. Robert White succeeded him at Ely.

Some of Tye's music has been lost, especially some of the Latin vocal music he wrote before the Reformation and in Mary's reign. Most of his English-texted music was written during the reign of Edward VI. These include some substantial anthems such as *I have loved* and *My trust, O Lord.* No keyboard music by Tye survives but he was a prolific writer of In Nomines, some of which are experimental with unusual metre and descriptive titles. Tye must have been an accomplished viol player and his consort music was likely written for musicians at court.

Thomas Tallis (*c.*1505–1585)

Nothing is known about Tallis's early life but it is likely like he was a chorister at a major choral foundation. By 1530 he was working as organist at Dover Priory, one of the wealthiest religious foundations in England, Dover being the gateway to Europe. In 1536 Tallis joined the musicians at St Mary-at-Hill, a wealthy London parish, noted for its music. From here in 1538, he moved to Waltham Abbey, where he was the highest paid musician. This Abbey was also wealthy; run by the Augustinians, it was used by English royalty as a hunting lodge. It was the last monastery to be dissolved in 1540. Following this, Tallis returned to Kent to join a new team of professional musicians at Canterbury Cathedral, where he remained for a short period of time. By 1543 he had joined the Chapel Royal; he remained there for the rest of his life until his death in 1585. Tallis served four monarchs, Henry VIII, Edward VI, Mary Tudor and Elizabeth I. It is not known if he was a Catholic, but he was certainly sympathetic to the Catholic cause. If he was Catholic, he managed to hide it and live without problem in protestant England.

Tallis was organist at the Chapel Royal, and as well as being a singing man, taught keyboard and composition and was probably involved in training boy choristers. He was foremost an organist and keyboard player. Tallis must have met the young Byrd in the 1550s, a relationship that became even closer after Byrd's return to London in 1572. They collaborated on the *Cantiones Sacrae* of 1575 and in 1576, Tallis became godfather to Byrd's son Thomas.

Tallis's compositions encompass Latin-texted church music, English church music, Latin motets, partsongs, keyboard music and a small amount of consort music. He wrote anthems and canticles for the earliest years of English services between 1549-1553, the beginning of an almost unbroken tradition of English church music. They served as models for the next generation of English composers working in the second half of the sixteenth century. The majority of the music he wrote for the Chapel Royal has probably been lost and his Latin motets were largely forgotten until the eighteenth century. Most of Tallis's surviving instrumental compositions are liturgical keyboard music, though one keyboard fantasy survives. Three of his consort compositions survive, two In Nomines and *A Solfing Song*.

Much of Tallis's music is restrained and his English settings have syllabic word settings. The four-part anthem *If ye love me*, dating from the 1540s is probably the most performed of Tallis's anthems. The words have historic significance being found at the beginning of the Gospel reading for Whit Sunday, on which day in 1549 the new English rites were implemented in the Church of England. The anthem lasts for approximately two minutes but the simple setting resulted in a much-loved piece of music. There are however exceptions to Tallis's restrained compositions, in particular his seven-part mass *Puer natus est nobis*, the six-part votive antiphon *Gaude gloriosa* and the forty-part motet *Spem in alium*. The latter was completely unprecedented in Tudor music. Written for eight five-part choirs, it may have been performed in the round. No records survive to tell us why Tallis wrote *Spem in alium*, but the number 40 has great significance in the bible, for example Christ spent forty days in the wilderness. It is thought to date from around 1570 and one theory is that Tallis wrote it to celebrate Elizabeth I's fortieth birthday in 1573.

After Byrd, Tallis is probably the most well-known, respected and loved English composer of the sixteenth century. His death was much mourned; his epitaph, recorded one month after his death stated

'In modest virtuous life he did excel.'

'As he dyd lyve, so also did he dy,
In myld and quyet Sort (O! happy man).'

Robert White (*c.*1530–1574)

White succeeded Christopher Tye as organist and master of choristers at Ely Cathedral and married Tye's daughter. Like many of his contemporaries, very little is known about his early life. He was known to be a lay clerk at Trinity College Cambridge, where he became master of choristers in 1559. White moved to Ely in 1562 and from there to Chester Cathedral in 1566. Finally he became organist and master of choristers at Westminster Abbey, where he remained until his death from the plague in 1574.

Most of White's surviving music is in Latin for unaccompanied voices, including Latin psalms and Lamentations. His small number of consort compositions are unadventurous but include six four-part fantasias, these being among the earliest fantasias composed by an English composer, as well two settings of *Christe qui lux* and four In Nomines.

Robert Parsons (*c.*1535–1572)

Nothing is known about Parsons's early life. His name first appears in documents from 1560/61 relating to service in the Chapel Royal. His name appears again in October 1563 and he was sworn in as a Gentleman in January 1563/4. He possibly served as assistant to Richard Bower, who was Master of the Choristers from 1545–1561. In 1567 Parsons acquired Crown leases for three properties near Lincoln, which he was possibly visiting when he died in the River Trent at Newark in 1572. Byrd was sworn into Parson's position at the Chapel Royal at apparent haste, four weeks after Parsons's death. The urgency could suggest that Parsons was expected to replace Tallis, then in his late sixties.

Only a small number of compositions by Parsons have survived. These consist of Latin settings and motets, at least one English service, English anthems, secular songs and instrumental consort music. The songs may have been written for choir boy plays, suggesting he assisted in teaching the choristers. His sacred English music was likely written in the 1560s for the Chapel Royal. The quality of some of the music illustrates what might have been if Parsons had lived longer, in particular that of his First Service, the five-part *Ave Maria* and three of his consort pieces, *De la court, The Song called trumpets* and his In Nomine a 5.

Like Byrd, Parsons explored writing instrumental music without a cantus firmus. His consort music was likely written for Chapel Royal musicians able to play demanding music. Parsons's five-part In Nomine became the most copied In Nomine illustrating the esteem in which it was held and the frequency with which it was performed.

Robert Dow's epitaph for Parson, found in partbooks written in the 1580s, states:-
'Qui tantus primo Parsone in flore fuisti
Quantus in autumn ni morer fores.'
Which translates as,
Parsons, you who were in the springtime of life,
How great you would have been in the autumn, had death not come.

Alfonso Ferrabosco I (1543–1588)

Ferrabosco I was born and died in Bologna. He was the eldest son of Domenico Maria Ferrabosco, a singer and composer who worked in Bologna and Rome. Ferrabosco probably spent time in Rome as a child and then accompanied his father when he moved the family to Paris. He became a chorister under the patronage of Charles de Guise, Cardinal of Lorraine. Between 1562 and 1578 Ferrabosco was the highest paid musician at the court of Elizabeth I and became highly respected as a composer in England, where he was better known than in Italy. His music includes 110 madrigals, 73 motets, 5 French chansons and 11 consort pieces.

Ferrabosco was acquainted with Byrd and there was friendly rivalry between them including a competition between them writing canons, which sadly do not survive. He brought continental imitative polyphony to the attention of contemporary English composers but he was also influenced by English style and polyphony; his consort works include three In Nomines. His word setting was much admired in his vocal music.

In 1578, Ferrabosco left England for Paris, with his wife, on the pretext of returning to Bologna following his mother's death. As a Catholic, his life had been complicated in England. His two young children were left behind in the care of one of the Queen's musician, probably as a hostage to ensure his return. From Paris he went to Rome, where he was imprisoned by the pope for his apparent lack of commitment to his Roman Catholic faith. On his release, for which Elizabeth I had asked Catherine de Medici to intercede, he entered the service of the Duke of Savoy. His son remained in England (Alfonso Ferrabosco II). Two books of madrigals by Ferrabosco I were published in Venice in 1587.

Ferrabosco I may have been a spy, possibly a double agent, but Elizabeth I valued him for his diplomatic skills as well as his musical skill. His music remained popular in England well into the seventeenth century.

Appendix Four

Web addresses for manuscripts available online at time of publication

GB-Lbl Add. MSS 30480–84 (AM1) www.diamm.ac.uk/sources/1885/#/

GB-Lbl Add MS 31390 (AM2) www.diamm.ac.uk/sources/1888/#/

GB-Ob Tenbury 1464 (AM3) www.diamm.ac.uk/sources/2334/#/

GB-Och MMS 979–83 (AM4) www.diamm.ac.uk/sources/2348/#/

GB-Och MMS 984–8 (Dow) (AM5) www.diamm.ac.uk/sources/2353/#/

GB-Ob MS Mus. Sch. e. 423 (AM6) www.diamm.ac.uk/sources/2294/#/

GB-Lbl Add MS 22597 (AM7) www.diamm.ac.uk/sources/1877/#/

GB-Lbl Add. MS 32377 (AM8) www.diamm.ac.uk/sources/1890/#/

US-Ws MS V.a.408 (AM9) www.diamm.ac.uk/sources/2677/#/

GB-Lbl MS Mus 1591 *My Ladye Nevell's Booke* (AM10) www.bl.uk/manuscripts/Viewer.aspx?ref=ms_mus._1591

GB-Ob MS 389 (AM11) www.diamm.ac.uk/sources/2325/#/

GB-Ob MSS Tenbury 341–4 (AM13) www.diamm.ac.uk/sources/2296/#/

GB-Lbl Add MS 29246 (AM14) www.diamm.ac.uk/sources/4189/#/

GB-Lbl Add MS 29996 (AM35) www.diamm.ac.uk/sources/4129/#/

Index

D

E

F

G

M

R

S

T

Z

www.ingramcontent.com/pod-product-compliance
Lightning Source LLC
Chambersburg PA
CBHW041156100726
47911CB00016B/764

* 9 7 8 1 9 1 4 9 3 4 5 3 7 *